Self-Declaration in the Legal Recognition of Gender

Self-Declaration in the Legal Recognition of Gender examines the impact of legislation premised upon the principle of 'self-declaration' of legal gender status.

Existing doctrinal and comparative analyses have tended to come out strongly in favour of, or against, self-declaration. This book offers a socio-legal alternative which focuses on how self-declaration is experienced, on an embodied level, by trans and gender diverse people. It presents research conducted in Denmark, which became the first European state to adopt self-declaration in June 2014. By analysing Danish law through a Foucauldian framework which brings together socio-, feminist, and trans legal scholarship on embodiment and jurisdiction, the book offers the first empirically based and theoretically informed analysis of self-declaration. It draws upon legal consciousness, affect theory, vulnerability, and governmentality literatures to argue that the jurisdictional boundaries which existed between law and medicine were maintained throughout the reform process. This limited the impact of the legislation, enabling access to health care to be restricted in the same year in which amending legal gender status was liberalised. As the list of states that have adopted self-declaration increases, this intervention offers activists and policymakers insights which might shape how they respond to similar reform proposals in the future.

A timely and important assessment, this book will appeal to researchers and practitioners working in trans, gender, feminist legal, and socio-legal studies.

Chris Dietz is Lecturer at the Centre for Law & Social Justice, University of Leeds, UK.

Part of the SOCIAL JUSTICE series

series editors

Sarah Keenan, Birkbeck College, University of London, UK
Davina Cooper, University of Kent, UK
Sarah Lamble, Birkbeck College, University of London, UK

For information about the series and details of previous and forthcoming titles, seehttps://www.routledge.com/Social-Justice/book-series/RCSOCJ

a GlassHouse book

Self-Declaration in the Legal Recognition of Gender

Chris Dietz

Routledge
Taylor & Francis Group
a GlassHouse Book

First published 2023
by Routledge
4 Park Square, Milton Park, Abingdon, Oxon OX14 4RN

and by Routledge
605 Third Avenue, New York, NY 10158

Routledge is an imprint of the Taylor & Francis Group, an informa business

a GlassHouse book

British Library Cataloguing-in-Publication Data
A catalogue record for this book is available from the British Library

ISBN: 978-0-367-25516-9 (hbk)
ISBN: 978-1-032-36484-1 (pbk)
ISBN: 978-0-429-28820-3 (ebk)

DOI: 10.4324/9780429288203

Typeset in Bembo
by Deanta Global Publishing Services, Chennai, India

Contents

Acknowledgements

Though the title page of this book indicates that I am its sole author, this does not reflect how it was written in practice. Ultimately, I would not have written the book were it not for the support and guidance of a number of people (many of whom I will neglect to mention here). Some offered me financial, practical, or emotional assistance. Others discussed ideas or invited me for tea or a beer. Each contribution was, in its own way, important and valuable. I am grateful for each one.

I will first acknowledge the School of Law at the University of Leeds, and the Economic and Social Research Council, for deciding my PhD proposal was worthy of financial and administrative support. I also wish to acknowledge the unparalleled support of my doctoral supervisors: Julie Wallbank, who saw the PhD through from its conception as a plan for an undergraduate dissertation, and Michael Thomson, who joined soon after and contributed too much for me to cover here. There was laughter, and occasional tears, but I was privileged to have been supervised in a way which was challenging only in an intellectual sense throughout.

I owe so many thanks to the people who agreed to be interviewed by me in Denmark, for giving up their time and providing such interesting material to form the basis of this book. These thanks extend to the exciting thinkers that I have been lucky enough to meet on my travels. To Vika Kirchenbauer, for being a source of inspiration (and pessimism). To Kate Hardy and Tom Gillespie, for advice about wage labour and 'all-inclusive' party hosting. To Simon Felgendreher and Verena Kurz, for Fusion and other holidays. To Sølve Storm and Morten Bjørner, for your thoughtfulness and generosity. To Sam de Boise, for keeping me in check. And to Olga Cielemęcka and Marianna Szczygielska, for *the* gig, and for injecting a bit of 'shimmer' into my Linköping summer, and to Olga in particular for the regular calls during lockdown.

To Mons Bissenbakker, for being a welcoming host in Copenhagen. To Silje Lundgren and Wibke Straube, for making my visits to Linköping and Karlstad happen. And to Nina Lykke, for helping me to think forwards. To the old PECANS Committee (Emily Jones, Arturo Sánchez García, Charlotte Bendall, Kay Lalor, Nayeli Urquiza, and Alex Dymock), for being my academic community at the early stages of my research. To the Nordic Trans Studies Network (and France Rose Hartline, Max van Midde, and Luca Tainio in particular) for giving me the chance to discuss my findings with likeminded scholars. And to the members of the Centre for Law & Social Justice, past (Jess Mant, Katie Cruz, Stu Marvel, Craig Purshouse) and present (Amanda Keeling, Mitch Travis, Jen Hendry, Imogen Jones, Carrie Bradshaw, Marie-Andrée Jacob, Jose Miola, Bev Clough, Ilias Trispiotis, and the rest), for the laughs and encouragement. To Ruth Pearce, for being an ace collaborator and colleague for a short but sweet period. And to my PhD examiners, Sally Hines and John Harrington, who took my thesis seriously before, during, and after, the *viva*.

To Colin Perrin and Naomi Round Cahalin at Routledge, whose hard work ensured that the book was published. And to the editors of the Social Justice book series, Sarah Lamble, Davina Cooper, and Sarah Keenan, for offering insightful comments at multiple stages of the drafting process – which the book would have been worse off without.

To Nicoline Joy Haas and Peter Vinum, for helping me let off steam in Copenhagen. To Linda Lund Pedersen and Carlos Reyes, for making me feel at home in their flat while conducting my research. To Rosie and Kasper Arltoft, for hosting me on arrival in Denmark. To the Kurtzweil/Cooks: Karin, Per, Benjamin, JP, Tine, and Sally, for being my second family in an unfamiliar country.

To the old Leeds gang: Ed Dodson, Tim Gallagher, Nick Jackson, Jack Morrice, Joe Armstrong, Joanna Sawkins, Phil Wallbank, Simon Rowbotham, Nikki Burland, Sam Lewis, Tim Inman, Jonny Cotton, and Nevan Meghani, for getting me through my LLB. To Ed, Florence Stencel-Wade, Sam, and Jasmine Mitchell, for the visits since. To Lora Evans and Joanna Lane, for welcoming me into their friendship group. To Harald Braun and Anne Sophie Schulin-Zeuthen, for hosting in Berlin. To Rebecca Holmberg, Sofia Edstrand, Irene Rossetti, Rhianna Ketley, Fikir Assefa, Alex Schafran, Muck Meylan, João Maio, and Inari Hulkkonen, for being ideal neighbours. To Carli Jones, Kate Cox, and Marie-Avril Berthet, for being tolerant housemates while I was writing the PhD. To Harry Woolner, for the walks and the chats. To Kate Brennan, Barry Vardy, and Seb O'Connor, for the dancing and dal. To Tora Hed and Elspeth McKeever, for being the best people to share my house with on my return to Leeds. And to Marianne Tuckman, for being a lovely guest in a difficult period. To Jack Howe, Andy Burrell, Matt Whitney, and the rest of the Sheffield crew/Barang FC team, for keeping me sane on dancefloors and 4G pitches across Yorkshire.

To my late grandparents, Margaret and Geoffrey Cartmell, who didn't fully understand what I was doing but were proud nonetheless. To my late dad, Micky Dietz, for the times we did have. To Carole, Mike, and Rachel Storey,

Giles Connolly, and Rob and Libby Dietz, for putting up with me even at my most obnoxious. And to my mum, Helen Dietz, for supporting me unfailingly in every way she has.

To Alice, for making me smile during the tough times. To Amanda, for the kindness and generosity of spirit. To Jodi Dublon, for being the first person to read through the first draft of this manuscript – and tell me to shorten the sentences – and for allowing me to be myself. Finally, to Sarah Maria Cook, for '?', and everything else besides.

This book is dedicated to the loving memory of Stuart Michael Pearson, who left us far too soon.

Chapter 1

Introduction

This book is about gender. It is also about sex, to the extent the two can be distinguished from one another. It focuses upon how legal regulation shapes experiences of sex/gender, and what those experiences mean for law. The book does this by discussing how sex and gender are registered, and how this affects legal subjects. Most nation-states register sex or gender at birth and retain this information throughout a person's life.[1] This causes problems for those who do not identify with the sex/gender they have been legally assigned. Even though they only constitute a small minority of the wider population, I contend in this book that the experiences of administrative and practical complexity faced by trans and other gender diverse people tell us as much about the registration and regulation of gender as the experiences of 'cis' (non-trans) people, who do identify to some extent with the sex or gender that was assigned to them at birth.[2]

In 2013, when I began researching trans legal issues, the regulation of gender was considered by many to be a relatively marginal concern. Yet over the course of writing this book, interest in trans issues has grown exponentially in mainstream media, politics, and academia across the world. The question of what distinguishes women from men, and vice versa – a problem which once primarily troubled feminist theorists – now features prominently in newspaper articles, television shows, and media debates. The issue of trans rights has become a key site for 'culture war' debates in the United States (US) and beyond.[3] 'Sex wars' rifts have re-emerged between groups holding opposing positions on the question of who ought and ought not to be recognised as

1 Some languages, including Danish, do not always distinguish clearly between sex and gender. In this book, I translate the Danish term '*køn*' as 'sex/gender' whenever the conceptual distinction is unclear. (This does not apply where its use is clarified with a prefix; such as '*biologiske køn*' or '*fysisk køn*' – 'sex' – or '*kønsidentitet*' – 'gender'.)

2 Other people, e.g. non-trans feminists, may also not identify with the sex/gender they were assigned at birth, in terms of the gendered expectations that are associated with this assignation.

3 C McLean, 'The Growth of the Anti-Transgender Movement in the United Kingdom. The Silent Radicalization of the British Electorate' (2021) 51(6) International Journal of Sociology 473.

DOI: 10.4324/9780429288203-1

a woman.[4] Trans people have, historically, been both included within, and excluded from, women-only spaces.[5] But as proposals to reform the way in which gender status is recognised have been mooted, and implemented, in numerous states, the question of how this affects women and women-only spaces has resurfaced. Though it considers reform proposals, this book does not directly address the debate about gender-segregated space and the extent to which women's rights stand to be affected by gender recognition laws.[6] I eschew purely theoretical speculation about what gender 'is',[7] and consider the ontology of gender only in relation to the epistemological question of how sex/gender is regulated – within and beyond legal systems – instead.

Gendering processes affect all legal subjects, to a greater and lesser extent. But this caveat is important in a world of unequal power relations. Certain bodies are regulated in specific ways, which can lead to them becoming more marginalised than others. Theoretical developments emerging from ethnomethodology,[8] and philosophy,[9] indicate that we all 'do' gender in different ways. But this should not obscure the feminist interjection that this is more difficult for some bodies than others.[10] This of course applies to cis women, who have throughout history been treated as socially inferior to men, and exploited for their unpaid labour in most societies.[11] But it also applies to trans people and others who do not identify with the gender that they were assigned at birth and embark upon some sort of transition across or beyond normative gender categories. Yet trans people have been treated as exhibiting a pathology or illness – i.e. pathologised – for 'doing' gender somewhat differently to their cis peers.

To access gender recognition, some states require that trans people undergo surgical or hormonal treatment.[12] Others, like the United Kingdom (UK),[13] currently necessitate proof of a psychiatric diagnosis such as 'transsexualism', 'gender incongruence', or 'gender dysphoria'. A small number, including the Netherlands,[14] demand approval by civil gatekeepers. Many offer no

4 S Hines, 'Sex Wars and (Trans) Gender Panics: Identity and Body Politics in Contemporary UK Feminism' (2020) 68(4) The Sociological Review Monographs 699.
5 J Halberstam, *Trans** (University of California Press 2018) ch 6.
6 see A Sharpe, 'Will Gender Self-Declaration Undermine Women's Rights and Lead to an Increase in Harms?' (2020) 83(3) Modern Law Review 539.
7 See S Hines, *Is Gender Fluid?* (Thames & Hudson 2019).
8 SJ Kessler and W McKenna, *Gender: An Ethnomethodological Approach* (Wiley 1978).
9 J Butler, *Gender Trouble: Feminism and the subversion of identity* (Routledge 2008).
10 J Butler, *Bodies That Matter: On the discursive limits of 'sex'* (Routledge 2011).
11 S Federici, *Caliban and the Witch* (2nd edn, Autonomedia 2014) 13.
12 P Dunne, 'Transgender Sterilisation Requirements in Europe' (2017) 25(4) Medical Law Review 554.
13 The Gender Recognition Act 2004 is currently good law in England, Scotland, Wales, and Northern Ireland. But as I acknowledge, below, it looks likely to be amended in Scotland in the near future.
14 New Netherlands Civil Code (*Nieuw Burgerlijk Wetboek*), Art 1:28 (NL).

legal gender recognition at all, reflecting the view that sex/gender is fixed at birth. A more recent trend – reflecting a backlash against trans inclusion – has also seen some states, including in the US, prohibit trans people from using facilities (such as bathrooms) not designated for use by people of the sex/gender they were assigned at birth.[15] By contrast, gender recognition laws based upon the principle of self-declaration offer trans people the chance to amend their gender status via statutory declaration, without further gatekeeping. For this reason, self-declaration has been celebrated as 'the optimal gender recognition model'.[16] It has been implemented in Argentina,[17] Denmark,[18] Malta,[19] Colombia,[20] the Republic of Ireland,[21] Norway,[22] Belgium,[23] Brazil,[24] Pakistan,[25] Portugal,[26] Uruguay,[27] Luxembourg,[28] Switzerland,[29] and New Zealand,[30] with Spain,[31] Sweden,[32] and Scotland,[33] apparently on course to follow in the near future. Yet no in-depth qualitative assessment of the impact

15 For example, see North Carolina's House Bill 2: the Public Facilities Privacy and Security Act 2016 (US).

16 P Dunne, 'Ten Years of Gender Recognition in the United Kingdom: Still a "Model for Reform"?' [2015] Public Law 530, 539.

17 Gender Identity Law 2012 (*Ley de Identidad de Genero 26.743*) (AR).

18 L 182 Law amending the Act on the Central Person Registry (11 June 2014) (*L 182 Lov om ændring af lov om Det Centrale Personregister*) (DK).

19 Gender Identity, Gender Expression and Sex Characteristics Act 2015 (MT).

20 Order #1227 of 2015 (*Decreto 1227 de 2015*) (CO).

21 Gender Recognition Act 2015 (ROI).

22 74 L Law amending the legal gender 2016 (*74 L Lov om endring av juridisk kjønn*) (NO).

23 Act reforming regulations relating to transgender persons concerning amendment of the registration of sex in civil status records and its effects 2017 (*Loi réformant des régimes relatifs aux personnes transgenres en ce qui concerne la mention d'une modification de l'enregistrement du sexe dans les actes de l'état civil et ses effets 2017*) (BE).

24 Direct Action of Unconstitutionality No 4275-DF (*Ação Direta de Incosntitucionalidade No 4275*) (BR).

25 Transgender Persons (Protection of Rights) Act 2018 (PK).

26 Decree (XIII 3 105) Right to self-determination of gender identity and expression of gender and protection of the sexual characteristics of each person (PT).

27 Comprehensive Law for Trans Persons 2018 (*Ley Integral Para Personas Trans 2018*) (UR).

28 Law of 10 August 2018 relating to the modification of the mention of the sex and the name or names in the civil status and modifying the Civil Code (*Loi du 10 août 2018 relative à la modification de la mention du sexe et du ou des prénoms à l'état civil et portant modification du Code civil*) (LU)

29 Explanatory report relating to the preliminary draft concerning the revision of the Swiss Civil Code (change of sex in civil status) 2018 (*Rapport explicatif relatif à l'avant-projet concernant la révision du Code civil suisse (changement de sexe à l'état civil) 2018*) (CH).

30 Births, Deaths, Marriages, and Relationships Registration Act 2021 (NZ).

31 Preliminary bill for the real and effective equality of trans people and for the guarantee of the rights of LGTBI people 2021 (*Anteproyecto de ley para la igualdad real y efectiva de las personas trans y para la garantía de los derechos de las personas LGTBI 2021*) (ES).

32 Government Enquiry, *Juridiskt kön och medicinsk könskorrigering: Betänkande av Utredningen om åldersgränsen för fastställelse av ändrad könstillhörighet* (SOU 2014: 91) (SE).

33 Gender Recognition Reform (Scotland) Bill 2022.

of self-declaration has been published for the benefit of international scholars and policymakers.

Legal research has mostly considered trans issues from human rights and anti-discrimination perspectives.[34] Such approaches risk implying that if laws were more inclusive, this would ensure the 'self-determination' of trans people.[35] This ignores the distinction between formal and substantive equality, where the former demands only equal treatment (and not equitable access to resources, as in the latter).[36] They also risk presenting self-declaration as a panacea. Trans studies literatures have eschewed legalistic perspectives in favour of a range of theoretical approaches; including care ethics,[37] relationality,[38] citizenship,[39] and phenomenology.[40] Research exploring issues which affect trans people's experiences of regulation, including access to health care,[41] have added depth to this area. I bring this research into conversation with feminist theories of embodiment and socio-legal work on jurisdiction and legal consciousness in this book. I centre legal embodiment, rather than law, to account for the power dynamic established between trans people, law, and medicine. The reason for this is that legal embodiment highlights the importance of both ontological and epistemological dimensions of regulation – both who and what I am, and how I identify and am identified. Legal embodiment supplements the Foucauldian understanding that bodies are always already regulated by codes and norms with the feminist insight that experiences of this governance are constitutive of both that subject and the legal system.[42] Legal embodiment should be understood as an ongoing process which produces normative bodies and practices while also shaping forms of embodied resistance. Though this

34 S Whittle, *Respect and Equality: Transsexual and Transgender Rights* (Cavendish 2002); A Sharpe, *Transgender Jurisprudence: Dysphoric Bodies of Law* (Cavendish 2002); A Sharpe, *Foucault's Monsters and the Challenge of Law* (Routledge 2010); A Sharpe, *Sexual Intimacy and Gender Identity 'Fraud': Reframing the Legal and Ethical Debate* (Routledge 2018); DA Gonzalez-Salzberg, *Sexuality and Transsexuality Under the European Convention on Human Rights: A Queer Reading of Human Rights Law* (Hart 2019).

35 P Dunne, 'Rethinking Legal Gender Recognition: Recent Reforms in Argentina, Denmark and the Netherlands' (2015) 1 International Family Law 41; DA Gonzalez-Salzberg, 'An Improved Protection for the (Mentally Ill) Trans Parent: A Queer Reading of *AP, Garçon and Nicot* v *France*' (2018) 81(3) Modern Law Review 526; P Cannoot, 'The Pathologisation of Trans* Persons in the ECtHR's Case Law on Legal Gender Recognition' (2019) 37(1) Netherlands Quarterly of Human Rights 14.

36 S Fredman, 'Substantive Equality Revisited' (2016) 14(3) International Journal of Constitutional Law 712.

37 S Hines, *TransForming Gender* (Polity Press 2007).

38 T Sanger, *Trans People's Partnerships: Towards an Ethics of Intimacy* (Palgrave Macmillan 2010).

39 S Hines, *Gender Diversity, Recognition and Citizenship* (Palgrave Macmillan 2013).

40 Z Davy, *Recognizing Transsexuals: Personal, Political and Medicolegal Embodiment* (Ashgate 2011).

41 R Pearce, *Understanding Trans Health: Discourse, Power and Possibility* (Policy Press 2018); B Vincent, *Non-Binary Genders: Navigating Communities, Identities, Healthcare* (Policy Press 2020).

42 C Dietz, 'Governing Legal Embodiment: On the Limits of Self-Declaration' (2018) 26(2) Feminist Legal Studies 185.

de-centres law, I stop well short of seeking to account for the comprehensive complexity of trans embodiment. The specific focus of this book is instead limited to exploring the power dynamic between law, trans people, and medical professionals, and how this is affected by regulatory governance.

By reading embodiment and jurisdiction literatures alongside one another, I explore how legal embodiment is shaped by jurisdiction – a legal 'technicality' which structures the relationships between regulatory authorities, including civil administrative bureaucracies and health institutions.[43] Jurisdiction helps form legal relations,[44] underscoring the authority 'to declare the law'.[45] Attention to jurisdiction has become more common among legal scholars over recent years, thanks to its ability to frame interrogations of conflict of laws, legal sovereignty, and property disputes.[46] Illuminating conflicts which take place on jurisdictional boundaries has enabled legal scholars to map challenges to, or between, state sovereignty. Yet such challenges are uncommon in trans contexts, as gender diverse peoples are just as likely to have their embodiment shaped by interactions with their doctor, employer, or even their family, as they are with administrative state authorities.[47] This insight has become established in the trans studies literature, and yet most legal scholarship on trans issues continues to focus upon the treatment of trans people by authorities of the state. This ignores the 'internal legal pluralism' at play within all regulatory systems.[48] I agree with Mariana Valverde that the jurisdictional conflict which takes place between nation-states can be less interesting than the everyday exchanges which occur between different governing authorities *within* a national legal system.[49] While this does include civil bureaucracies – such as those which record legal gender status – it extends to other institutions, including the national health care systems which also do the work of governing the boundaries of normative gendered embodiment.

Jurisdiction facilitates the practical work of governance by authorising and limiting institutional competences, sorting and ordering different types and levels of authority.[50] Valverde's work on jurisdiction has been adapted to

43 M Valverde, 'Jurisdiction and Scale: Legal 'Technicalities' as Resources for Theory' (2009) 18 Social & Legal Studies 139, 153–154.

44 S Dorsett and S McVeigh, *Jurisdiction* (Routledge 2012).

45 T Hobbes, 'A Dialogue of the Common Law', in W Molesworth (ed), *The English Works of Thomas Hobbes*, vol 6 (Bohn 1839) 118. The etymology is the genitive of *jūs* ('law') and *dictio*; a noun of action ('to declare').

46 Dorset and McVeigh (n 43); S Pasternak, 'Jurisdiction and Settler Colonialism: Where Do Laws Meet?' (2014) 29(2) Canadian Journal of Law and Society 145.

47 A notable exception might be the experience of trans migrants, who will be considered later in Chapter 5.

48 M Valverde, *Chronotopes of Law: Jurisdiction, Scale and Governance* (Routledge 2015) 180.

49 ibid.

50 ibid. 83.

various fields, including housing law,[51] criminology,[52] family law,[53] and medical law.[54] In this book, I explore relations between governing institutions and trans people to illuminate the interplay between legal and medical norms in the regulation of gendered embodiment. As I have noted, this can highlight the subtle processes through which law orders and contains the knowledge claims, politics, and embodied effects of legal and medical institutions.[55] To evidence these embodied effects, I employ a legal consciousness approach. This understands consciousness as 'formed within and by social action'.[56] Legal consciousness research explores experiences of law, questioning how and why people decide to turn to the legal system for assistance (or not). For this reason, it is well-suited to determining the success of a law reform project.

Jurisdictional analysis of legal embodiment allows me to assess the impact of self-declaration in a way which breaches the divide between the critical and policy-oriented research into reform proposals. In the UK, this gap has become an issue as scholars producing critical analyses of the Gender Recognition Act (GRA) 2004 have tended to focus upon practical and formal limitations of this legislation rather than how these might be reformed. In the absence of empirically based analyses of reform possibilities, it has been left to comparative scholars to chart the increasing number of states to have adopted self-declaration.[57] While this offers a useful overview of such developments, it has been harder to gain substantive insight into how self-declaration works in practice. This book addresses this deficit by presenting a theoretically informed and empirically driven assessment of how self-declaration was implemented and experienced in Denmark, the first European state to adopt it, in June 2014.

Research

The book presents original empirical material collected during my doctoral studies, which were funded by the UK Economic and Social Research Council

51 D Cowan, C Hunter, and H Pawson, 'Jurisdiction and Scale: Rent Arrears, Social Housing, and Human Rights' (2012) 39(2) Journal of Law and Society 269.

52 A Crawford, 'Temporality in Restorative Justice: On time, Timing and Time-Consciousness' (2015) 19(4) Theoretical Criminology 1.

53 J Mant and J Wallbank, 'The Mysterious Case of Disappearing Family Law and the Shrinking Vulnerable Subject: The Shifting Sands of Family Law's Jurisdiction' (2017) 26(5) Social & Legal Studies 629.

54 F Garland and M Travis, 'Making the State Responsible: Intersex Embodiment, Medical Jurisdiction, and State Responsibility' (2020) 47(2) Journal of Law and Society 298.

55 C Dietz, 'Jurisdiction in Trans Health' (2020) 47(1) Journal of Law and Society 60.

56 P Ewick and S Silbey, 'Conformity, Contestation, and Resistance: An Account of Legal Consciousness' (1992) 26 New England Law Review 731, 742.

57 Dunne, 'Rethinking Legal Gender Recognition' (n 35); ME Castro-Peraza, JM García-Acosta, N Delgado, AM Perdomo-Hernández, MI Sosa-Alvarez, R Llabrés-Solé, and ND Lorenzo-Rocha, 'Gender Identity: The Human Right of Depathologization' (2019) 16 International Journal of Environmental Research and Public Health 978.

(ESRC) between October 2013 and December 2016. This material was collected with a view to assessing the impact of self-declaration in Denmark for the benefit of researchers, policymakers, legislators, and activists who might be tasked with drawing up and responding to proposals to adopt a similar model elsewhere. To address this empirical and policy-oriented socio-legal problem, and to understand the impact of self-declaration on an institutional and embodied level, I answer the following research questions:

1. How is jurisdiction mobilised in the governance of legal embodiment?
2. How do law reforms register on an embodied level?
3. How are jurisdictional boundaries between institutions such as law and medicine affected by self-declaration?

Working from the embodied to the institutional level, these questions address the impact of the Danish reforms in a way which would benefit scholars and activists across the globe. Rather than undertaking a comparative analysis between Denmark and the UK (for example), I present an in-depth investigation of how gender is being regulated in the Danish context instead. And though this book advocates investigating legal embodiment, it does not present a 'grand' theory of embodiment, self-declaration, or gender recognition. Instead it develops an analytical framework to consider specific issues which are currently emerging out of the embodiment and gender recognition literatures. My objective in doing so has been to provide a frame which generates the questions linked to embodied concerns which ought to be considered when conducting jurisdictional analysis, legal consciousness research, and other forms of socio-legal study.

Denmark is a Nordic European country with an estimated population of just under six million people. The majority of this population reside on the mainland peninsula of Jutland, and the two larger islands of Zealand and Funen.[58] Around one-third live in the region surrounding the capital city, Copenhagen, on Zealand. The Danish government manages its population through a Central Person Registry (CPR). Established in 1968 to facilitate pay-as-you-earn taxation,[59] the CPR allocates each registered resident in Denmark a ten-digit number. The final digit of this CPR number indicates its holder's legal sex/gender. This binary system follows an 'odd/even rule' whereby an even final digit indicates that the holder is female, and an odd final digit indicates that they are male.[60] Access to personal identification documentation

58 Statistics Denmark, 'Population at the First Day of the Quarter by Region, Sex, Age and Marital Status' <www.statbank.dk/FOLK1A> accessed 26 July 2016.

59 AV Ebbesen, 'The Creation of the Central Person Registry in Denmark' in C Gram, P Rasmussen, and SD Østergaard (eds), *History of Nordic Computing 4* (Springer 2015) 50.

60 Order regarding the Central Person Registry no 1153 (2006) (*Bekendtgørelse om folkeregistrering mv*) (DK), s 1.

including passports,[61] driving licences, and birth certificates, as well as certain names,[62] is restricted in accordance with this legal status. Numbering residents might seem bureaucratic, and perhaps even authoritarian, when viewed from a non-Scandinavian perspective. But it is accepted as normal by most Danish residents. Trust of the Danish state is relatively high among its citizens, in a social democratic context where an unparalleled high tax rate is used to generate funds to guarantee access to health care and subsidise nurseries, schools, universities, and nursing homes, as well as to provide generous social support in case of unemployment, sickness, or retirement.[63]

Before 2014, legal gender recognition in Denmark involved being allocated a new CPR number whose final digit indicates a new sex/gender status. The two numbers have remained linked on the CPR system to ensure that administrators and other authorised personnel could join up past and present activity. Before Denmark adopted self-declaration in 2014, a practice had been established whereby trans people could be allocated a new CPR number in accordance with a provision in the Act on the Central Person Registry permitting the correction of 'errors' included on the previous one.[64] However, this was only available to people who could demonstrate that they had been castrated 'for the purposes of sex/gender modification'. This required an applicant to submit evidence that they had undergone removal of their uterus (hysterectomy) and both ovaries (bilateral oophorectomy), or penis (penectomy) and both testicles (orchiectomy).[65] Genital reconstruction surgery was not a pre-requisite.[66] Even after 2014, it remains the case that access to such procedures is dependent upon having been diagnosed with 'transsexualism'.[67]

61 It is possible to apply for an unspecified gender designation ('X') in Danish passports, provided the applicant has been diagnosed with 'unspecified transsexualism' at the Sexological Clinic in Copenhagen; Ministry of Justice, *Rapport fra arbejdsgruppen om juridisk kønsskifte* (27 February 2014) <http://justitsministeriet.dk/sites/default/files/media/Pressemeddelelser/pdf/2014/Rapport%20om%20juridisk%20k%C3%B8nsskifte.pdf> accessed 21 July 2016, 26.

62 The Name Act 2012 (*Navneloven*) (DK), s 13 para 2, states that a first name 'may not denote the opposite sex/gender to the one that will bear the name'. The National Appeals Board (*Ankestyrelsen*) keeps a list of approved male and female names. Approved gender-neutral names appear on both lists, though it is possible to apply to take on a gender-neutral name which does not feature on both lists; see Ministry of Justice (n 61) 23.

63 MN Svendsen, LE Navne, IM Gjødsbøl, and MS Dam, 'A Life Worth Living: Temporality, Care, and Personhood in the Danish Welfare State' (2018) 45(1) American Ethnologist 20, 23.

64 Order regarding the Act on the Central Person Registry (9 January 2013) (*Bekendtgørelse af lov om Det Centrale Personregister*) (DK), s 3 para 5.

65 NV Munkholm, 'Legal Status of Transsexual and Transgender Persons in Denmark' in JM Scherpe (ed), *The Legal Status of Transsexual and Transgender Persons* (Intersentia 2015) 153.

66 ibid.

67 'Transsexualism' is currently defined in the World Health Organization's tenth 'International Statistical Classification of Diseases and Related Health Problems' as 'A desire to live and be accepted as a member of the opposite sex, usually accompanied by a sense of discomfort with, or inappropriateness of, one's anatomic sex, and a wish to have surgery and hormonal treatment

Denmark is a constitutional monarchy governed by representative parliamentary democracy. The legislature, the Danish Parliament (*Folketinget*), is based in Copenhagen.[68] Its 179 members (including 4 members from the Faroe Islands and Greenland) are elected by proportional representation in general elections that must be held at 4-year intervals.[69] In the period from 2011 to 2015, when self-declaration was adopted, the Parliament was led by a minority centre-left coalition government of the Social Democrats (*Socialdemokratiet*), the Social Liberal party (*Radikale Venstre*) and the Socialist People's party (*Socialistisk Folkeparti*). This coalition ruled with support from the left-wing Red-Green Alliance (*Enhedslisten*), and three of the four parties representing the Faroe Islands and Greenland. This comprised the 'Red Bloc' (*rød blok*) of parliamentary parties.[70] From 2011 to 2015, the official opposition was provided by the 'Blue Bloc' (*blå blok*): the Liberals (*Venstre*), the Danish People's party (*Dansk Folkeparti*), the Liberal Alliance (*Liberal Alliance*), and the Conservative People's party (*Det Konservative Folkeparti*).

The legal process in Denmark is such that any member of the Parliament – from governing or opposition parties – can propose a Bill (*Beslutningsforslag*) for consideration. Yet the possibility of such a Bill being passed is dependent upon it gaining a parliamentary majority in support of it. So although the issue of gender recognition law reform has been on the Danish parliamentary agenda for almost a decade (with Bills tabled in 2007, 2008, 2009, and 2010),[71] it was not until the 2011 general election – when the incumbent centre-right coalition government of the Liberals and the Conservative People's party lost power to the Red Bloc – that it became likely that any of these would become law. Gender recognition law reform was all but confirmed when the new centre-left coalition government policy agreement document (*Regeringsgrundlaget*) included the first ever section on 'sex/gender equality'.[72] Here, the government expressed a comprehensive commitment to 'examine the rules concerning sex/gender modification treatment, including opportunities to change legal sex/gender without the need for surgical intervention.'[73]

---

to make one's body as congruent as possible with one's preferred sex'; WHO ICD-10, 'F64.0 Transsexualism' <http://apps.who.int/classifications/icd10/browse/2015/en#/F64> accessed 22 May 2015.

68 'About the Danish Parliament' (*Folketinget*) <www.thedanishparliament.dk/About_the_Danish_Parliament.aspx> accessed 26 September 2016.

69 '179 Members' (*Folketinget*) <www.thedanishparliament.dk/About_the_Danish_Parliament/179_Members.aspx> accessed 26 September 2016

70 Though the Red Bloc was bolstered by the addition of The Alternative party (*Alternativet*) in the 2015 General Election, this was not enough to retain control of the Parliament, after the Blue Bloc secured 90 of the 179 seats.

71 Munkholm (n 65) 151–152.

72 Prime Minister's Office, 'Et Danmark, Der Står Sammen' (October 2011) <www.stm.dk/publikationer/Et_Danmark_der_staar_sammen_11/Regeringsgrundlag_okt_2011.pdf> accessed 20 August 2015.

73 ibid. 66.

Trans issues coincidentally gained attention in the Danish media in the same month that the government published this policy commitment. This was thanks to a story which became known as the 'Caspian case' (even though no formal legal proceedings actually took place),[74] in which a 15-year-old trans boy (named Caspian Drumm) underwent a mastectomy at a private hospital in Odense, on the island of Funen, in May 2011. In response to the media controversy that followed, Astrid Krag, the Minister of Health at the time, called for the Danish Health and Medicines Authority (DHMA) to investigate existing health care regulation and practice concerning trans people's access to body modification technologies, and to determine whether the private hospital had 'acted responsibly'.[75] By November 2012, the surgeon who performed Caspian's mastectomy had been reprimanded by a DHMA disciplinary committee for failing to subject his patient to sustained psychiatric assessment prior to the operation.[76] The DHMA issued new interim guidelines which stated that, while they were working on the investigation demanded by the government, medical practitioners were to refer all new trans patients, and all existing patients below the age of 18, to the Sexological Clinic in Copenhagen.[77] This closed the legal loophole through which trans people in Denmark had been granted access to body modification technologies other than those associated with surgical castration through a small number of medical practitioners, working in the private sector, who had been willing to prescribe hormones and perform minor surgeries on an informed consent basis.[78] A state monopoly was established in its place whereby all new and underage trans patients seeking access to body modification technologies would have to first undergo psychiatric assessment at the Sexological Clinic.

After the interim guidelines were published, an 'inter-ministerial working group on legal sex/gender change' (the working group) was established, in January 2013, to investigate how the government's policy commitment to 'examine the rules concerning sex/gender modification treatment, including opportunities to have a legal sex/gender change without the need for surgical

74 T Raun, 'The "Caspian Case" and Its Aftermath: Transgender People's use of Facebook to Engage Discriminatory Mainstream News Coverage in Denmark' in J Björklund and U Lindqvist (eds), *New Dimensions of Diversity in Nordic Culture and Society* (Cambridge Scholars Publishing 2016) 79.

75 ibid., citing 'Minister går nu ind i Caspian-sag' (*TV2 Nyhederne*, 15 October 2011) <http://nyhederne.tv2.dk/article.php/id-44674432:minister-går-nu-ind-i-caspiansag.html>.

76 Patients' Ombudsman, 'Kritik for behandling – speciallæge i plastikkirurgi Jens Pilegaard Bjarnesen' (1 November 2012) <www.patientombuddet.dk/Afgoerelser_og_domme/Afgoerelser_fra_Sundhedsvaesenets_Disciplinaernaevn/Afgoerelser_med_navn/2012/1294528.aspx> accessed 16 September 2015.

77 Danish Health and Medicines Authority, 'Behandling af transseksuelle' (23 November 2012) <https://sundhedsstyrelsen.dk/da/nyheder/2012/behandling-af-transseksuelle> accessed 30 November 2015.

78 The creation, development, and closure of this legal loophole will be discussed in detail in Chapter 5.

intervention' could be put into practice.[79] This working group was made up of representatives from the Ministry of Justice (*Justitsministeriet*), the Ministry of Health (*Ministeriet for Sundhed og Forebyggelse*), the Ministry of Equality and the Church (*Ministeriet for Ligestilling og Kirke*), the Ministry of the Economy and the Internal Affairs (*Økonomi- og Indenrigsministeriet*), and the Ministry of Social, Children and Integration Affairs (*Social-, Børne- og Integrationsministeriet*). It was given a mandate to 'develop and evaluate possible models for achieving legal sex/gender recognition in Denmark'.[80] One year later, in the same month as Amnesty International released a report criticising both the diagnostic process at the Sexological Clinic and the requirement that trans people had to be castrated before they could access legal gender recognition,[81] the working group published its report. This considered four different models for granting legal gender recognition – including one based upon the principles of self-declaration of legal gender status.[82]

When the government decided to implement this self-declaration model, a Bill was drafted for the purpose of 'assigning a new personal number to people who experience themselves as belonging to the other sex/gender'.[83] In June 2014, the Bill passed through the Danish Parliament, and a new subsection was inserted into the Act on the Central Person Registry:[84]

> The Ministry of the Economy and the Interior will issue, after a written application, a new CPR number to a person who experiences themselves as belonging to the other sex/gender. Assigning a new CPR number is conditional upon the person concerned making a written declaration that the desire for a new personal identity is based upon an experience of belonging to the other sex/gender, and that they confirm, in writing, this application following a reflection period of six months from the filing date. It is a further condition that, at the time of the application, the applicant is 18 years old.[85]

79 Prime Minister's Office (n 72) 66.

80 Ministry of Justice, 'Kommissorium for tværministeriel arbejdsgruppe om udmøntning af regeringsgrundlagets afsnit om kønsskifte' (17 May 2013) <https://panbloggen.files.wordpress.com/2013/05/kc3b8nsskifte-kommissorium-jm.pdf&usg=ALkJrhjLszn-4IJPOaQMon8NdRzCGtYKSA> accessed 10 September 2015.

81 Amnesty International, 'The State Decides Who I Am: Lack of Legal Gender Recognition for Transgender People in Europe' (4 February 2014) <www.amnesty.org/en/documents/EUR01/001/2014/en> accessed 8 April 2015.

82 Ministry of Justice (n 61).

83 Bill for amending the Act on the Central Person Registry (30 April 2014) (*Forslag til Lov om ændring af lov om Det Centrale Personregister*) (DK).

84 After para 5 (which provides for the assigning of a new CPR number for individuals who have errors in the information contained in their current one); Order regarding the Act on the Central Person Registry (n 64).

85 L 182 (n 18), s 1; Order regarding the Act on the Central Person Registry (n 64), s 3 para 6.

The L 182 Law amending the Act on the Central Person Registry ('the CPR law') permits Danish residents to self-declare their legal gender status – irrespective of whether they have undergone medical treatment or been granted a 'transsexualism' diagnosis. Campaigners in the UK,[86] and Europe,[87] immediately celebrated its adoption. The CPR law was said to constitute the first European gender recognition legislation to respect the 'self-determination of the individual'.[88] It was described as 'something revolutionary, yet very sensible' for making Danish trans people 'the sole decision makers on their gender and body, without any conditions imposed by the state.'[89] Denmark was congratulated for having 'pioneered another significant change in Europe';[90] and 'other countries' were encouraged to 'follow the Danish example'.[91]

Denmark's reputation as a pioneer of 'sexual liberalism', which has been said to constitute an important aspect of Danish 'self-understanding',[92] was thus augmented. Denmark was the first state to legalise pornographic texts and images (in 1967 and 1969, respectively),[93] and to introduce civil partnership legislation for gay and lesbian couples (in 1989).[94] But in a trans context, its reputation for sexual liberalism is based primarily upon its association with two of the most widely reported instances of genital reconstruction surgery. The first involved the Danish artist Lili Elbe, who travelled to Germany to undergo a series of procedures in the 1920s and 1930s.[95] The second involved former US soldier Christine Jorgensen, who underwent two widely reported

86 N Gale, 'Denmark Leads Europe on Gender Recognition' (*Scottish Trans*, 18 June 2014) <www.scottishtrans.org/denmark-leads-europe-on-gender-recognition> accessed 14 November 2014.

87 TGEU, 'Denmark Goes Argentina! Denmark Passes Best Legal Gender Recognition Law in Europe' (11 June 2014) <http://tgeu.org/denmark-goes-argentina> accessed 8 February 2016.

88 A Voipio, Co-Chair of TGEU, cited in ibid.; TGEU, 'Historic Danish Gender Recognition Law Comes into Force' (1 September 2014) <www.tgeu.org/TGEU_statement_Historic_Danish_Gender_Recognition_Law_comes_into_Force> accessed 26 November 2014.

89 D de Jong, Vice-President of the LGBT Intergroup, cited in LGBT Press Network, 'Denmark Becomes Europe's Leading Country on Legal Gender Recognition' (*GayAsUs.com*, 14 June 2014) <http://gayasus.com/pub/2014/06/14/denmark-becomes-europes-leading-country-legal-gender-recognition/17> accessed 26 November 2014.

90 G Calleja, Co-Chair of ILGA-Europe's Executive Board, cited in ILGA Europe, 'Denmark Becomes the First European Country to Allow Legal Change of Gender without Clinical Diagnosis' (11 June 2014) <www.ilga-europe.org/home/news/for_media/media_releases/denmark_becomes_the_first_european_country_to_allow_legal_change_of_gender_without_clinical_diagnosis> accessed 26 November 2014.

91 Ehrt, TGEU Executive Director, cited in TGEU (n 87); see also: Amnesty International, 'World Must Follow Denmark's Example after Landmark Transgender Law' (12 June 2014) <www.amnesty.org/en/latest/news/2014/06/denmark-transgender-law> accessed 25 September 2016.

92 Raun (n 74), citing MN Petersen, 'Somewhere Over the Rainbow: Biopolitiske rekonfigurationer af den homoseksuelle figure' (PhD thesis, University of Copenhagen 2012).

93 C Graugaard and others, 'Denmark' in RT Francoeur and RJ Noonan (eds), *The Continuum Complete International Encyclopaedia of Sexuality* (Continuum 2004) 330.

94 ibid. 332.

95 Raun (n 74).

operations while visiting relatives in Denmark in 1951 and 1952.[96] The international reception of the CPR law as 'the best' of its kind in Europe can be construed as playing into the same liberal narrative. Yet domestic controversies – including around the Caspian case, and the restriction of access to body modification technologies that followed, as well as seemingly unrelated anti-migration policies – mount a significant challenge to what Tobias Raun has called 'the myth of liberal Denmark'.[97] In December 2014, only months after the CPR law had been enacted, the DHMA replaced the interim guidelines that had been established following the Caspian case with new formal guidelines 'on the evaluation and treatment of transgender' ('the 2014 guidelines').[98] These 2014 guidelines codified that 'sex/gender modification' treatments (such as hormone replacement treatment and various surgical operations)[99] could only be administered by a 'multidisciplinary team of collaborating specialists in psychiatry, obstetrics/gynaecology and plastic surgery, who have special knowledge of transgender patients'.[100] The result was that the *de jure* monopoly established following the Caspian case was abolished – as no explicit reference is made to the Sexological Clinic. Yet a *de facto* state monopoly was effectively retained – as the Sexological Clinic was at the time the only clinic with sufficient capacity to put together this multidisciplinary team and meet these requirements. This situation persisted until the Danish Health Authority approved treatments at a new Sexological Centre (*Sexologisk Center*) at the Aalborg University Hospital in September 2017 – five years after the monopoly at the Sexological Clinic had been established, and three years after self-declaration had been adopted.[101]

When I refer to 'the 2014 reforms', I mean to cover both civil and medical regulations concerning trans embodiment. This includes the celebrated reforms of civil registration that were made by the CPR law,[102] but also the new 2014 guidelines concerning the processes authorising access to body modification technologies.[103] I also include the less well-reported reforms of medical legislation by the L 189 Law amending the Health Act and the Act on Assisted Reproduction in connection with treatment, diagnosis, and research, etc. ('the amendment to the Health Act') introduced, as an independent Bill,

96 ibid.

97 ibid.

98 Guideline no 10353 on the treatment of transgender (19 December 2014) (*Vejledning nr 10353 om udredning og behandling af transkønnede*) (DK).

99 ibid. s 1.

100 ibid. s 2.

101 Guideline no 9921 on health care related to gender identity (22 September 2017) (*Vejledning nr 9921 om sundhedsfaglig hjælp ved kønsidentitetsforhold*) (DK); since updated by Guideline no 9658 on health care related to gender identity (16 August 2018) (*Vejledning nr 9921 om sundhedsfaglig hjælp ved kønsidentitetsforhold*) (DK).

102 L 182 (n 18).

103 Guideline no 10353 (n 98).

Table 1.1 Activist and campaigner interviewees by organisation

Organisation	*Members*	*Interviewees*
Amnesty International	89,620	Claus Juul
Social Democrats	85,838	Flemming Møller Mortensen
Red-Green Alliance	74,144	Camilla Tved
AIDS-Foundation	15,380	Ole Møller Markussen
Danish Institute for Human Rights	12,353	Peter Ussing, Maria Ventegodt Liisberg, Sofie Aviaja Bünger
LGBT Denmark	10,638	Søren Laursen, Linda Thor Pedersen
Trans Political Forum	723	Elvin Pedersen-Nielsen, Elias Magnild
FATID	245	Irene Haffner

Membership figures are based upon Facebook 'likes' as of 7 December 2016.

after the CPR law in June 2014.[104] It is imperative from a socio-legal perspective that such reforms are analysed in relation to each other.

Methods

In this book, the main doctrinal sources that I will draw upon will be the legislative materials cited above, as well as the parliamentary debates and explanatory comments that accompanied the 2014 reforms. The book is also informed by semi-structured qualitative interviews that I undertook with 33 respondents over the course of a 3-month fieldwork visit to Denmark in 2015. Interviews were conducted with 14 trans people, 1 intersex person, 11 activists and campaigners, 1 politician, and 6 other stakeholders (including 4 civil servants, and 2 medical practitioners). Twenty-five interviews took place in person, and eight by telephone. I began by interviewing activists, campaigners, politicians, and other stakeholders, to develop a hypothesis as to how the 2014 reforms were supposed to work in practice. These interviewees were drawn from organisations including human rights groups (LGBT Denmark, Amnesty International (Denmark), and the AIDS-Foundation), political parties (the Social Democrats, and the Red-Green Alliance), a governmental monitoring body (the Danish Institute for Human Rights), and trans rights activists (Trans Political Forum, and FATID – the Association for Transgender People in Denmark) (see Table 1.1).

Beginning with activists and campaigners enables the researcher to ask respondents if they can recommend any professional contacts whom it would also be worth interviewing. It also gave me the opportunity to ask if they would be willing to share my call for interviewees on their mailing list and

104 L 189 Law amending the Health Act and the Act on Assisted Reproduction in connection with treatment, diagnosis, and research, etc. (11 June 2014) (*L 189 Lov om ændring af sundhedsloven og lov om assisteret reproduktion i forbindelse med behandling, diagno stik og forskning m.v.*) (DK).

social media pages. Much is made of the distinction between 'gatekeepers' and 'participants',[105] but here the line blurred. After interviews, respondents became gatekeepers to their colleagues and members of their organisations.

The initial stages of the access process are said to be characterised as involving a 'negotiation' between the researcher, gatekeepers, and research subjects.[106] I was fortunately able to advertise my call for respondents on the Facebook and information pages of several of the groups included in Table 1.1 (including LGBT Denmark, Trans Political Forum, and FATID), as well as other, more grassroots organisations' social media pages (including LGBT Denmark's 'T-Gruppen', the KaPow Collective, activist Tina Thranesen's 'knowledge database on gender identity', and 'TransFAQ'). Membership of all of these organisations is more or less fluid. Some provide a platform for discussion that takes place exclusively on social media. Others host regular events such as cafes and meetings in spaces local to their membership. One or two campaign for trans and LGBT rights on a national level. Advertising with such a range of groups ensured that the call could be seen by people across Denmark, with different levels of experience of activism and organising, and varying degrees of access to trans communities.

In the absence of a permanent trans social space in Denmark,[107] the above organisations tended at this time to communicate almost exclusively via the social media platform Facebook. An effect of positioning early interviewees as gatekeepers to future respondents was to exclude prospective interviewees who did not have access to Facebook (or the internet generally). Not translating the call for participants into Danish also excluded those who did not speak English. Given the strong English language proficiency of those educated in Denmark in the post-war era,[108] this appeared – alongside recruiting primarily via Facebook – to have had a marked effect mainly on the recruitment of older people (of whom, out of 15 respondents, there was only 1 over the age of 50, and none over 60) and migrants (of whom there were 2, from other countries within the EU).

Writing the call for participants in English might also have affected the recruitment of non-white interviewees, who were not well represented within my research (with only one interviewee classifying their ethnicity as 'Asian'). Yet I based the decision to publicise the call for participants in English on my feeling that it was important to be clear that the interview could not be conducted in Danish from the outset (due to a lack of resources to pay for audio translation in the fieldwork budget). Still, the fact that one older activist did turn down my

105 A Bryman, *Social Research Methods* (4th edn, OUP 2012) 151.

106 R Madden, *Being Ethnographic: A Guide to the Theory and Practice of Ethnography* (Sage 2011) 59.

107 Copenhagen has a vast array of gay bars which cater primarily to gay people more than trans people (though the two groups are not mutually exclusive, as is indicated by the demographic data laid out in Table 1.2).

108 Denmark was ranked third in the world in the Education First English Proficiency Index 2015; Education First, 'The World's Largest Ranking of Countries by English Skills' (2015) <www.ef.edu/epi> accessed 2 September 2016.

Table 1.2 Demographics

Gender		*Sexuality*		*Ethnicity*	
Male	5	Pansexual	7	Caucasian	14
Female	3	Heterosexual	6	Asian	1
Non-binary	3	Homosexual	1		
Transman	2	Bisexual	1		
Transwoman	1				
Intersex woman	1				
Employment		*Age*		*Location*	
Paid employment	5	18–30	8	Zealand	8
Unemployed	3	31–40	3	Jutland	4
Student	3	41–50	3	Funen	3
Retired	2	51–60	1		
Self-employed	1				
Care work	1				

interview request on the grounds of their own perceived lack of English-speaking skills indicates that self-selecting respondents may well have been deterred from responding to the call, highlighting problems that future researchers seeking to conduct interviews overseas in English ought to be aware of.

Aside from limitations in terms of age and ethnicity, my sample was relatively mixed. This was particularly evident in respect of gender (self-)identification, sexual orientation, and employment status (see Table 1.2). My concern that being based in Copenhagen, on the island of Zealand, could constitute a geographical barrier for trans people living elsewhere in Denmark also appeared unfounded. One unanticipated reason for this may have been explained, in part, by a side-effect of the 2014 medical guidelines. Before the Sexological Centre at the Aalborg University Hospital was authorised to assess trans people in September 2017, the 2014 guidelines required all trans people who wished to undergo body modification to undergo psychiatric evaluation at the Sexological Clinic in Copenhagen. And those that were required to travel there from other regions were entitled to have their travel expenses covered by the region in which they live. This enabled at least one respondent, who lived on the Danish peninsula of Jutland, to meet me for an in-person interview in Copenhagen immediately after their appointment at the Sexological Clinic. For others located outside Copenhagen, the possibility of an online interview using video-calling software was utilised on several occasions. In the end, this enabled geographic variation, with almost half of those interviewed located outside of the most populous island of Zealand.[109]

109 Almost 2.5 million people – around 43% of the population – were registered as residing on Zealand as of 1 January 2016; Statistics Denmark, 'Population by island and date' <www.statbank.dk/BEF4> accessed 13 December 2016.

I designed my call for respondents to be as inclusive as possible, addressing anyone who did not identify with the gender they were assigned at birth rather than specifying a specific identity category (such as 'trans people') as the subject of the study. This responded to Zowie Davy's reflection upon the difficulties of recruiting 'stealth' trans people (i.e. those who are not 'out' – or do not openly identify as trans) as interviewees.[110] My call was phrased as follows: 'Do you identify with the gender you were assigned at birth? If not, you are invited to participate in a project that helps a researcher from the UK understand how gender identity is recognised in Denmark'.

Formulating the call in this way did have the intended effect of enabling the recruitment of eight interviewees that self-identified as 'male' or 'female' (see Table 1.2), rather than 'trans' (including one who noted that they lived their day-to-day life in a manner which might be understood as 'stealth'). But it also led to the recruitment of one intersex woman,[111] who felt that she could contribute to a project which sought to explore 'how gender is recognised in Denmark' – as she did not identify with the gender she was assigned at birth. At the time – and in the spirit of inclusion – I decided to interview her to see what insights she could offer. And yet while she did offer many, it could equally be argued that interviewing 1 intersex person alongside 14 trans people was not the best methodological decision. The reason for this is that the under-representation of intersex people in the research made it difficult to make any assumptions about how intersex people had been affected by the 2014 reforms as a population group. While I took care to ensure that this one intersex person's concerns were not taken as representative of all intersex people in Denmark, I acknowledge that this issue raises some general questions about research design when targeting non-specific marginalised groups (as it would have been as difficult to exclude this interviewee as it was to include them). This is something that future researchers ought to be wary of.

Alongside activists, campaigners, and trans people, this book draws upon interviews conducted with respondents who were professionally involved in the design and implementation of the 2014 reforms. In doing so, it seeks to develop a more comprehensive picture of the intentions and rationalities which shaped the 2014 reform process. Supplementing the perspectives of

110 Z Davy, 'Transsexual Recognition: Embodiment, Bodily Aesthetics and the Medicolegal System' (PhD thesis, University of Leeds 2008) 91.

111 The term 'intersex' refers to people born with chromosomal, gonadal, hormonal, or anatomical characteristics that challenge the bio-medical sex/gender binary; FR Ammaturo, 'Intersexuality and the "Right to Bodily Integrity": Critical Reflections on Female Genital Cutting, Circumcision, and Intersex "Normalizing Surgeries" in Europe' (2016) 25(5) Social & Legal Studies 591. Intersex embodiment coincides with trans experience in some respects, as many intersex people do not identify with the gender they were assigned at birth. Yet there are points of distinction in how this dis-identification is experienced, hence intersex being afforded a discreet category in academic and activist literature.

Table 1.3 Regulator interviewees by organisation

Employer during reform process	*Name*	*Role in working group*
CPR Office	Grethe Kongstad	Secretary to member
Ministry of Health	John Erik Pedersen	Member
Danish Health and Medicines Authority	Anne Mette Dons	Member
Sexological Clinic	Annamaria Giraldi	Not officially involved
Department for Gender Equality	Trine Ingemansen	Member

those personally affected by the reforms with the professional insights of regulators enables me to add depth to my initial findings as to how these reforms were working in practice. Interviewing regulators as well as trans people and activists and campaigners provides an opportunity to draw insights from the opposite 'pole' of the regulatory arrangement. It allows me to develop a point of contrast between those tasked with designing and implementing the regulations and those who are governed in accordance with them. In this book, these testimonies are at times contrasted or corroborated, enhancing the 'concreteness' of the study, and alleviating the concerns developed in relation to exploring only the embodied dimension of this governance project (discussed in more detail in Chapter 3) to the detriment of the institutional perspective.

Of the five regulators I interviewed, four had been professionally involved in the working group tasked with amending the civil legislation (see Table 1.3). As the process of reforming the medical guidelines was less transparent than legislative reforms, it is not completely clear which institutions were actively involved in this process (and to what extent).

When recruiting these regulators, I again relied upon snowball sampling, and upon the professional connections between the civil servants involved in the reform process. On one specific occasion, my request that one professional interviewee recommend me to their colleague revived an email exchange that had previously stagnated. While I was aware that access is not necessarily comprehensive even after it had been partially granted by professional bureaucracy,[112] it appeared to help, as with the activists and campaigners, when my call came with a recommendation from a previous interviewee.

Chapter outline

The book is split into six chapters. In Chapter 1, I have introduced my research, describing how this sits in relation to relevant academic scholarship and legal practice, as well as contemporary debates around legislative reform. I have argued for in-depth investigation of how laws such as those based upon self-declaration of legal gender status work in practice. I have explained why my

112 M Hammersley and P Atkinson, *Ethnography: Principles in Practice* (3rd edn, Routledge 2009) 41.

research took me to Denmark, describing the mixed context that I found upon arriving there. I introduced my theoretical approach which brings together a legal embodiment perspective and jurisdictional analysis. I finally mentioned some of the methods I employed and reflected upon some of the issues that I encountered as I conducted my research.

In Chapter 2, I will lay out my theoretical perspective more comprehensively. In it, I will argue for a conception of legal embodiment as it is socially experienced; that is, encompassing its subjective, intersubjective, material, symbolic, and institutional elements. Drawing upon trans legal studies and sociological literatures, before adding insights from feminist theory and feminist legal scholarship, I will develop a conceptual framework which is well-suited to interrogating gender recognition law reforms. In centring institutional dimensions of legal embodiment, I stress the importance of acknowledging how powerful institutions like law and medicine shape embodied experiences of regulation. Following Valverde, I employ jurisdictional analysis to help me do this.

Chapter 3 offers some methodological detail as to how I brought legal embodiment and jurisdiction together in my research. This required me to supplement both approaches with a legal consciousness methodology. Legal consciousness centres and probes conscious experience, allowing researchers insight into the impact of regulation on people's everyday lives. For theoretical reasons, it might not seem at first glance to be perfectly compatible with legal embodiment and jurisdictional approaches, which look beyond subjective experience. Yet when employed critically, and with attention to context and structures, legal consciousness is a useful method through which to explore embodied experience. Experience is a tricky concept. But, as feminist theorists have noted, it is also an excellent starting place to begin empirical analysis – particularly as I seek to build a coherent picture of how institutional regulations including gender recognition laws and medical guidelines affect gendered embodiment. After exploring the conceptual basis of my methodology in the first half of Chapter 3, I go on to discuss some of the practical issues that I encountered as I implemented it in the second.

I present the substantive findings from my research in Chapters 4–6. Chapter 4 discusses ideas of visibility and progress, and the commonplace notion that the former is a necessary precondition of the latter. By considering the experience of adopting self-declaration in Denmark, I challenge the assumption that trans visibility is a precursor to progress in the context of gender recognition. Unlike in nation-states such as the US and the UK, trans people were not particularly visible in Danish mainstream media before 2014. Yet this did not stop Denmark adopting self-declaration as early as it did. With reference to affect theory, I seek to understand why. In the second part of the chapter, I discuss the idea of 'progress' itself. I consider how far the 2014 reforms substantively increase the rights of trans people in Denmark, when they were limited from the outset to avoid contention or significant material consequence.

A conclusion that many trans people, in Denmark and elsewhere, have drawn from processes of failed or limited reform projects is that too much power remains concentrated in medical institutions. Without a re-distribution of this power, reforms will continue to be watered down and neglect the health, and other basic needs, of trans people. While such an argument is compelling, I complicate this picture in Chapter 5 with reference to Martha Fineman's vulnerability theory. Rather than demonstrating omnipotence, I suggest that the risk-averse practices of medical regulators and clinics would be better understood as a defensive response to their institutional vulnerability. I present the effects of these practices from the perspective of the trans people subjected to them, before returning to vulnerability theory to call for a more response state, which seeks to actively meet trans people's health care needs instead.

Chapters 4 and 5 could be said to concern themselves with the gap between what law claims to be doing, and what it is actually doing in practice. In Chapter 6, I distance myself from this perspective by presenting a governmentality analysis of the Danish reforms. Influenced by the work of Foucault and others, I address how different governmental priorities were given preference over the needs and demands of trans people in Denmark during the 2014 reform process. Rather than criticising the Danish adoption of self-declaration for the ways in which it failed, I consider the possibility that it was always expected to fall short of the transformative gains trans people hoped for. I address the disciplinary effects of the Danish reforms, which include the exclusion of non-binary trans people from gender recognition – with a risk of criminalisation for non-compliance. I then move on to the regulatory effects of the 2014 reforms, to broaden my perspective and elucidate how reforms including self-declaration play into broader political currents – from historical eugenics to contemporary border controls.

This informs the conclusion of Chapter 6, which reflects upon the significance of governmentality for legal studies of gender recognition laws and other reform projects. If gender recognition reforms can be enacted at little governmental expense, without significantly affecting population management technologies, and while doing nothing to improve the material circumstances of trans people's lives – including health care, employment, housing, and migration – it is worth asking how much energy activists and scholars ought to invest in pushing for them. Some policymakers may be influenced enough to achieve more transformative reforms than the ones adopted in Denmark: such as those adopted in Argentina, which guarantee access to health care on an informed consent basis;[113] or in Uruguay, which, in addition to this, also create quotas for employment and access to education and offer reparations to trans peo-

113 MDM Rucovsky, 'The Travesti Critique of the Gender Identity Law in Argentina' (2019) 6(2) TSQ: Transgender Studies Quarterly 223, 230.

ple persecuted under Uruguay's 1973–1985 military dictatorship.[114] But even then, self-declaration will only amount to a partial solution to the embodied problems faced by trans and other gender diverse people. How prominently they should feature within trans studies and activism becomes an important question.

It is my intention that this book can be read as a collection of distinct essays, or as a more conventional research project (building from one chapter to the next). What all the chapters share is a focus on the regulation of trans and other gender diverse people, and specifically on the research that I conducted in Denmark in 2015. While I have acknowledged that there is no such thing as a perfect case study above, I do think that the Danish experience raises numerous issues which ought to be considered more widely by trans people, activists, and scholars who are considering the potential of legal reforms including self-declaration. The wider points that this research allows me to make about regulation and embodiment will also interest researchers including (but not limited to) those interested in trans studies, feminist legal scholarship, and socio-legal studies more broadly.

Before I begin, though, I ought to acknowledge my own social situation as an able-bodied, white, English, middle-class, cis man. I have been fortunate enough to take advantage of numerous privileges in my education and wider life. These life experiences will have inevitably shaped my research into and writing of this book. On the occasions where it has appeared possible to account for the effect of my own background on my research, I have sought to. On others, the effect of my demographics may have been more imperceptible, at least to me (which is, of course, how privilege works).[115] In this book, I have tried to do as much as I could to acknowledge and address my privilege, but I accept that there is always more to be done. At no point in this book do I intend to 'speak for' or 'on behalf of' trans people. (In my limited experience, trans people are more than capable of speaking for, and representing, themselves.) Yet I accept that my assumption that I have something to offer in researching this area is a reflection of my own privileged upbringing. Still, I hope that the book will be seen as a useful interjection, as the fight for gender recognition law reforms – and the discussion of their benefits and limitations – continues.

Bibliography

Ammaturo FR, 'Intersexuality and the "Right to Bodily Integrity": Critical Reflections on Female Genital Cutting, Circumcision, and Intersex "Normalizing Surgeries" in Europe' (2016) 25(5) Social & Legal Studies 591

114 C Dietz and R Pearce, 'Depathologising Gender: Vulnerability in Trans Health Law' in C Dietz, M Travis, and M Thomson (eds), *A Jurisprudence of the Body* (Palgrave Macmillan 2020) 189.

115 MS Kimmel, 'Introduction: Toward a Sociology of the Superordinate' in MS Kimmel and AL Ferber (eds), *Privilege: A Reader* (4th edn, Routledge 2018).

Amnesty International, 'The State Decides Who I Am: Lack of Legal Gender Recognition for Transgender People in Europe' (4 February 2014) <https://www.amnesty.org/en/documents/EUR01/001/2014/en> accessed 8 April 2015

——— 'World Must Follow Denmark's Example after Landmark Transgender Law' (12 June 2014) <https://www.amnesty.org/en/latest/news/2014/06/denmark-transgender-law> accessed 25 September 2016

Bryman A, *Social Research Methods* (4th edn, OUP 2012)

Butler J, *Gender Trouble: Feminism and the Subversion of Identity* (Routledge 2008)

——— *Bodies that Matter: On the Discursive Limits of 'Sex'* (Routledge 2011)

Cannoot P, 'The Pathologisation of Trans* Persons in the ECtHR's Case Law on Legal Gender Recognition' (2019) 37(1) Netherlands Quarterly of Human Rights 14

Castro-Peraza ME, García-Acosta JM, Delgado N, Perdomo-Hernández AM, Sosa-Alvarez MI, Llabrés-Solé R, and Lorenzo-Rocha ND, 'Gender Identity: The Human Right of Depathologization' (2019) 16 International Journal of Environmental Research and Public Health 978

Cowan D, Hunter C, and Pawson H, 'Jurisdiction and Scale: Rent Arrears, Social Housing, and Human Rights' (2012) 39(2) Journal of Law and Society 269

Crawford A, 'Temporality in Restorative Justice: On Time, Timing and Time-Consciousness' (2015) 19(4) Theoretical Criminology 1

Danish Health and Medicines Authority, 'Behandling af Transseksuelle' (23 November 2012) <https://sundhedsstyrelsen.dk/da/nyheder/2012/behandling-af-transseksuelle> accessed 30 November 2015

Davy Z, 'Transsexual Recognition: Embodiment, Bodily Aesthetics and the Medicolegal System' (PhD thesis, University of Leeds 2008)

——— *Recognizing Transsexuals: Personal, Political and Medicolegal Embodiment* (Ashgate 2011)

Dietz C, 'Governing Legal Embodiment: On the Limits of Self-Declaration' (2018) 26(2) Feminist Legal Studies 185

——— 'Jurisdiction in Trans Health' (2020) 47(1) Journal of Law and Society 60

——— and Pearce R, 'Depathologising Gender: Vulnerability in Trans Health Law' in Dietz C, Travis M, and Thomson M (eds), *A Jurisprudence of the Body* (Palgrave Macmillan 2020)

Dorsett S and McVeigh S, *Jurisdiction* (Routledge 2012)

Dunne P, 'Ten Years of Gender Recognition in the United Kingdom: Still a 'Model for Reform'?' [2015] Public Law 530

——— 'Rethinking Legal Gender Recognition: Recent Reforms in Argentina, Denmark and the Netherlands' (2015) 1 International Family Law 41

——— 'Transgender Sterilisation Requirements in Europe' (2017) 25(4) Medical Law Review 554

Ebbesen AV, 'The Creation of the Central Person Registry in Denmark' in Gram C, Rasmussen P, and Østergaard SD (eds), *History of Nordic Computing 4* (Springer 2015)

Education First, 'The World's Largest Ranking of Countries by English Skills' (2015) <http://www.ef.edu/epi> accessed 2 September 2016

Ewick P and Silbey S, 'Conformity, Contestation, and Resistance: An Account of Legal Consciousness' (1992) 26 New England Law Review 731

Federici S, *Caliban and the Witch* (2nd edn, Autonomedia 2014)

Fredman S, 'Substantive Equality Revisited' (2016) 14(3) International Journal of Constitutional Law 712

Gale N, 'Denmark Leads Europe on Gender Recognition' (*Scottish Trans*, 18 June 2014) <http://www.scottishtrans.org/denmark-leads-europe-on-gender-recognition> accessed 14 November 2014

Garland F and Travis M, 'Making the State Responsible: Intersex Embodiment, Medical Jurisdiction, and State Responsibility' (2020) 47(2) Journal of Law and Society 298

Gonzalez-Salzberg DA, 'An Improved Protection for the (Mentally Ill) Trans Parent: A Queer Reading of *AP, Garçon and Nicot* v *France*' (2018) 81(3) Modern Law Review 526

——— *Sexuality and Transsexuality under the European Convention on Human Rights: A Queer Reading of Human Rights Law* (Hart 2019)

Graugaard C, Eplov LF, Giraldi A, Kristensen E, Munck E, Møhl B, Owens AF, Risør H, and Winther G, 'Denmark' in Francoeur RT and Noonan RJ (eds), *The Continuum Complete International Encyclopaedia of Sexuality* (Continuum 2004)

Halberstam J, *Trans** (University of California Press 2018)

Hammersley M and Atkinson P, *Ethnography: Principles in Practice* (3rd edn, Routledge 2009)

Hines S, *TransForming Gender* (Polity Press 2007)

——— 'Sex Wars and (Trans) Gender Panics: Identity and Body Politics in Contemporary UK Feminism' (2020) 68(4) The Sociological Review Monographs 699

——— *Gender Diversity, Recognition and Citizenship* (Palgrave Macmillan 2013)

——— *Is Gender Fluid?* (Thames & Hudson 2019)

Hobbes T, 'A Dialogue of the Common Law' in Molesworth W (ed), *The English Works of Thomas Hobbes*, vol 6 (Bohn 1839)

ILGA Europe, 'Denmark Becomes the First European Country to Allow Legal Change of Gender without Clinical Diagnosis' (11 June 2014) <http://www.ilga-europe.org/home/news/for_media/media_releases/denmark_becomes_the_first_european_country_to_allow_legal_change_of_gender_without_clinical_diagnosis> accessed 26 November 2014

Kessler SJ and McKenna W, *Gender: An Ethnomethodological Approach* (Wiley 1978)

Kimmel MS, 'Introduction: Toward a Sociology of the Superordinate' in Kimmel MS and Ferber AL (eds), *Privilege: A Reader* (4th edn, Routledge 2018)

LGBT Press Network, 'Denmark Becomes Europe's Leading Country on Legal Gender Recognition' (*GayAsUs.com*, 14 June 2014) <http://gayasus.com/pub/2014/06/14/denmark-becomes-europes-leading-country-legal-gender-recognition/17> accessed 26 November 2014

Madden R, *Being Ethnographic: A Guide to the Theory and Practice of Ethnography* (Sage 2011)

Mant J and Wallbank J, 'The Mysterious Case of Disappearing Family Law and the Shrinking Vulnerable Subject: The Shifting Sands of Family Law's Jurisdiction' (2017) 26(5) Social & Legal Studies 629

McLean C, 'The Growth of the Anti-Transgender Movement in the United Kingdom. The Silent Radicalization of the British Electorate' (2021) 51(6) International Journal of Sociology 473

Ministry of Justice, 'Kommissorium for tværministeriel arbejdsgruppe om udmøntning af regeringsgrundlagets afsnit om kønsskifte' (17 May 2013) <https://panbloggen.files.wordpress.com/2013/05/kc3b8nsskifte-kommissorium-jm.pdf&usg=ALkJrhjLszn-4IJPOaQMon8NdRzCGtYKSA> accessed 10 September 2015

——— 'Rapport fra arbejdsgruppen om juridisk kønsskifte' (27 February 2014) <http://justitsministeriet.dk/sites/default/files/media/Pressemeddelelser/pdf/2014/Rapport%20om%20juridisk%20k%C3%B8nsskifte.pdf> accessed 21 July 2016

Munkholm NV, 'Legal Status of Transsexual and Transgender Persons in Denmark' in Scherpe JM (ed), *The Legal Status of Transsexual and Transgender Persons* (Intersentia 2015)

Pasternak S, 'Jurisdiction and Settler Colonialism: Where Do Laws Meet?' (2014) 29(2) Canadian Journal of Law and Society 145

Patients' Ombudsman, 'Kritik for behandling – speciallæge i plastikkirurgi Jens Pilegaard Bjarnesen' (1 November 2012) <https://www.patientombuddet.dk/Afgoerelser_og_domme/Afgoerelser_fra_Sundhedsvaesenets_Disciplinaernaevn/Afgoerelser_med_navn/2012/1294528.aspx> accessed 16 September 2015

Pearce R, *Understanding Trans Health: Discourse, Power and Possibility* (Policy Press 2018)

Prime Minister's Office, 'Et Danmark, Der Står Sammen' (October 2011) <http://www.stm.dk/publikationer/Et_Danmark_der_staar_sammen_11/Regeringsgrundlag_okt_2011.pdf> accessed 20 August 2015

Raun T, 'The 'Caspian Case' and Its Aftermath: Transgender People's Use of Facebook to Engage Discriminatory Mainstream News Coverage in Denmark' in Björklund J and Lindqvist U (eds), *New Dimensions of Diversity in Nordic Culture and Society* (Cambridge Scholars Publishing 2016)

Rucovsky MDM, 'The Travesti Critique of the Gender Identity Law in Argentina' (2019) 6(2) TSQ: Transgender Studies Quarterly 223

Sanger T, *Trans People's Partnerships: Towards an Ethics of Intimacy* (Palgrave Macmillan 2010)

Sharpe A, *Transgender Jurisprudence: Dysphoric Bodies of Law* (Cavendish 2002)

——— *Foucault's Monsters and the Challenge of Law* (Routledge 2010)

——— *Sexual Intimacy and Gender Identity 'Fraud': Reframing the Legal and Ethical Debate* (Routledge 2018)

——— 'Will Gender Self-Declaration Undermine Women's Rights and Lead to an Increase in Harms?' (2020) 83(3) Modern Law Review 539

Statistics Denmark, 'Population by Island and Date' <http://www.statbank.dk/BEF4> accessed 13 December 2016

Svendsen MN, Navne LE, Gjødsbøl IM, and Dam MS, 'A Life Worth Living: Temporality, Care, and Personhood in the Danish Welfare State' (2018) 45(1) American Ethnologist 20

TGEU, 'Denmark Goes Argentina! Denmark Passes Best Legal Gender Recognition Law in Europe' (11 June 2014) <http://tgeu.org/denmark-goes-argentina> accessed 8 February 2016

——— 'Historic Danish Gender Recognition Law Comes into Force' (1 September 2014) <http://www.tgeu.org/TGEU_statement_Historic_Danish_Gender_Recognition_Law_comes_into_Force> accessed 26 November 2014

Valverde M, 'Jurisdiction and Scale: Legal 'Technicalities' as Resources for Theory' (2009) 18 Social & Legal Studies 139

——— *Chronotopes of Law: Jurisdiction, Scale and Governance* (Routledge 2015)

Vincent B, *Non-Binary Genders: Navigating Communities, Identities, Healthcare* (Policy Press 2020)

Whittle S, *Respect and Equality: Transsexual and Transgender Rights* (Cavendish 2002)

Chapter 2

Theorising legal embodiment

Introduction

In this chapter I locate trans people within their institutional and interpersonal relations, offering a conceptualisation of legal embodiment as it is socially experienced. Previous approaches, including those formulated around human rights and anti-discrimination perspectives,[1] have tended to centre an individualised legal subject whose concerns are abstracted from the everyday issues trans people face. This chapter presents a grounded alternative, which moves beyond concerns with rights and discrimination. It explores subjective, intersubjective, material, symbolic, and institutional dimensions of legal embodiment. In locating trans people within institutional as well as interpersonal relations, I draw upon citizenship,[2] intimate relations,[3] care ethics,[4] and phenomenological perspectives;[5] the main alternatives to legalistic theoretical frameworks in the sociology and trans studies literature. Bringing trans legal studies and sociological scholarship together, and considering them alongside feminist theory and feminist legal scholarship, I construct a theory of legal embodiment upon which to base an assessment of the impact of gender recognition laws such as the Danish reforms of 2014.

This chapter takes the UK Gender Recognition Act (GRA) 2004 as a point of departure. This constituted one of the first legislative instruments to crystallise a gender recognition law reform project, as before 2004 few states sought to enable access to gender recognition without numerous pre-requisites (often including sterilisation).[6] Drawing upon critiques of the GRA 2004, I identify

1 S Whittle, *Respect and Equality: Transsexual and Transgender Rights* (Cavendish 2002); A Sharpe, *Transgender Jurisprudence: Dysphoric Bodies of Law* (Cavendish 2002); A Sharpe, *Foucault's Monsters and the Challenge of Law* (Routledge 2010); DA Gonzalez-Salzberg, *Sexuality and Transsexuality under the European Convention on Human Rights: A Queer Reading of Human Rights Law* (Hart 2019).
2 S Hines, *Gender Diversity, Recognition and Citizenship* (Palgrave Macmillan 2013).
3 T Sanger, *Trans People's Partnerships: Towards an Ethics of Intimacy* (Palgrave Macmillan 2010).
4 S Hines, *TransForming Gender* (Polity Press 2007).
5 Z Davy, *Recognizing Transsexuals: Personal, Political and Medicolegal Embodiment* (Ashgate 2011).
6 A Sharpe, *Transgender Jurisprudence* (n 1).

DOI: 10.4324/9780429288203-2

the aspects of legal embodiment which could help determine the success or failure of a gender recognition law. In the subsequent chapters of this book, I use this to shape my analysis of the specific law reform project designed and implemented in Denmark in 2014, one decade on. To date, no scholar has synchronised existing critiques of the GRA 2004 to develop a conceptual framework capable of interrogating contemporary reforms. This is in spite of the fact that the GRA 2004 has been criticised for, inter alia: reproducing binary understandings of gender as male or female;[7] authorising psychiatric discourses that distinguish between an internally gendered mind and an externally sexed body;[8] and requiring gender and sexuality to align if applicants for gender recognition are to retain recognition of their intimate relationships.[9] The effect of these provisions is to authorise particular ways of 'passing' as trans,[10] to the detriment of those who are unable or unwilling to meet the normative standards developed by medical and legal authorities.

Each of the above critiques is worthy of attention in its own right. But I consider them as collectively indicating a failure of the GRA 2004 to come to terms with what Sharon Cowan calls the 'problem of the body'.[11] Trans people are embodied, and this experience of embodiment will be shaped by their sex/gender identity. But rather than addressing this, the GRA 2004 seeks to reproduce binary dualisms between mind and body, gender and sex, male and female, hetero- and homosexuality. In this chapter, I enhance Cowan's critique, supplementing it with feminist theories of embodiment which draw different spheres of experience together into one category of analysis. The idea of being 'born in the wrong body' is highlighted in many critiques of the GRA 2004, drawing attention to how trans narratives are developed in relation to experiences of physicality. But such critiques have only rarely been theorised in relation to the critiques of mind/body dualism that have been developed in feminist theories of embodiment more generally.[12] In this chapter, I

7 R Sandland, 'Running to Stand Still' (2009) 18 Social & Legal Studies 253, 254.

8 S Cowan, 'Looking Back (To)wards the Body: Medicalization and the GRA' (2009) 18 Social & Legal Studies 247.

9 B Tirohl and IR Bowers, 'Opposite Sex – A Discussion of Rights Under the Gender Recognition Act' (2006) 15(1) Journal of Gender Studies 83. Though this requirement has been voided by the Marriage (Same Sex Couples) Act 2013, schedule 5 still requires trans people to include 'a statutory declaration by the applicant's spouse that the spouse consents to the marriage continuing after the issue of a full gender recognition certificate' when applying for gender recognition; F Renz, 'Consenting to Gender? Trans Spouses after Same-Sex Marriage', in N Barker and D Monk (eds), *From Civil Partnership to Same-Sex Marriage: Interdisciplinary Reflections* (Routledge 2015).

10 'Passing' is a term used to describe when a trans person is assumed not to be trans. On controversy around its use, see K Roen, '"Either/Or" and "Both/Neither"': Discursive Tensions in Transgender Politics' (2002) 27(2) Signs 501.

11 S Cowan (n 8) 247.

12 C Dietz, 'Governing Legal Embodiment: On the Limits of Self-Declaration' (2018) 26(2) Feminist Legal Studies 185.

consider different embodiment literatures emerging from feminist theory and feminist legal studies. After drawing on their insights, I address their limitations – including the tendency to underplay the extent to which institutions affect embodiment. This is particularly problematic for my present purpose of defining a specifically legal embodiment. In response, I argue for greater emphasis to be placed upon the institutional dimension of embodiment in the legal regulation of gender.

To emphasise the institutional dimension of embodiment, I draw upon Mariana Valverde's work on jurisdiction. Jurisdictional analysis offers clear insight into how institutional authorities shape embodied experience. By bringing together embodiment and jurisdiction literatures, I highlight how jurisdiction can be mobilised to investigate the interplay between rules and bodies, legality, and embodiment. In the process of doing so, the chapter develops a theory of legal embodiment which moves beyond concerns with rights and discrimination in legal studies. This argument is premised upon an understanding of legal embodiment which encompasses identity and recognition, subjectivity, and regulation. It also reaffirms my definition of legal embodiment as the process through which ontology (what I am) meets epistemology (how I identify and am identified) in the construction of the legal subject.[13]

In the first part of this chapter, I review the ways in which feminist scholars have sought to encapsulate 'the problem of the body'. To structure this review, I adopt a taxonomy developed by Marie Fox and Thérèse Murphy; working through conceptions of 'the body', and 'bodies', before settling upon 'embodiment' as the analytical lens best suited to the critical interrogation of self-declaration. In the second part of the chapter, I review the key dimensions of legal embodiment raised in feminist legal scholarship, before suggesting that this should be reoriented somewhat to consider the ways in which institutional regulations saturate and produce certain modes of embodiment by regulating forms of embodied action and reaction. I conclude by suggesting that these institutional factors could be illuminated by considering how the regulation of gendered embodiment is structured through jurisdiction. In identifying this point of focus, and what it can offer to putative feminist governance studies, I lay the theoretical ground for the rest of the book.

The problem of 'the body'

The body

'The body' has long constituted 'a conceptual blind spot' for mainstream and feminist philosophy, positioned in opposition to 'the mind'.[14] Where body

13 ibid.
14 E Grosz, *Volatile Bodies: Toward a Corporeal Feminism* (Indiana University Press 1994) 3.

and mind are construed as separate entities, theorists and legislators alike have failed to acknowledge the two as co-constitutive. Furthermore, dualistic conceptions of mind and body have rarely arisen in isolation from other dualisms. Just as mind/body dualism absorbs other binaries (including sex/gender, male/female, hetero-/homosexual) in the GRA 2004, Elizabeth Grosz describes a dualistic conception of mind and body being mapped onto other dichotomies in the history of philosophy: 'thought and extension, reason and passion, psychology and biology'.[15] What's more, such divisions have not been drawn between equals. Grosz sees this as an issue with binary thought:

> The problem of dichotomous thought is not the dominance of the pair …; rather, it is the *one* which makes it problematic, the fact that the one can allow itself no independent, autonomous other. All otherness is cast in the mould of sameness, with the primary term acting as the only autonomous or pseudo-autonomous term. The one allows no twos, threes, fours. It cannot tolerate any *other.* The one, in order to be a one, must draw a barrier or boundary around itself, in which case it is necessarily implicated in the establishment of a binary – inside/outside, presence/absence.[16]

Though she traces the practice of separating mind and body back to the conception of philosophy as a self-contained discipline in ancient Greece, Grosz notes that it was René Descartes – with whom the mind/body split is more famously associated – who first dichotomised them.[17] This led to contents of the mind becoming privileged over and above the concerns of the body.

The clearest legacy of such Cartesian thinking can be found in theoretical conceptions which construe the body as a means to an end; as an object, instrument or tool, or a 'vehicle for public expression'.[18] Emily Grabham refers to this as 'a propertied or sovereigntist understanding of embodiment as the subject's ownership and determination of the soma'.[19] Within sovereigntist conceptions, the body does little more than put into effect the mind's will and bidding. Such understandings are identified with what Catriona Mackenzie calls the 'maximal choice' conception of autonomy; popularly represented in political slogans such as 'Whose body is it, anyway?' and 'My body, my property'.[20] Maximal choice conceptions of autonomy respond to instances in which marginalised

15 ibid.
16 ibid. 211 fn 1.
17 ibid. 6.
18 ibid. 8–9.
19 E Grabham, 'Bodily Integrity and the Surgical Management of Intersex' (2012) 18(2) Body & Society 1, 3.
20 C Mackenzie, 'Conceptions of the Body and Conceptions of Autonomy in Bioethics' in J Scully, L Baldwin-Ragaven, and P Fitzpatrick (eds), *Feminist Bioethics: At the Center, On the Margins* (Johns Hopkins University Press 2010) 73.

subjects are reduced to their bare physicality, with a view to increasing their capability to choose how 'their' body is intervened upon.

A propertied or sovereigntist understanding of the body crops up relatively frequently within law and legal theory. As Ngaire Naffine and Rosemary Owens note,[21] legal scholarship and practice has focused on the content of minds, first and foremost, and only later to the actions of bodies.[22] Yet law also asserts a claim to objectivity, distancing itself from bodily concerns including those relating to intersections of age, class, disability, ethnicity, gender, and sexuality.[23] Hence law has been criticised both for seeking, and failing, to divorce itself from the body. This paradox has been said to constitute the 'founding concern' of feminist legal scholarship – which sought to challenge law for facilitating discrimination against women and thus 'falling short in meeting its own claims about gender-neutrality and objectivity'.[24] The response from early feminist legal scholarship was to argue that women – and women's values – ought to be taken into account more systematically within legal analysis; or, 'adding women and stirring'.[25] Women were understood to be essentially different from men; for biological,[26] or psycho-social,[27] reasons. This motivated a desire to incorporate repressed aspects of 'women's culture' into legal structures (perhaps best represented by scholarship which sought to re-frame legal policy to fit an 'ethic of care').[28] It also formed the basis of attempts to protect women-only spaces; and even to oppose trans rights, in some instances.

Such approaches have had a 'profound influence on feminist thinking'.[29] Yet Fox and Murphy understand them as constituting an attempt to *insert the body* into legal studies – to contest the ways in which it had hitherto been misrepresented, excluded, or simply omitted.[30] In certain circumstances, such as when assessing the impact of equal pay legislation, this approach seems highly intuitive. But conceptually, any attempt to relocate the emphasis of law – from mind onto body – still works from within the mind/body dichotomy. Evoking Audre Lorde's famous assertion that 'the Master's tools will never dismantle the

21 N Naffine and RJ Owens (eds), *Sexing the Subject of Law* (LBC 1997).
22 N Naffine and RJ Owens, 'Sexing Law' in ibid. 12.
23 M Neave, 'foreword' in N Naffine and RJ Owens (n 21) v.
24 ibid.
25 E Jackson and N Lacey, 'Introducing Feminist Legal Theory' in JE Penner, D Schiff, and R Nobles (eds), *Jurisprudence and Legal Theory: Commentary and Materials* (Butterworths 2002) 781.
26 R West, 'Jurisprudence and Gender' (1988) 55(1) University of Chicago Law Review 1.
27 C Gilligan, *In a Different Voice* (Harvard University Press 1982).
28 ibid.
29 V Munro, *Law and Politics at the Perimeter: Re-Evaluating Key Debates in Feminist Theory* (Hart 2007) 23–24.
30 M Fox and T Murphy, 'The Body, Bodies, Embodiment: Feminist Legal Engagement with Health' in M Davies and VE Munro (eds), *The Ashgate Research Companion to Feminist Legal Theory* (Ashgate 2013) 250.

Master's House',[31] Nicola Lacey warns that any attempt to redistribute privilege from mind onto body within feminist legal studies risks leaving unchallenged 'the priority of the mental over the material' in other fields and disciplines.[32]

Where dualism is understood to be part of the problem in itself, the mind/body split ought to be deconstructed rather than inverted. Attempts to re-appropriate the languages of 'mind' and 'body' risk reducing the former to wistful idealism and the latter to blunt materiality.[33] Fox and Murphy suggest that the central limitation of early feminist legal scholarship on the body was that it concerned itself with questions of *difference* rather than *differences*. *The* body that early feminist legal scholars sought to insert into law was a singular body; assuming unity, boundedness, and coherency. It was also a female body, with reproductive capacity. While debates over the political utility of the category 'women' are ongoing,[34] purely deconstructionist perspectives have been criticised for threatening to marginalise women within even feminist legal scholarship.[35] Yet focusing law reform around a conception of *the body* as represented by a reproductive woman would not only exclude most trans people,[36] but also 'cis' (non-trans) women who are infertile, or too old or young to reproduce; non-binary people, and, of course, men.[37] It could also obstruct intersecting issues faced by ethnic minority, disabled, lesbian, and/or working class women.

Deconstructive approaches, such as those employed by Judith Butler, have also been criticised for neglecting material realities,[38] including those faced by trans people.[39] Yet the same charge could be made of scholarship that centres the experiences and concerns of white, able-bodied, straight, and middle-class, mothers. Fox and Murphy describe this as 'feminism without flesh.'[40] Critiquing gender recognition legislation from the perspective of 'the body' would come up against conceptual limitation for similar reasons. Uncritical

31 A Lorde, *Sister Outsider: Essays and Speeches* (Crossing Press 2007) 110.

32 N Lacey, 'On the Subject of Sexing the Subject' in N Naffine and RJ Owens (n 21) 73.

33 ibid.

34 L Gunnarsson, 'A defence of the category "women"' (2011) 12(1) Feminist Theory 23.

35 Jackson and Lacey (n 25) 781.

36 This is apparent in Grosz's own work, where trans embodiment is dismissed as an impossibility; Grosz (n 14) 207; cf R Connell, 'Transsexual Women and Feminist Thought: Toward New Understanding and New Politics' (2012) 37(4) Signs: Journal of Women in Culture and Society 857, 863.

37 Fox and Murphy (n 30) 252.

38 N Fraser, *Justice Interruptus: Rethinking Key concepts of a Post-Socialist Age* (Routledge 1997); cf E Loizidou, 'The Body Figural and Material in the Work of Judith Butler' (2008) 28 Australian Feminist Legal Journal 29.

39 J Prosser, *Second Skins: The Body Narratives of Transsexuality* (Columbia University Press 1998); V Namaste, 'Undoing Theory: The 'Transgender Question' and the Epistemic Violence of Anglo-American Feminist Theory' (2009) 24(3) Hypatia 11; cf G Salamon, *Assuming a Body: Transgender and Rhetorics of Materiality* (Columbia University Press 2010).

40 Fox and Murphy (n 30) 253, citing T Murphy, 'Feminism on Flesh' (1997) 8 Law and Critique 37.

attempts to centre *the body* in legal scholarship could also neglect the question of whether the body even needs to be included – when in many cases it is already there (however implicitly). Michel Foucault's work has evidenced how the construct of the body has been woven into various paradigms of science and law since the birth of the modern state.[41] Certainly, the body is rarely absent from gender recognition legislation. In the GRA 2004, the requirement to declare a trans history before getting married,[42] or the limitation of recognition to those in receipt of a psychiatric diagnosis,[43] evidence the presence of a pathologised trans body that 'acquires' a new gender. By aligning medical and legal understandings of trans phenomena, the GRA 2004 simply adjusts the legal precedent that gender is 'fixed at birth',[44] to render mind and body conceptually distinct. This distinction may allow for subjective change of the former (mind), but the objective determinacy of the latter (body) remains.

Bodies/embodiment

If *the body* does not constitute a strong starting point for law reform projects and the researchers analysing them, then what might? Fox and Murphy describe a more recent shift in the trajectory of feminist legal scholarship towards *bodies*. This has seen a range of bodies – including, but no longer limited to, the reproductive woman's body – brought within the frame of feminist legal scholarship. This shift from the body to bodies has enabled researchers to explore 'not only how different bodies are legally regulated in differing ways, but [also] how the same body is regulated differently at different stages of its life course.'[45] Along with younger, ageing, or otherwise marginalised bodies, bodies that were deemed anomalous and in need of correction, modification, or prohibition came to the fore.[46] It was at this point that feminist legal scholars began to explicitly consider the regulation of trans bodies.[47]

Focusing upon *bodies* signals multiplicity. It sheds connotations of unitary boundedness and coherency that marked consideration of *the body*. Yet it could still underplay the extent to which bodies change over time. Starting with 'bodies' still comes with an implicit association with the objectifying tendencies of biological determinism (and the 'reality' of what bodies 'are' or 'can be'). This risks underestimating the plasticity of our bodies, which are both pliable and resistant – a site of agency and resistance. Linguistic associations with

41 M Foucault, *The Birth of Biopolitics: Lectures at the Collège de France 1978–1979* (M Senellart ed, G Burchell tr, Picador 2008).

42 A Sharpe, 'A Return to the 'Truth' of the Past' (2009) 18 Social & Legal Studies 259.

43 Cowan (n 8) 247.

44 *Corbett v Corbett* [1970] 2 All ER 33 [1971] P 83, 104.

45 Fox and Murphy (n 30) 253.

46 ibid. 255.

47 ibid.

the term 'bodies' also offers only a slight point of distinction from the language of 'the body'. The shift to bodies thus harbours only a partially mitigated risk of reproducing mind/body dualism in comparison with previous feminist legal scholarship on the body.[48]

As they enter the third phase of their taxonomy, Fox and Murphy describe how, after having brought bodies back into view, feminist legal scholarship has sought to move 'beyond bodies'.[49] One strand of contemporary scholarship which they identify as seeking to do so avoids construing the body (or bodies) as an object of analysis by positioning *embodiment* as a category of analysis instead.[50] Foregrounding embodiment mandates 'a broader focus on lived experience and the question of how we inhabit and experience the world through our bodies.'[51] Rather than theorising *about* the body (or bodies) in an incongruously disembodied manner, embodiment requires scholars to theorise *from* an embodied position instead.[52] One advantage is that the distance between the researcher and that which is researched can be reduced – and in some cases even eliminated (in the rise of auto-ethnographical studies of embodiment, for instance)[53] – as embodied concerns are inserted into analytical frameworks.[54] The distance between mind and body can also be limited; if the distinction is even retained once a more dynamic interrelation between subjectivity and physicality is allowed to emerge.

The language of embodiment has been advocated by various scholars as a promising lens through which to challenge mind/body dualism within feminist legal theory and feminist theory more generally. Lacey notes that while 'an adequate linguistic framework has yet to be attained', it is preferable to frame arguments in the language of 'embodied experience' than of the body or bodies – as this better captures 'continuity between the corporeal, the psychic and the emotional.'[55] Grosz admits that within our Western 'intellectual heritage' there is no language which completely avoids mind/body dualism, but suggests an attempt should be made to develop some kind of understanding of '*embodied subjectivity*'.[56] I concur that scholarship conducted through a lens of embodiment is better placed to interrogate how law values and validates certain bodies, as well as embodied forms of action or reaction, as it is contests

48 R Fletcher, M Fox, and J McCandless, 'Legal Embodiment: Analysing the Body of Healthcare Law' (2008) 16 Medical Law Review 321, 335.
49 Fox and Murphy (n 30) 256.
50 Fletcher, Fox, and McCandless (n 48) 321.
51 Fox and Murphy (n 30) 256.
52 SJ Williams and G Bendelow, *The Lived Body: Sociological Themes, Embodied Issues* (Routledge 1998) 3.
53 See PB Preciado, *Testo Junkie: Sex, Drugs, and Biopolitics in the Pharmacopornographic Era* (Feminist Press 2013).
54 I address my own subject position briefly in the next section, and more comprehensively in Chapter 3.
55 Lacey (n 32) 73–74.
56 Grosz (n 14) 21–22.

representations of legal subjectivity 'as universal and disembodied'.[57] In theory, at least, embodiment acknowledges inconsistency and unpredictability, plasticity and difference. It could help researchers move away from, and even work against, mind/body dualism.[58]

To 'start with embodiment' admittedly allows for many different approaches, which vary considerably in practice.[59] And though embodiment issues have arisen in the existing literature on gender recognition, they have mainly been read through other theoretical lenses. This has led to the relationship between the existing socio-legal and sociological research into gender recognition being under-theorised in relation to feminist legal scholarship and wider feminist theory on embodiment. For instance, when Zowie Davy considers the effects of the GRA 2004 in relation to trans people's bodily aesthetics, she does so through a framework built around phenomenology. Phenomenology has had a strong influence on feminist theories of embodiment.[60] Yet Davy does not explore how this relationship has been developed within feminist legal scholarship (despite her interest in the embodied effects of the GRA 2004). Sally Hines, meanwhile, engages with legal scholarship on the GRA 2004 in her research which seeks to assess the law's sociological impact. When issues of embodiment arise in Hines's study, they are not explicitly theorised in relation to the embodiment literature, but alongside care and citizenship literatures instead.[61] Building upon this sociological research, this book demonstrates how feminist legal scholarship on embodiment can be used as a bridge between feminist theories of embodiment and legal critiques of the GRA 2004. This has helped me meet my objective of analysing the socio-legal impact of this legislation and other gender recognition law reforms, including the Danish reforms of 2014.

In what remains of this chapter, I lay out the most important dimensions of embodiment; which must be considered in assessing the embodied impact of a gender recognition law reform project. I do this by taking the feminist legal studies literature as a point of departure, before reading this alongside wider feminist theoretical literature on embodiment and socio-legal critiques of the GRA 2004. Ruth Fletcher, Fox, and Julie McCandless have suggested that the 'four key dimensions' of legal embodiment are subjectivity, intersubjectivity, materiality, and symbolism.[62] This example from the embodiment literature will be supplemented by my suggestion that it ought to be slightly re-orientated to consider institutional, and even jurisdictional, aspects of embodiment more explicitly. To this end, I develop a definition of legal embodiment that

57 Fox and Murphy (n 30) 256.

58 R Fletcher, 'Embodied Practices' (2009) 17 Feminist Legal Studies 315, 316.

59 Fox and Murphy (n 30) 257.

60 Davy (n 5).

61 Hines (n 4); Hines (n 2).

62 Fletcher, Fox, and McCandless (n 48) 321.

will be employed in the rest of this book, before laying down some pointers as to how this will be mobilised in Chapter 3.

Legal embodiment

Subjectivity

Subjectivity addresses the ways in which legal subjects value their bodies.[63] In health law, challenges to subjectivity have arisen most frequently when subjects have been forced to undergo, or prohibited from undergoing, certain forms of treatment. In a trans health context, the importance of access to body modification technologies depends upon the subjective value a trans person places on their embodied characteristics – vis-à-vis the possibility of having these modified in one way or another.[64] It can also affect the accessibility of gender recognition laws in nation-states that require sterilisation as a pre-requisite for legal recognition.[65] Traditionally, law has struggled to incorporate subjective value, in part because its drive to claim objectivity. This is particularly apparent in legislation, which seeks to establish and maintain legal norms. Fletcher, Fox, and McCandless suggest that it is 'the impossibility of resolving epistemological questions about how to substantiate claims about subjective value, which partly explains why law remains wedded to objective standards.'[66]

The question of what does or does not constitute a legitimate subjective claim has been addressed by scholars of both embodiment and gender recognition. While subjectivity and experience may be taken as synonyms, distinctions between the two have been contested for decades in the feminist theory. In challenging how experience has been used as 'evidence', Joan Scott warns against taking experience as self-evident or constitutive of 'truth'.[67] If we are to better understand difference as structurally and relationally constituted, we must study the historical processes that produce subjective experiences: 'It is not individuals who *have* experience, but subjects who are constituted *through* experience.'[68] This contains two lessons. The first is that while experience is something clearly worth identifying and exploring, it is not something that can be reified and taken as 'knowledge'.[69] The second is that subjectivity is not commensurate with experience – it exceeds it.

63 ibid. 335–336.

64 ibid. 336.

65 J Honkasalo, 'In the Shadow of Eugenics: Transgender Sterilisation Legislation and the Struggle for Self-Determination' in R Pearce, I Moon, K Gupta, and DL Steinberg (eds), *The Emergence of Trans: Cultures, Politics and Everyday Lives* (Routledge 2020).

66 Fletcher, Fox, and McCandless (n 48) 336.

67 JW Scott, 'The Evidence of Experience' (1991) 17 Critical Inquiry 773.

68 ibid. 779 (emphasis added).

69 ibid. 780.

Subjectivity encompasses various structural and relational processes which affect the subject (and their subjective experience). Like Scott, Grosz is careful not to conflate subjectivity and experience, distinguishing them through engagement with Maurice Merleau-Ponty. Merleau-Ponty's work occupies 'a unique position to provide a depth and sophistication to feminist attempts to harness experience in political evaluation.'[70] This is because while he 'refuses to relegate experience to an ineffable, unquestionable, given category', outside of the influence of other (social, political, historical, cultural, etc.) fields, Merleau-Ponty still values experience 'as something to be explained'.[71] As Grosz explains:

> Merleau-Ponty locates experience midway between mind and body. Not only does he link experience to the privileged locus of consciousness; he also demonstrates that experience is always necessarily embodied, corporeally constituted, located in and as the subject's incarnation.[72]

Subjectivity must therefore be considered from different angles and perspectives, to incorporate structural constraints alongside potential and agency.

Positioning embodied experience between mind and body highlights a tension which has arisen within trans studies between narratives of personal experience and other factors that have shaped subjectivity. Relying too straightforwardly upon reports of trans experience may even lead to it becoming complicit in replicating the mind/body dichotomy. The example of the 'wrong body' narrative, which frames current medical (and some legal) understandings of trans phenomena, is worthy of consideration here. Cowan notes:

> Feeling that one's mind and body do not match, that one is in the 'wrong body' is not an uncommon way for transsexual people, or for those psychiatrists and other medial [*sic*] professionals who police the transgender boundaries, to understand and speak about the experience of what it means to be transsexual.[73]

But bringing trans people's experiences of embodiment into this equation complicates any straightforward attempt to develop a non-dualistic conception of embodiment. If trans people report experiencing their mind and body as in conflict, and their experience is taken as indisputable, this could reproduce mind/body dualism. This demands a return to the first lesson of Scott's intervention. Experience cannot be taken as self-evident or straightforward, but

70 Grosz (n 14) 94.
71 ibid. 94–95.
72 ibid. 95.
73 Cowan (n 8) 247.

instead – like all categories of analysis – ought to be understood as 'contextual, contested, and contingent';[74] and 'always therefore political.'[75]

Developing new conceptions of embodiment requires a careful and politically-sensitive contextualisation of experience. Yet the politics around analysing experience, and specifically trans experience, are by no means uncontroversial. Traumatic personal experiences have been used to justify positions both for and against the self-declaration of gender status in the UK and the US, in a way which has tended to obscure more structural dynamics.[76] The question of how to conduct analysis of trans phenomena with 'respectful curiosity' has been discussed at length.[77] The need to acknowledge 'the embodied experience of the speaking subject' is considered a normative imperative,[78] particularly when that research is being conducted by a researcher who, like myself, is a cis man.[79] Without this, Tobias Raun suggests, the researcher risks neglecting

> an analysis of the individual renegotiation of self and body, or why one of the tropes is used (maybe strategically) or feels right, and not the other. To explore what function these different narratives serve in these people's life-projects would not only be analytically interesting, but also allow for the individual story 'to breathe.'[80]

Henry Rubin suggests researchers 'should be wary of simple attempts to dismiss all experience as false consciousness'.[81] A 'respectful' and politically-informed analysis of experience ought to consider how such subjectivities interrelate with, and are shaped by, structures and relations instead.[82]

Medical regulations feature prominently within the structures which shape experiences of trans embodiment. Cowan cites Hines's empirical research as indicative of the extent to which the 'wrong body narrative' is complicated by the power dynamics in trans people's relationships with medical gatekeepers to

74 Scott (n 67) 796.

75 ibid. 797.

76 A Phipps, 'Whose Personal Is More Political? Experience in Contemporary Feminist Politics' (2016) 17(3) Feminist Theory 303.

77 T Raun, 'Trans as Contested Intelligibility: Interrogating how to Conduct Trans Analysis with Respectful Curiosity' [2014] (1) Lambda Nordica 13.

78 S Stryker, '(De)Subjugated Knowledges: An Introduction to Transgender Studies' in S Stryker and S Whittle (eds), *The Transgender Studies Reader* (Routledge 2006) 12.

79 This is not so much because cis researchers have no insight into trans experience, but because deconstructing trans identities without identifying as trans can involve an element of 'othering' which may leave the researcher's own biases unexamined; Raun (n 77) 18–19.

80 ibid. 18.

81 ibid. 19, citing H Rubin, *Self-Made Men: Identity and Embodiment Among Transsexual Men* (Vanderbilt University Press 2003) 12.

82 Phipps (n 76).

hormones and surgery.[83] As her interviewees portrayed keen awareness of the medical notions underpinning access to body modification, Hines found that the 'wrong body' narrative associated with gender dysphoria was not a straightforwardly personal emotion but given at least partial meaning by social and political factors.[84] This finding has subsequently been supplemented by Davy, whose research suggests that while trans people do exhibit agency in their pragmatic responses to medical discourses, this agency is notably 'reflexive'.[85] In demonstrating an understanding of the conditions and requirements that would affect their access to body modification technologies or legal gender recognition, participants in Davy's study acknowledged that their biographies would often require manipulation if they were to secure practical benefits.[86] Situating trans embodiment between the extremes of voluntariness and internal fixity, Davy describes her participants' agency and desire as 'imaginatively adapted through intersubjective validation by others and the social contexts in which people find themselves.'[87]

Intersubjectivity

The importance of structural influences upon subjectivity, and validation through relation, is apparent in Fletcher, Fox, and McCandless's second dimension of embodiment. Here, embodiment is valued for facilitating connection with other people and living entities; 'it has intersubjective or relational value.'[88] This focus on intersubjectivity qualifies without opposing previous consideration of subjectivity. By recognising that various kinds of bodily interventions require the help of others,[89] relationality challenges the individualisation of trans embodiment inherent in the 'wrong body' narrative that medicine itself promulgates, as Cowan has noted:

> Treating the transsexual person as a medical subject, whose mind requires psychiatric intervention and whose body should if possible be surgically adjusted to reflect the deep-rooted internal sense of self, avoids the more pressing issue of the socio-political construction of the sexual self.[90]

83 Cowan (n 8) 248, citing S Hines, '(Trans)forming Gender: Social Change and Transgender Citizenship' (2007) 12(1) Sociological Research Online.

84 ibid.

85 Z Davy, 'Transsexual Agents: Negotiating Authenticity and Embodiment within the UK's Medicolegal System', in S Hines and T Sanger (eds), *Transgender Identities: Towards a Social Analysis of Gender Diversity* (Routledge 2010) 123.

86 ibid. 107, 123.

87 Davy (n 5) 170.

88 Fletcher, Fox, and McCandless (n 48) 337.

89 ibid.

90 Cowan (n 8) 248.

Stressing the importance of intersubjectivity situates medicine *within* the (relational) practice of embodiment. It locates trans people in relation to medical discourse and practice.

In an early predecessor to embodiment and affect theory, Elspeth Probyn addresses relationality as an important starting point for feminist theorising. Though Probyn insists that gender 'must be represented as processes that proceed through experience',[91] she also stresses that this conception of experience cannot stand alone. Instead, it is important to understand experience as constituted by ontologically informed accounts of existence *and* their epistemological limitations. Rejecting any opposition between ontology and epistemology, Probyn sees the self 'as a theoretical manoeuvring, not as a unifying principle',[92] which must be understood as a mode of holding ontological and epistemological accounts of experience together.[93]

In her study of how the GRA 2004 has been experienced by trans subjects, Hines explores this tension between epistemological and ontological experience.[94] She addresses the positives of legal recognition, noting that a majority of her participants reported feelings of social acceptance after having been awarded with a gender recognition certificate.[95] Yet this positivity is tempered by a scepticism which emerged when participants were asked to reflect on what Hines calls the 'cause and effect' model of legal reformism; which expects cultural understandings and practices to shift in response to, and in direct accordance with, official changes in law and policy.[96] Most of Hines's participants suggest that 'they were not so naive to think that the law would create total social harmony.'[97] Hines's methodological decision to employ qualitative interviews thus enabled her to probe *how* participants responded when asked to reflect on the actual benefits of legal recognition.

After asking a more general question as to why participants saw the GRA 2004 as important, Hines went on to ask why that interviewee had themselves sought recognition.[98] Most articulated strategic rather than symbolic reasons.[99] This prompted Hines's conclusion that while the promotion of equality and diversity registered as a benefit of recognition for trans people on an abstract level, applicants focused more pragmatically on the practical legal benefits of the GRA 2004 on a more grounded, affective, level.[100] In a manner which

91 E Probyn, *Sexing the self: gendered positions in cultural studies* (Routledge 1993) 3.
92 ibid. 106.
93 ibid. 4.
94 Hines (n 2).
95 ibid. 22.
96 ibid. 97.
97 ibid. 23.
98 ibid. 56.
99 ibid.
100 ibid.

concurs with Davy's characterisation of the process of engagement with legal and medical authorities as a 'negotiation',[101] Hines construes her respondents as well-informed and capable of demonstrating 'reflexive awareness of legal restraints'.[102] One participant who rejected binary gender classification on a personal level applied for and acquired official recognition nonetheless.[103] Explaining this apparent contradiction, the interviewee explained that while she would not have ruled out 'elements of masculinity' on a personal level, the fact that she 'identifies more as female than male' enabled her to present a more coherent account which separates official classification from her otherwise 'gendered 'moods''.[104] Hines describes other participants distancing their subjective gender identity from that which is recorded on official documents. This suggests that trans people do find themselves 'checking' official epistemological classification with ontological accounts of gender as subjectively experienced.[105]

Hemmings agrees that researchers should avoid prioritising either ontology or epistemology lest this result in 'an over-individualising account of subjectivity, or a determinist account of the social world and the modes through which it may be transformed'.[106] The two philosophical lenses should be used *with* and *against* each other if a theory is to be elaborated in which social experiences are central.[107] On an ontological level, experience is instrumental in identifying the disjuncture that can appear between material and discursive aspects of the social. On an epistemological level, experience draws forth an analysis of the material-discursive relations formed between that which is lived and that which is articulated.[108] Meanwhile, ontological moments of recognition are not left as self-evidently constitutive of knowledge, but are 'checked' by what Probyn calls 'the epistemological insistence precisely on theoretical exigency and social conjecture from and for which the self is spoken'.[109]

Materiality

In the context of legal embodiment, materiality refers to the physical and tactile world.[110] The 'material value' of embodiment is defined as 'the particular

101 Davy (n 85) 125.
102 Hines (n 2) 56.
103 ibid.
104 ibid.
105 Hines (n 2) 57.
106 C Hemmings, 'Affective Solidarity: Feminist Reflexivity and Political Transformation' (2012) 13(2) Feminist Theory 147, 149.
107 E Probyn (n 91) 21 (emphasis added).
108 ibid. 22.
109 ibid. 30–31.
110 This is not to be confused with, for example, the Marxist practice of historical materialism; see P Anderson, *In the Tracks of Historical Materialism: The Wellek Library Lectures* (Verso 1983).

characteristics of objects whose value derives from their particularity and capacity to be developed.'[111] This dynamic definition of materiality allows it to sit alongside, without opposing, (inter)subjective dimensions of embodiment. The key here is avoiding the temptation to use materiality as a justification for re-asserting the need to return to a reductive conception of biology.[112] Instead, it is important to emphasise materiality as it is socially experienced – i.e. (inter)subjectively. Insisting on the interdependency of materiality and sociality allows the embodiment literature to challenge mind/body dualism, rather than merely asserting the importance of the body. Chris Beasley and Carol Bacchi argue that just as the mind cannot be considered separate from the body, neither can the self that emerges thereafter: '"we" do not "control" our bodies, [...] "we" are not separable from our bodies. Indeed *we are our bodies*.'[113]

Rather than considering this material perspective in isolation, Beasley and Bacchi immediately politicise the material body. They admit that the association with bodily material should be considered a resource rather than a limitation, but also concur with care ethics that 'sociality *is* embodied'.[114] They construe 'embodied interconnection' as 'the pre-existing condition of human life and therefore of sociality.'[115] Beasley and Bacchi thus look forward – stressing that what is done with this 'thin' social starting point will always be political.[116] In response to the critique of frameworks based around 'the body', they argue not for *any* body to be brought into citizenship theory, but for a 'grounded' notion of the body as both plural (bodies) and lodged within its material and social particularities (embodiment).[117] Bodies that have been 'conventionally regarded as mired in biology, marginal or 'lacking'',[118] appear well-suited to being made part of citizenship's participating subject.[119] To facilitate their inclusion, Beasley and Bacchi posit a metaphor of 'social flesh' which highlights 'embodied interdependence', and 'mutual reliance'.[120] This

111 Fletcher, Fox, and McCandless (n 48) 338.
112 C Beasley and C Bacchi, 'Making Politics Fleshy: The Ethic of Social Flesh' in A Bletsas and C Beasley (eds), *Engaging with Carol Bacchi: Strategic Interventions and Exchanges* (University of Adelaide Press 2012) 103. This does not dismiss the value of new materialist approaches to biology in, for example, feminist science and technology studies; see L Skewes and SW Adrian, Interview with N Lykke, 'Epistemology, Activism and Entanglement – Rethinking Knowledge Production' (2018) 27(1) Women, Gender & Research 15, 22.
113 C Beasley and C Bacchi, 'Citizen Bodies: Embodying Citizens – A Feminist Analysis' (2000) 2(3) International Feminist Journal of Politics 337, 344 (emphasis added).
114 C Beasley and C Bacchi, 'Envisaging a New Politics for an Ethical Future: Beyond Trust, Care and Generosity – Towards an Ethic of "Social Flesh"' (2007) 8(3) Feminist Theory 279, 287.
115 Beasley and Bacchi (n 112) 107.
116 ibid.
117 Beasley and Bacchi (n 113) 349.
118 ibid. 350.
119 ibid. 349.
120 Beasley and Bacchi (n 114) 280.

could capture the (inter)subjectivity and materiality of embodiment without foreclosing transformative political possibilities, as, they argue:

> Insistence upon this shared reliance underpins a profoundly levelling perspective, a radical politics, challenging the inadequacy of meliorist reforms that tinker at the edges of inequality.[121]

This vision is both ontological and utopian; it is 'both about "what *is*" and "what *might be*"'.[122] Social flesh constitutes 'a strategic political intervention' which challenges normative understandings of the body in society,[123] and a piece of utopian imagery which opens up a realm of political possibilities. It accords with Fox and Michael Thomson's understanding that bodies are both

> 'a constitutive part of who we are', and who we may become. It [an embodiment perspective] accommodates more fluid visions of bodily integrity which, far from being static, accommodate the mutability and plasticity of bodies.[124]

In highlighting plasticity, Fox and Thomson place an important caveat on attempts to understand the importance of embodied materiality. Like Beasley and Bacchi, they are wary that structuralist and materialist attempts to lodge bodies within their material and social particularities have often been misunderstood or co-opted to stress biological determinism or fixity. The examples of trans and intersex people, excluded from citizenship as their bodies are somehow 'too' material to fit within legislative categories,[125] warn against biological determinism. In contrast, social flesh's mutable and fluid conception of embodiment appears well-suited to going 'beyond bodies'.[126]

Drucilla Cornell's work on personhood chimes with a critical conception of embodiment which reflects (inter)subjective materiality. Cornell illustrates the importance of dynamism by tracing the etymology of the word 'person' back to the Latin *persona* (which literally means 'a shining-through').[127] Drawing upon this tradition, Cornell defines 'a person' as something which 'shines through a mask', despite the fact that the concept of the 'mask' is often most commonly

121 ibid. 280.
122 Beasley and Bacchi (n 112) 107.
123 ibid. 103.
124 M Fox and M Thomson, 'Bodily Integrity, Embodiment, and the Regulation of Parental Choice' (2017) 44(4) Journal of Law and Society 501, 519, citing EF Kittay, 'Forever Small: The Strange Case of Ashley X' (2011) 26(3) Hypatia (2011) 610, 617.
125 E Grabham, 'Citizen Bodies, Intersex Citizenship' (2007) 10(1) Sexualities 29, 43.
126 Fox and Murphy (n 30) 256.
127 D Cornell, *The Imaginary Domain: Abortion, Pornography & Sexual Harassment* (Routledge 1995) 4.

associated with the word 'persona'.[128] Cornell's understanding of personhood – as a process rather than an end state – challenges any attempt to objectify the material body. On these terms, a person can never be an object or *thing* which acts or is acted upon. It constitutes instead 'a possibility, an aspiration which, because it is that, can never be fulfilled once and for all. The person is, in other words, implicated in an endless process of working through personae.'[129] 'We', Cornell concludes, are not 'persons from the beginning', but rather 'creatures whose equal worth is postulated as personhood.'[130]

Cornell's work fits the phenomenological frameworks discussed above in the context of trans embodiment. By theorising the trans body through a framework based on bodily aesthetics rather than gender identity, Davy situates the trans body 'sociohistorically'; avoiding the mistake of understanding trans embodiment as resulting from a purely internal identity.[131] Trans embodiment emerges through a process of negotiation, rather than from an alignment between mind and body. Materiality meets subjectivity meets relationality, in the process of construing a holistic understanding of embodiment. Though both Davy and Hines consider the 'wrong body' narrative as resulting from a limited framing of mind/body dualism, they are careful not to deny the powerful effects that it may have when experienced subjectively. In addition to material, subjective, and intersubjective processes of embodiment, they accept that bodies will inevitably be shaped by cultural understandings. At some stage of the embodiment process, symbolic meanings become culturally embodied.[132]

Symbolism

Embodiment relies upon symbolic value – and bodily perceptions are not only constructed in the material realm, but involve symbolic reflection on, and perception of, the body. Fletcher, Fox, and McCandless argue that symbolic understandings of the body must be recognised, even where they exceed or conflict with other values.[133] Cornell agrees that the symbolic realm – or the 'imaginary domain' – is central to the process of 'shining-through' personae: 'For a person to be able to shine through, she must first be able to imagine herself as whole even if she knows that she can never truly succeed in becoming whole.'[134] This process of 'becoming a person' therefore depends on the 'psychic space of the imagination'.[135]

128 ibid.
129 ibid. 5.
130 ibid. 18.
131 Davy (n 5) 5.
132 Fox and Thomson (n 124).
133 Fletcher, Fox, and McCandless (n 48) 342.
134 Cornell (n 127) 4–5.
135 ibid. 232.

The idea that personhood requires working through different personae is echoed in Davy's decision to consider trans embodiment across three fluid sites; the 'social', 'sexual', and 'phenomenological'.[136] The 'social body' is 'situated in various social spaces from which cultural meanings of other bodies may be incorporated.'[137] The importance of social symbolism is highlighted across the trans studies literature. Hines describes a majority of her participants reporting positive affective responses, including 'a renewed self-esteem and vitality',[138] after being granted legal gender recognition under the GRA 2004. Such affects remain significant, even where they are 'checked' by a scepticism over whether law reform will benefit them in any substantive way.[139] Davy's 'sexual body' presents itself in more intimate situations 'in which people have sex or try to procure sex'.[140] The 'phenomenological body' meanwhile refers to 'a semi-private site in which reflection; ideals, imagination and intentionality are grounded or fantasized.'[141]

In her work on 'imaginary anatomies', Catherine Waldby finds that the morphology of the body – or, in Cornell's terms, the form that the body takes as it works through personae – cannot be dissociated with the 'psychic investment' of the subject who 'lives that body.'[142] Imaginations produce anatomies which are positioned

> in relation both to its love objects, those whom it desires, and to socially generated 'imaginary anatomies', to ideas about bodies which circulate in the culture. The 'imaginary anatomies' of sexual difference can be regarded as indicative of certain historically available forms of desire.[143]

This argument is used to illustrate Waldby's point that the animation of the physical body can only take place in a particular historical and social context.[144] Davy augments this understanding by engaging with Merleau-Ponty's claim that 'subjectivity is only possible through the construction of a coherent body image'.[145] Yet Davy takes care to note that a 'coherent' body image does not necessarily mean a normative one.[146] Coherency will rather be contextually

136 Davy (n 5) 10.
137 ibid. 10.
138 Hines (n 2) 23.
139 ibid. 97.
140 Davy (n 5) 10.
141 ibid. 11.
142 C Waldby, 'Destruction: Boundary Erotics and Refigurations of the Heterosexual Male Body' in E Grosz and E Probyn (eds), *Sexy Bodies: The strange carnalities of feminism* (Routledge 1996) 268.
143 ibid.
144 ibid. 268.
145 Davy (n 5) 66, citing M Merleau-Ponty, *Phenomenology of Perception* (C Smith tr, Routledge Classics 2002).
146 ibid.

dependent. In the 'wrong body' narrative, for example, it is unclear what the coherent opposite of the 'wrong body' would be. Challenging the idea of a 'right body', Davy asks: 'At what point is the body right? Can embodiment ever feel right?'[147]

A defence of the wrong body narrative has been offered in the trans studies literature on the basis that mind/body dualism 'feels right' to those trans people who identify with it.[148] In feminist legal studies, Nicolette Priaulx suggests that symbolic conceptions of bodily integrity, such as 'the right body', or a propertied or sovereigntist understanding of embodiment 'as the subject's ownership and determination of the soma',[149] are not valuable in themselves. Instead their value lies in the opportunities that they may open up for people 'to craft their own sense of identity, to pursue their talents and quite simply, for fostering their 'own' sense of the good life.'[150] While in contemporary legal systems, the wrong body narrative may or may not open up such opportunities for trans people, it is at least possible to conceive of a reformed system which acknowledges (inter)subjective, material, and symbolic aspects of trans embodiment. In such a system, trans people could be granted enough space to develop a personal narrative of embodiment without having to dwell on the question of whether their body is 'right' or 'wrong'. They could be supported to take their body 'more or less for granted (quite irrespective of what one's existing physical state actually is)', instead of being 'conscious of and consumed by' their physicality all the time.[151]

Legal embodiment, in this conception, provides 'a sense of self, a stable platform for pursuing one's plans, [rather] than an actual descriptor of our physicality.'[152] Instead of offering false optimism, seeking to provide a 'stable platform' restricts itself to a minimum standard marked by the understanding that legal protections can only ever be partial and limited – particularly in the absence of wider social and systemic change. Yet it still looks beyond present conditions, offering a mandate for legal intervention in situations where authorities require (or simply leave) subjects to become 'consumed by' their physicality. Fox and Thomson endorse a conception of 'embodied integrity' that encompasses 'not only decisions to modify our bodies but highlight the importance of transcending our bodies.'[153] In the trans context, it is clear that the possibility of forgetting the body, and simply *being* embodied, may or may not be achieved via gender recognition or body modification. But it implies

147 ibid. 53.

148 Prosser (n 39); Raun (n 77) 18.

149 Grabham (n 19) 3.

150 N Priaulx, 'Rethinking Progenitive Conflict: Why Reproductive Autonomy *Matters*' (2008) 16 Medical Law Review 169, 183.

151 ibid. 185.

152 ibid.

153 Fox and Thomson (n 124).

that those regulating access to gender recognition or body modification technologies ought to aim to support decision-making through 'reflection and dialogue';[154] rather than entrenching the current default of pathologisation and sustained psychiatric assessment.

Embodied integrity, as a stable platform, also touches on an important aspect of embodiment not explicitly stressed within Fletcher, Fox, and McCandless's typology (or much of the embodiment literature). This concerns the institutional aspects of embodiment, which address how institutions either support or encumber embodied subjects on their route to 'forgetting' about their bodies. In some scenarios, being granted institutional support may involve being granted authorisation to undertake some form of action, such as body modification. In others, supportive regulation could require institutions to refrain from one course of action or another, by way of acknowledging how certain modes of governance adversely affect embodiment. In the next section, I emphasise the importance of these institutional dimensions, concluding that they should be explicitly inserted into any definition of legal embodiment.

Institutions

As Foucault established, the individual subject is not bound by regulation in the classical liberal sense.[155] Instead he drew upon the Nietzschean insight that the individual is *made free* by regulation to suggest that the subject is more accurately understood as *constituted by* regulation.[156] For, it is impossible to identify the existence of 'an' individual before the concept of 'the individual' was discursively constructed. This draws upon the understanding of power as productive, which Foucault developed through analysing the medicalisation of homosexuality in the 19th century.[157] Prior to this, civil and canon law had understood sodomy as constituting one of a range of forbidden practices. But once medical discourses around 'homosexuality' produced a 'homosexual' subject position, a range of 'scattered sexualities rigidified' and became stuck to *the* homosexual body.[158] The idea that embodiment is always already regulated – in that forms of embodied action or reaction are permitted or prohibited, supported or discouraged, within regulatory frameworks – is a useful premise.[159]

154 J Harrington, 'Time as a Dimension of Medical Law' (2012) 20 Medical Law Review 491, 514, citing AR Maclean, 'Autonomy, Consent and Persuasion' (2006) 13 EJHL 321.

155 As developed, for example, in J Locke, *Second Treatise of Government* (first published 1690, Hackett 1980).

156 M Foucault, *The Will to Knowledge: The History of Sexuality Volume One* (first published 1976, R Hurley tr, Penguin 1998) 48.

157 ibid. 42–43.

158 ibid. 48.

159 Though trans issues were not included in UK statute before 2004, trans people still sought to petition being denied rights (most commonly to marriage); R Reed, 'Transsexuals and European

Yet as I noted in Chapter 1, legal embodiment studies proceed from a slightly different point of departure. Inspired by feminist epistemology, legal embodiment looks beyond the discursive production of bodies to consider the regulatory processes which saturate bodies with meaning.[160]

The emphasis on the discursive realm is limited just enough to account for (inter)subjectivity (how discourse is structured and experienced) and materiality (how subjectivity will be affected by the matter that existed before the body was discursively produced). From this position, legal embodiment draws from the literature on legal pluralism to acknowledge that permission to perform embodied (re)actions must be sought not from some singular authority (such as 'the state'), but from one or more of a range of diverse formal and informal institutions.[161] These include public and private institutions, as well as hybrid organisations which blur the public/private distinction.[162] The trans studies literature indicates that it is in their relations with this level of institution, rather than a singular monolithic state, that trans people have reported experiencing discrimination and exclusion.[163] These include civil registration systems;[164] but also encompass the employment context,[165] the family,[166] and medical clinics.[167]

Institutions draw their influence from the way they mobilise both knowledge and power; characterised as plural and interdependent by the Foucauldian term 'power-knowledges'.[168] In practice, power-knowledges form 'governing assemblages', a term Valverde uses to acknowledge the 'combinations of capabilities and resources that do the work of governing', which, she adds, are often 'only partially planned'.[169] An example would be the dynamic interplay between different structures and agents governing trans embodiment; including psychiatric discourses, medical institutions, legislators, medical professionals, and individual trans people. Each inhibits power or resistance at different

Human Rights Law' in H Graupner and P Tahmindjis (eds), *Sexuality and Human Rights: A Global Overview* (Harrington Park Press 2005) 49, 56.

160 I am grateful to Olga Cielemęcka for helping me formulate this point.

161 R Harding, *Regulating Sexuality: Legal Consciousness in Lesbian and Gay Lives* (Routledge 2011) 29–30.

162 M Valverde, *Chronotopes of Law: Jurisdiction, Scale and Governance* (Routledge 2015) 83.

163 Connell (n 36) 865.

164 For a discussion of civil registration in the UK before the GRA 2004; see Sharpe, *Transgender Jurisprudence* (n 1). For evidence of discrimination thereafter; see Hines (n 2).

165 D Irving, 'Normalized Transgressions: Legitimizing the Transsexual Body as Productive' (2008) 100(1) Radical History Review 38.

166 T Flynn, 'The Ties That (Don't) Bind: Transgender Family Law and the Unmaking of Families' in P Currah, RM Juang, and SP Minter (eds), *Transgender Rights* (University of Minnesota Press 2006).

167 SJ Ellis, L Bailey, and J McNeil, 'Trans People's Experiences of Mental Health and Gender Identity Services: A UK Study' (2015) 19 Journal of Gay & Lesbian Mental Health 4.

168 Foucault (n 156).

169 Valverde (n 162) 51, citing S Sassen, *Territory, Authority, Rights* (Princeton University Press 2006) 5.

points, as all of them are constituted by power and resistance. Attempts to position disputes over gender as involving an 'individual' trans person and 'the' state thus appear over-simplistic.

This institutional dimension of embodiment demands consideration. In her study of the management of bodies that die in suspicious circumstances, Imogen Jones identifies the symbolic role of the body for those who are related to the deceased. She then addresses how this symbolism is affected by the institutional processes instigated once a body is sent for forensic autopsy.[170] One might assume that the shift from recognising the body as a (former) subject to an 'object of crime' would obscure any symbolism around. But Jones notes that this is deliberately preserved by forensic pathologists who switch between dispassion and compassion during their investigations. Irrespective of whether the key dimensions of legal embodiment are conceptualised as subjective, intersubjective, material, and symbolic, or more succinctly, (as they are within the wider feminist theoretical literature) as 'material-discursive',[171] the importance of such relations between subjects and institutions should not be ignored.

While the potential of institutional embodiment has not been realised within socio-legal studies, the relationship between embodiment and institutions has been explored by scholars of critical institutionalism. Frances Cleaver and Jessica de Koning suggest considering how agency is enacted through physical bodies, in relation to material structures.[172] They note that power can be linked to forms of 'dress, demeanour, and behaviour', which tends to be evident in public spaces, and that the bodily enactment of resource allocation has both symbolic and political significance.[173] And the ability to take up institutional space and to affect the distribution of resources 'depends upon physical presence.'[174] This can apply to the context of trans embodiment, as trans people seek recognition, and access to body modification technologies, from legal and clinical institutions. If institutions are formed 'in the interplay between the creative exercise of agency and the often constraining effects of social relationships, environments and the workings of power',[175] it is worth assessing how trans phenomena are shaped by legal and medical gatekeepers.

When we consider institutional power-knowledges such as medicine – which has quasi-legal, if not fully legal, authority in the regulation of embodiment – it would underplay the extent to which medical practices shape trans embodiment

170 I Jones, 'Objects of Crime: Bodies, Embodiment and Forensic Pathology' (2020) 29(5) Social & Legal Studies 679, 680.
171 K Barad, 'Posthumanist Performativity: Toward an Understanding of How Matter Comes to Matter' (2003) 28(3) Signs: Journal of Women in Culture and Society 801, 822–823.
172 F Cleaver and J de Koning, 'Furthering Critical Institutionalism' (2015) 9(1) International Journal of the Commons 1, 11.
173 ibid.
174 ibid.
175 ibid. 12.

to consider medicine as 'just' another discourse. It is not my intention to engage in theoretical debate around whether powerful discourses can be written off as 'merely' cultural, particularly when the effects of the discursive realm can be so far reaching.[176] I merely suggest that it is worth considering the institutional realm as somewhat distinct from the discourses that it is involved in producing, particularly when theorising a specifically *legal* embodiment.

Drawing upon the many insights of the feminist theoretical, feminist legal, and trans studies scholarship detailed above, I have expanded upon my definition of legal embodiment as a process of becoming at the intersection of subjective and intersubjective, material, symbolic, and institutional realms. In developing this definition, I have stressed that while consideration of 'the body' or 'bodies' may neglect subjective, intersubjective, material and symbolic experiences of law, a critical conception of embodiment is capable of holding these dimensions together. In emphasising the institutional realm, I have developed a specifically 'legal' (albeit legally pluralist) framework, which can attend to the regulatory practices governing gendered embodiment. This definition is capable of moving beyond the theoretical constraints of mind/body dualism, developing an alternative (political) conception of embodiment as the process through which people are or are not granted a stable platform upon which to achieve legal subjectivity. It demands consideration of material (physical and relational), discursive (social and symbolic), *and* institutional (financial and practical) elements of legal embodiment.

In insisting upon this institutional dimension, I re-orientate existing literature on legal embodiment. Cornell's argument that legal provisions are required to guarantee 'the equivalent bases for this chance to transform ourselves into the individuated beings we think of as persons' is important.[177] So is her understanding of embodiment as 'an endless process of working through', which requires each legal subject to be granted 'the chance to take on this struggle in his or her own unique way.'[178] The equal worth of each subject must 'be legally guaranteed, at least in part, in the name of the equivalent chance to take on that project.'[179] This stresses the need for law to provide a stable platform for each subject, either directly or through the regulation of institutions. Understanding how embodiment is affected by institutional power-knowledges thus demands analysis of the enactment and enforcement of institutional regulations.

Scholars of sociological institutionalism define institutions 'as formal and informal collections of interrelated norms, rules, and routines, understandings and frames of meaning that define "appropriate" action and roles and acceptable

176 Fraser (n 38).
177 Cornell (n 127) 5.
178 ibid.
179 ibid. 4–5.

behavior of their members.'[180] This reflects a Foucauldian influence, as according to Valverde, what distinguishes Foucault's approach to governance from previous analyses of institutions is that he focuses on their practices: 'Institutions are only coagulations or 'densifications' of certain assemblages of practices which are also found in other institutions'.[181] This promotes a focus upon the actual practices promoted and shaped by institutional power-knowledges, more than on the particularities of the specific institutions themselves. Feminist institutionalism scholars are advised by Meryl Kenny to map the formal architecture and informal practices of the institutions under study, while remaining attentive to the ways in which gender is reformulated in those institutions.[182]

Centring institutional practices gains support from the various literatures upon which I draw in this book. It is endorsed by feminist theory, in the work of those who consider institutional practices in their analyses of embodiment. This approach is also supported by wider feminist research into institutions, including within feminist political science and policy studies.[183] Institutional practices have even been discussed in trans studies by those who wish to move beyond exploring trans as an identity formation.[184] Approaching legal embodiment from an institutional perspective is also advocated by feminist legal scholars engaging with the position of law within the wider regulatory environment. Fox and Murphy implore researchers to reach 'beyond law reform', and even beyond the state, to consider the role of institutions that 'act as, or instead of, the state'.[185] They cite the informal and increasingly participatory decision-making about access to treatment and health as an example.[186] These issues invite further questions about resource allocation – both for treatment and research.[187] Fox and Murphy note that feminist legal scholarship

> faces a future where not just law but also governance must be an object of inquiry. One might even say that the broader field of feminist governance studies rather than FLS [feminist legal studies] is where we ought to be headed.[188]

180 F Mackay, S Monro, G Waylen, 'The Feminist Potential of Sociological Institutionalism' (2009) 5(2) Politics & Gender 253, 255.

181 M Valverde, 'Genealogies of European States: Foucauldian Reflections' (2007) 36(1) Economy and Society 159, 161, citing M Foucault, *Sécurité, territoire, population: cours au Collège de France 1977–1978* (Gallimard 2005) 121.

182 M Kenny, 'A Feminist Institutional Approach' (2014) 10(4) Politics & Gender 679, 679–680.

183 M Sawer, 'Feminist Political Science and Feminist Politics' (2014) 29 Australian Feminist Studies 137; W Pillow, '"Bodies Are Dangerous": Using Feminist Genealogy as Policy Studies Methodology' (2003) 18(2) Journal of Education Policy 145.

184 Connell urges researchers to concentrate instead upon the institutional relations in which trans people (and, specifically, transsexual women) are embedded; (n 36) 863–866.

185 Fox and Murphy (n 30) 259.

186 ibid.

187 ibid.

188 ibid.

Considering how embodiment intersects with institutional power-knowledges fits within this research agenda. On the one hand, in emphasising the role of institutions within processes of embodiment, it centres questions of regulation more clearly than in existing embodiment literatures. Analyses of embodiment can therefore become more legal (in a pluralist sense, of being both normative and regulatory) than those conducted to date. On the other hand, maintaining focus on institutional practices allows researchers to go beyond what is often understood as law, including other institutional power-knowledges. To facilitate this, I turn to emerging governance studies literature on jurisdiction. Jurisdictional analysis centres upon the qualitative aspects of decision-making processes, illuminating how governance is carried out in practice. In addition, by emphasising governance, rather than law or legislation, jurisdictional analysis is attentive to law's place within the regulatory frameworks, and thus also identifies the practices of the institutional power-knowledges.

Feminist governance studies

Jurisdiction

Jurisdiction is a practical mechanism which organises legal relations.[189] It has been defined in various ways, but is generally understood as underscoring the authority 'to declare the law'.[190] Jurisdiction is discussed increasingly in socio-legal studies, and I have previously asserted its utility for health law analysis.[191] My interest in this legal mechanism can be traced back to the work of Valverde, who advocates attending to jurisdiction rather than sovereignty when analysing regulatory arrangements.[192] Searching for sovereignty risks over-emphasising the unifying power of law as that which delineates distinct territories before allocating the responsibility to govern these to discrete, identifiable, authorities.[193] This is in spite of the fact that a Hobbesian sovereign – a 'Leviathan'[194] with 'unified, compete jurisdiction' – has never existed, even in a dictatorship.[195] Jurisdictional analysis constitutes a weak form of legal

189 S Dorsett and S McVeigh, *Jurisdiction* (Routledge 2012) 4, 14.

190 T Hobbes, 'A Dialogue of the Common Law', in W Molesworth (ed), *The English Works of Thomas Hobbes,* vol 6 (Bohn 1839) 118. The Latin etymology is the genitive of *jūs* ('law') and *dictio*; a noun of action ('to say, declare').

191 C Dietz, 'Jurisdiction in Trans Health' (2020) 47(1) Journal of Law and Society 60.

192 Valverde has developed other modes for analysing governance, including a comprehensive understanding of scale (which encompasses spatial, temporal, affective, and aesthetic dimensions); (n 162).

193 M Valverde, 'Jurisdiction and Scale: Legal "Technicalities" as Resources for Theory' (2009) 18 Social & Legal Studies 139, 145.

194 T Hobbes, *Leviathan* (first published 1651, Oxford University Press 1996).

195 M Valverde, 'Studying the Governance of Crime and Security: Space, Time and Jurisdiction' (2014) 14(4) Criminology & Criminal Justice 379, 387. For: 'Even in States that Have by and Large Marginalized or Even Suppressed Alternative or Specialized Jurisdictions, a Variety of Overlapping Jurisdictions Still Exist'; Valverde (n 162) 57.

pluralism,[196] as it charts which institutions are tasked with (or challenge for) the right to govern within regulatory frameworks.

Centring sovereignty, rather than attending to the fragmented and plural practice of jurisdiction, may underestimate the extent to which contestation bubbles beneath what might seem at first glance to be a 'smoothly' functioning governance arrangement.[197] Though critics of the GRA 2004 have been attentive to the complexities of power relations elsewhere, they have tended to emphasise the authority of medical and legal power-knowledges. Cowan describes medical institutions being granted a 'stamp of statutory authority' when the diagnosis of gender dysphoria was included as a pre-requisite to being granted gender recognition.[198] Davy agrees that a 'medicolegal alliance' was bolstered by the GRA 2004's enactment into law.[199] Yet conceiving of 'stamps' and 'alliances' cannot capture how various institutions compete for, or avoid, the responsibility for governing at different times and places. Jurisdictional analysis provides an alternative through which latent conflicts may be illuminated:

> governing projects and the power-knowledges that make them work are differentiated from one another and kept from overtly clashing by the workings of the machinery of 'jurisdiction', which instantly sorts governance processes, knowledges, and powers into their proper slots as if by magic, and sets up a chain by which (most of the time) deciding who governs where effectively decides how governance will happen.[200]

Jurisdiction can distinguish not only territories and authorities (the *where* and the *who* of governance), but also objects (the *what* of governance) and, importantly, governing rationalities and capacities (the *how* of governance).[201] To exemplify this, Valverde considers jurisdiction over a hypothetical supply of fish. If these fish are located in Canadian (rather than international) waters, they would 'automatically' come under the jurisdiction of Canadian authorities. Valverde notes that this would probably see them governed in accordance with a logic of 'natural resources', with extraneous factors such as unemployment in coastal fishing villages factored into the equation.[202] The decision of *where* the fish are located, then, determines not only *who* they will be governed by, but also as *what* they are, and *how* they will be governed. Once jurisdiction has been allocated to an authority within a certain territory, questions of *what* the

196 I am grateful to the editors of the Routledge Social Justice Book Series for noting this.
197 Valverde (n 162) 84.
198 Cowan (n 8) 247.
199 Davy (n 85) 119.
200 Valverde (n 193) 145.
201 ibid. 144.
202 ibid.

object of governance is, and *how* it ought to be conducted tend to be decided quietly – almost as though they are assumed not to merit much discussion.[203]

A similar tendency can be identified within a trans context. Many people exhibit gender-diverse practices of embodiment, but it is only when they are diagnosed as suffering from 'gender dysphoria' that they come into the regulatory orbit of medical systems of governance. Through sustained psychiatric assessment, medical professionals diagnose whether the patient is trans, or otherwise. This will in turn affect their chances of being offered access to body modification technologies, including hormones and surgeries, via official medical routes. And it states like the UK, it will have the knock-on effect of determining whether they are eligible to apply for legal gender recognition or not. The importance of where the gender-diverse person is located in relation to psychiatric diagnoses and medicolegal authorities (the *where* and *who* of governance) will hereby influence *what* they are considered to be (trans, or cis) and *how* they might be treated (as eligible for legal recognition and health care, or not).

Shaunnagh Dorsett and Shaun McVeigh understand jurisdiction as forming 'part of the technique and craft of legal ordering and the art of creating legal relations.'[204] As it primarily concerns 'how to do things with law', jurisdiction is, in their view, 'the most technical and prosaic ordering of legal authority.'[205] Jurisdiction can determine the scope of an authority, how this authority will be technically represented, or address 'the proper form of legal relations.'[206] It has an everyday impact on people's lives, in that it both 'tells us how to do things with and against law.'[207] Dorsett and McVeigh add that jurisdiction might even 'inaugurate' law; in that it can bring law into being.[208] In this case, it must also 'in some sense' precede law.[209] As they note,

> This raises a number of conceptual and institutional questions about the nature and sources of authority. In particular, the idea that jurisdiction inaugurates law brings with it subsequent questions of transmission – how authority gets passed from one place to another – and the sense that each jurisdiction works as its own source of authority.[210]

In the context of legal gender recognition, questions about the transmission of authority between medical and legal discourses might be obscured by conceptualising their relationship as a sovereign 'alliance'. Such questions would even

203 Valverde (n 195) 388.
204 Dorsett and McVeigh (n 189) 4.
205 ibid.
206 ibid.
207 ibid.
208 ibid.
209 ibid. 11.
210 ibid.

appear misguided in the context of the 2014 reforms in Denmark, which at first glance appear to have untangled medical and legal regulation by removing medical gatekeepers from the gender recognition process. Jurisdictional analysis is suited to illuminating latent conflicts between different institutions that work within what might otherwise be read as an authoritative and settled governing assemblage. Contrasting positions on *how* governance should be practised – determined, for instance, by varying governing rationalities or capacities – will affect the subjects of governance. They could have significant consequences for the legal embodiment of trans people, for example, who are granted straightforward access to legal gender recognition in the Danish civil registration system, and yet continue to be subjected to sustained psychiatric assessment in the clinical setting.

An objection might be raised that what goes on in medical institutions is not strictly relevant for legal (or even socio-legal) analysis. But, as I have demonstrated, the clinic constitutes an important locus in the regulation of gendered embodiment, and medical guidelines constitute a form of 'law' themselves (albeit in the pluralist sense). If medical regulations can undermine the accessibility of legal gender recognition, this will have a domino effect for a trans person's legal embodiment. Indeed it would almost always be incorrect to state that medical institutions are *un*regulated. As Lacey notes, even when we can distinguish between regulation and an absence of regulation, the significance of this can be questioned by the fact that 'decisions *not* to regulate made state or other institutions with the power to do so are every bit as *political* decisions as are decisions to regulate.'[211] Even where institutions are granted wide discretion, the competences that they enjoy are always delineated, and often restricted, by jurisdiction.[212] Law may govern directly, but it also authorises the governance carried out by institutions.[213] As Dorsett and McVeigh have suggested, jurisdiction holds the ability to 'delimit the scope of authority, determine the technical means of its representation or adjudicate on the proper form of lawful relations.'[214] Hence the potential of jurisdictional analysis is not that it provides tools for 'overcoming the state', but rather those for 'putting the state in its place.'[215]

Conclusion

In this chapter, I have constructed a theory of legal embodiment which will frame the findings presented in what remains of this book. By reviewing the

211 N Lacey, 'Theory into Practice? Pornography and the Public/Private Dichotomy' (1993) 20(1) Journal of Law and Society 93, 96.

212 Hence why Valverde calls jurisdiction 'the governance of legal governance'; (n 193) 141.

213 Valverde (n 162) 83, citing M Valverde, 'Authorizing the Production of Urban Moral Order: Appellate Courts and their Knowledge Games' (2005) 29(1) Law and Society Review 419.

214 Dorsett and McVeigh (n 189) 4.

215 ibid. 51.

various ways in which bodies have been conceptualised in different feminist theories and feminist legal studies of embodiment, I brought these two literatures together to develop a definition of legal embodiment which concerns the ontological and epistemological experience of becoming a legal subject at the intersection of subjective, intersubjective, material, symbolic, and institutional realms. Legal embodiment illuminates the processes through which regulations constitute and saturate bodies, and where regulatory power meets embodied resistance. It addresses the question of how embodiment is affected by, and in turn affects, institutional power-knowledges and governing assemblages. Informed by the socio-legal and sociological literature on gender recognition, in the GRA 2004 and more widely, I suggested that these spheres are of paramount importance for those trying to capture the complexity of trans embodiment and construct a stable platform for legal subjects.

These insights accord to a great extent with the existing literature on embodiment and gender recognition. Yet in stressing the final, institutional, dimension of embodiment, I had to turn to recent governance studies and feminist institutionalism literature to suggest that jurisdictional analysis – which addresses how different institutional power-knowledges are authorised, sorted, and separated to enable them to do the work of governance – could be used to mobilise a study of legal embodiment. In emphasising how institutional practices affect experiences of becoming alongside the more readily acknowledged material and discursive realms, I have re-orientated the embodiment literature to cast greater light on how embodiment is affected by, and in turn affects, institutional power-knowledges and governing assemblages.

By conducting jurisdictional analysis at the moment when law constitutes and saturates bodies, I hope to de-mystify, and potentially even re-politicise, how embodiment is affected by, and in turn affects, these regulatory processes. This is the specific type of legal embodiment which I concern myself with in this book. Framed by my specific conceptualisation of legal embodiment, I have explained how jurisdictional analysis will be used to illuminate the various processes through which regulations constitute and saturate bodies, and where institutional regulations meet embodied resistance. Jurisdiction provides the necessary bridge between theory and methodology. In Chapter 3, my attention will turn to the question of exactly how, and in what contexts, this analysis will be conducted.

Bibliography

Anderson P, *In the Tracks of Historical Materialism: The Wellek Library Lectures* (Verso 1983)

Barad K, 'Posthumanist Performativity: Toward an Understanding of How Matter Comes to Matter' (2003) 28(3) Signs: Journal of Women in Culture and Society 801

Beasley C and Bacchi C, 'Citizen Bodies: Embodying Citizens – A Feminist Analysis' (2000) 2(3) International Feminist Journal of Politics 337

——— 'Envisaging a New Politics for an Ethical Future: Beyond Trust, Care and Generosity – Towards an Ethic of 'Social Flesh'' (2007) 8(3) Feminist Theory 279

——— 'Making Politics Fleshy: The Ethic of Social Flesh' in Bletsas A and Beasley C (eds), *Engaging with Carol Bacchi: Strategic Interventions and Exchanges* (University of Adelaide Press 2012)

Cleaver F and de Koning J, 'Furthering Critical Institutionalism' (2015) 9(1) International Journal of the Commons 1

Connell R, 'Transsexual Women and Feminist Thought: Toward New Understanding and New Politics' (2012) 37(4) Signs: Journal of Women in Culture and Society 857

Cornell D, *The Imaginary Domain: Abortion, Pornography & Sexual Harassment* (Routledge 1995)

Cowan S, 'Looking Back (To)wards the Body: Medicalization and the GRA' (2009) 18 Social & Legal Studies 247

Davy Z, 'Transsexual Agents: Negotiating Authenticity and Embodiment within the UK's Medicolegal System' in Hines S and Sanger T (eds), *Transgender Identities: Towards a Social Analysis of Gender Diversity* (Routledge 2010) 123

——— *Recognizing Transsexuals: Personal, Political and Medicolegal Embodiment* (Ashgate 2011)

Dietz C, 'Governing Legal Embodiment: On the Limits of Self-Declaration' (2018) 26(2) Feminist Legal Studies 185

——— 'Jurisdiction in Trans Health' (2020) 47(1) Journal of Law and Society 60

Dorsett S and McVeigh S, *Jurisdiction* (Routledge 2012)

Ellis SJ, Bailey L, and McNeil J, 'Trans People's Experiences of Mental Health and Gender Identity Services: A UK Study' (2015) 19 Journal of Gay & Lesbian Mental Health 4

Fletcher R, 'Embodied Practices' (2009) 17 Feminist Legal Studies 315

———, Fox M, and McCandless J, 'Legal Embodiment: Analysing the Body of Healthcare Law' (2008) 16 Medical Law Review 321

Flynn T, 'The Ties that (Don't) Bind: Transgender Family Law and the Unmaking of Families' in Currah P, Juang RM, and Minter SP (eds), *Transgender Rights* (University of Minnesota Press 2006)

Foucault M, *The Will to Knowledge: The History of Sexuality Volume One* (first published 1976, Hurley R tr, Penguin 1998)

——— *The Birth of Biopolitics: Lectures at the Collège de France 1978–1979* (Senellart M ed, Burchell G tr, Picador 2008)

Fox M and Murphy T, 'The Body, Bodies, Embodiment: Feminist Legal Engagement with Health' in Davies M and Munro VE (eds), *The Ashgate Research Companion to Feminist Legal Theory* (Ashgate 2013)

Fox M and Thomson M, 'Bodily Integrity, Embodiment, and the Regulation of Parental Choice' (2017) 44(4) Journal of Law and Society 501

Fraser N, *Justice Interruptus: Rethinking Key Concepts of a Post-Socialist Age* (Routledge 1997)

Gilligan C, *In a Different Voice* (Harvard University Press 1982)

Gonzalez-Salzberg DA, *Sexuality and Transsexuality under the European Convention on Human Rights: A Queer Reading of Human Rights Law* (Hart 2019)

Grabham E, 'Citizen Bodies, Intersex Citizenship' (2007) 10(1) Sexualities 29

——— 'Bodily Integrity and the Surgical Management of Intersex' (2012) 18(2) Body & Society 1

Grosz E, *Volatile Bodies: Toward a Corporeal Feminism* (Indiana University Press 1994)

Gunnarsson L, 'A Defence of the Category 'Women'' (2011) 12(1) Feminist Theory 23

Harding R, *Regulating Sexuality: Legal Consciousness in Lesbian and Gay Lives* (Routledge 2011)

Harrington J, 'Time as a Dimension of Medical Law' (2012) 20 Medical Law Review 491

Hemmings C, 'Affective Solidarity: Feminist Reflexivity and Political Transformation' (2012) 13(2) Feminist Theory 147
Hines S, *TransForming Gender* (Polity Press 2007)
——— *Gender Diversity, Recognition and Citizenship* (Palgrave Macmillan 2013)
Hobbes T, 'A Dialogue of the Common Law' in Molesworth W (ed), *The English Works of Thomas Hobbes*, vol 6 (Bohn 1839)
——— *Leviathan* (first published 1651, Oxford University Press 1996)
Honkasalo J, 'In the Shadow of Eugenics: Transgender Sterilisation Legislation and the Struggle for Self-Determination' in Pearce R, Moon I, Gupta K, and Steinberg DL (eds), *The Emergence of Trans: Cultures, Politics and Everyday Lives* (Routledge 2020)
Irving D, 'Normalized Transgressions: Legitimizing the Transsexual Body as Productive' (2008) 100(1) Radical History Review 38
Jackson E and Lacey N, 'Introducing Feminist Legal Theory' in Penner JE, Schiff D, and Nobles R (eds), *Jurisprudence and Legal Theory: Commentary and Materials* (Butterworths 2002)
Jones I, 'Objects of Crime: Bodies, Embodiment and Forensic Pathology' (2020) 29(5) Social & Legal Studies 679
Kenny M, 'A Feminist Institutional Approach' (2014) 10(4) Politics & Gender 679
Lacey N, 'Theory into Practice? Pornography and the Public/Private Dichotomy' (1993) 20(1) Journal of Law and Society 93
——— 'On the Subject of Sexing the Subject' in Naffine N and Owens RJ (eds), *Sexing the Subject of Law* (LBC 1997)
Locke J, *Second Treatise of Government* (first published 1690, Hackett 1980)
Loizidou E, 'The Body Figural and Material in the Work of Judith Butler' (2008) 28 Australian Feminist Legal Journal 29
Lorde A, *Sister Outsider: Essays and Speeches* (Crossing Press 2007) 110
Mackay F, Monro S, and Waylen G, 'The Feminist Potential of Sociological Institutionalism' (2009) 5(2) Politics & Gender 253
Mackenzie C, 'Conceptions of the Body and Conceptions of Autonomy in Bioethics' in Scully J, Baldwin-Ragaven L, and Fitzpatrick P (eds), *Feminist Bioethics: At the Center, on the Margins* (Johns Hopkins University Press 2010) 73
Munro V, *Law and Politics at the Perimeter: Re-Evaluating Key Debates in Feminist Theory* (Hart 2007)
Murphy T, 'Feminism on Flesh' (1997) 8 Law and Critique 37
Naffine N and Owens RJ (eds), *Sexing the Subject of Law* (LBC 1997)
——— 'Sexing Law' in Naffine N and Owens RJ (eds), *Sexing the Subject of Law* (LBC 1997)
Namaste V, 'Undoing Theory: The 'Transgender Question' and the Epistemic Violence of Anglo-American Feminist Theory' (2009) 24(3) Hypatia 11
Neave M, 'Foreword' in Naffine N and Owens RJ (eds), *Sexing the Subject of Law* (LBC 1997)
Phipps A, 'Whose Personal Is More Political? Experience in Contemporary Feminist Politics' (2016) 17(3) Feminist Theory 303
Pillow W, '"Bodies Are Dangerous": Using Feminist Genealogy as Policy Studies Methodology' (2003) 18(2) Journal of Education Policy 145
Preciado PB, *Testo Junkie: Sex, Drugs, and Biopolitics in the Pharmacopornographic Era* (Feminist Press 2013)
Priaulx N, 'Rethinking Progenitive Conflict: Why Reproductive Autonomy *Matters*' (2008) 16 Medical Law Review 169

Probyn E, *Sexing the Self: Gendered Positions in Cultural Studies* (Routledge 1993)
Prosser J, *Second Skins: The Body Narratives of Transsexuality* (Columbia University Press 1998)
Raun T, 'Trans as Contested Intelligibility: Interrogating How to Conduct Trans Analysis with Respectful Curiosity' (2014) (1) Lambda Nordica 13
Reed R, 'Transsexuals and European Human Rights Law' in Graupner H and Tahmindjis P (eds), *Sexuality and Human Rights: A Global Overview* (Harrington Park Press 2005)
Renz F, 'Consenting to Gender? Trans Spouses after Same-Sex Marriage', in Barker N and Monk D (eds), *From Civil Partnership to Same-Sex Marriage: Interdisciplinary Reflections* (Routledge 2015)
Roen K, '"Either/Or" and "Both/Neither": Discursive Tensions in Transgender Politics' (2002) 27(2) Signs 501
Salamon G, *Assuming a Body: Transgender and Rhetorics of Materiality* (Columbia University Press 2010)
Sandland R, 'Running to Stand Still' (2009) 18 Social & Legal Studies 253
Sanger T, *Trans People's Partnerships: Towards an Ethics of Intimacy* (Palgrave Macmillan 2010)
Sawer M, 'Feminist Political Science and Feminist Politics' (2014) 29 Australian Feminist Studies 137
Scott JW, 'The Evidence of Experience' (1991) 17 Critical Inquiry 773
Sharpe A, *Transgender Jurisprudence: Dysphoric Bodies of Law* (Cavendish 2002)
——— 'A Return to the 'Truth' of the Past' (2009) 18 Social & Legal Studies 259
——— *Foucault's Monsters and the Challenge of Law* (Routledge 2010)
Skewes L and Adrian SW, Interview with Lykke N, 'Epistemology, Activism and Entanglement – Rethinking Knowledge Production' (2018) 27(1) Women, Gender & Research 15
Stryker S, '(De)Subjugated Knowledges: An Introduction to Transgender Studies' in Stryker S and Whittle S (eds), *The Transgender Studies Reader* (Routledge 2006) 12
Tirohl B and Bowers IR, 'Opposite Sex – A Discussion of Rights under the Gender Recognition Act' (2006) 15(1) Journal of Gender Studies 83
Valverde M, 'Genealogies of European States: Foucauldian Reflections' (2007) 36(1) Economy and Society 159
——— 'Jurisdiction and Scale: Legal 'Technicalities' as Resources for Theory' (2009) 18 Social & Legal Studies 139
——— 'Studying the Governance of Crime and Security: Space, Time and Jurisdiction' (2014) 14(4) Criminology & Criminal Justice 379
——— *Chronotopes of Law: Jurisdiction, Scale and Governance* (Routledge 2015)
Waldby C, 'Destruction: Boundary Erotics and Refigurations of the Heterosexual Male Body' in Grosz E and Probyn E (eds), *Sexy Bodies: The Strange Carnalities of Feminism* (Routledge 1996)
West R, 'Jurisprudence and Gender' (1988) 55(1) University of Chicago Law Review 1
Whittle S, *Respect and Equality: Transsexual and Transgender Rights* (Cavendish 2002)
Williams SJ and Bendelow G, *The Lived Body: Sociological Themes, Embodied Issues* (Routledge 1998)

Chapter 3

Legal consciousness of embodiment

Introduction

In this chapter, I argue that a legal consciousness approach constitutes a useful method for conducting jurisdictional analyses of legal embodiment. I do so by explaining how I implemented it in my own research, as I sought to assess the impact of self-declaration of legal gender status in Denmark. In the socio-legal studies literature, legal consciousness is said to provide the necessary tools to interrogate the position of law in society. It enables researchers to uncover and probe how law and regulation affects interviewees' everyday lives. It is my contention that critical and contextual adaptation of legal consciousness enables researchers to chart embodied experiences of institutional regulation. This supplements existing modes of socio-legal research, including jurisdictional analysis. Finally, I demonstrate how I utilised this approach to assess the impact of the implementation of self-declaration of legal gender status in Denmark.

The chapter is split into two main parts. The first lays out my methodological approach, describing how legal consciousness can be moulded to fit the ontological and epistemological points of focus in jurisdictional analysis and legal embodiment research. As discussed in Chapter 2, this concerns the subjective, intersubjective, material, and symbolic dimensions of legal embodiment, and particularly how these are affected by institutional regulations. Supplementing jurisdictional analysis with a legal consciousness methodology, I consider how the effect of gender recognition law reforms on legal embodiment can be investigated. Jurisdictional boundaries can be identified by exploring the experiences of those directly involved in reforms processes – including both the regulators professionally involved in designing or enacting the reforms, and the legal subjects who have been personally affected by them.

The second part of the chapter presents my methodological framework, which explains how I put my methodological approach into practice within my research. This discusses how my research was planned and organised before I reflect upon the benefits and limitations of the approach I developed. I end the chapter by documenting some of the ethical concerns that I encountered when implementing legal consciousness methods; including negotiating outsider

DOI: 10.4324/9780429288203-3

status, soliciting informed consent, and seeking to ensure confidentiality and security. I then explain the methodological decisions I took to attempt to deal with these. I conclude by stating my intention to guide future researchers interested in exploring the embodied effects of law reform projects, including feminist and socio-legal scholars who are keen to address how people are affected by developments in institutional regulation.

Methodological approach

Studying jurisdictional practices

Existing analyses of gender recognition law reforms, as I noted in Chapters 1 and 2, have largely been developed from human rights and anti-discrimination perspectives. Research on self-declaration of legal gender status specifically has for the most part been conducted within comparative legal studies. Peter Dunne has, for example, considered how far different legislative 'models' meet 'international best practice standards.'[1] While insights are offered by comparative research, it has its limitations. Discussing the doctrinal content of gender recognition laws, and then comparing them with those adopted in different states, will not unveil the embodied effects of such reforms on the trans people governed by them. Though doctrinal studies can usefully summarise the content of formal laws enacted in various states, they also tend, at least to some extent, to take what law claims about itself at face value. This highlights a risk of neglecting the process of how law is implemented in practice and experienced on an embodied level. After developing similar concerns around debates in security studies, Valverde suggested that

> it may be time to move to a different type of project, one that instead of focussing on security as a noun, a thing – a choice that inevitably leads into normative discussions about good security versus bad security – turns the gaze not on a single word or a concept but rather on the very wide variety of *activities* and *practices* that are being carried out under the name of 'security'. [2]

Rather than starting from an 'abstract noun' – such as 'self-declaration' – and commencing doctrinal or theoretical analysis, Valverde proposes researching 'actually existing practices of governance'.[3] This shift from the 'Oxford tradition' of conceptual clarification to an epistemology centred on governing

1 P Dunne, 'Rethinking Legal Gender Recognition: Recent Reforms in Argentina, Denmark and the Netherlands' [2015] 1 International Family Law 41, 42.

2 M Valverde, 'Studying the Governance of Crime and Security: Space, Time and Jurisdiction' (2014) 14(4) Criminology & Criminal Justice 379, 383.

3 ibid. 383–384.

practices mimics Foucault's 'great intellectual move';[4] which spawned an entire field of 'governmentality' studies where the 'political thinkers' deemed worthy of analysis are the administrators and politicians who actively implement social policy rather than philosophers or theorists.[5]

Foucault's desire to examine the 'rationalities really at work' reflects his position that because the existence of universal abstractions has not yet been demonstrated, scholarship must proceed as if they do not.[6] He understood power to be dynamically produced in all relations; and '"minor" practices' of power are central to governmentality scholarship.[7] To investigate these minor practices of power, Bent Flyvbjerg proposes seeking 'practical knowledge' of 'the actual daily practices which constitute a given field of interest'.[8] Valverde also works at a 'concrete and empirically driven' scale, where 'the key object of study consists of governing mechanisms and the tools we have to analyse them'.[9] In-depth studies of concrete situations have greater epistemological value than those clarifying abstract principles.[10]

The decision to adopt one ontological perspective over another will have epistemological implications for any research project, as a whole.[11] Like the feminist theory discussed in Chapter 2, sociological research methods stress that ontology and epistemology must be considered in relation to one another if the researcher is to establish how they will produce valid knowledge about particular phenomena.[12] Valverde favours studying practices of governance – including the 'machinery' of jurisdiction – over legal doctrine and general principles.[13] Yet she offers little guidance on what a practice of governance is, or how it might be identified. Cues can be taken from her own research, or that which she cites approvingly. They could also be inferred from trends in governance studies. In all instances, the methods favoured tend to involve participant observation. This indicates that an investigation of the jurisdictional effect of a gender recognition project should focus on how boundaries between different power-knowledges are (re)drawn during law reform processes. Yet such boundaries would be extremely difficult to observe in any conventional

4 ibid. 383.
5 M Valverde, 'Genealogies of European States: Foucauldian Reflections' (2007) 36(1) Economy and Society 159, 168.
6 B Flyvbjerg, *Making Social Science Matter: Why Social Inquiry Fails and How It Can Succeed Again* (S Sampson tr, Cambridge University Press 2002) 100.
7 Valverde (n 5) 160.
8 Flyvbjerg (n 6) 134.
9 Valverde (n 2) 380.
10 B Flyvbjerg, 'Case Study' in NK Denzin and YS Lincoln, *The Sage Handbook of Qualitative Research* (4th edn, Sage 2011) 304.
11 J Mason, *Qualitative Researching* (2nd edn, Sage 2002) 15.
12 C Ramazanoğlu with J Holland, *Feminist Methodology: Challenges and Choices* (Sage 2002) 11.
13 M Valverde, 'Jurisdiction and Scale: Legal "Technicalities" as Resources for Theory' (2009) 18 Social & Legal Studies 139, 143–145.

sense. An immediate challenge would be gaining access to the relevant spaces – with many jurisdictional decisions made 'behind closed doors', away from public view.[14] Even this assumes that such boundaries are visibly managed within institutional spaces – an assumption which privileges the spatial scale over other important temporal, affective, and aesthetic, scales.[15] To suggest that jurisdictional divisions can be easily observed is doubtful, when their relative invisibility constitutes one of their facets in facilitating the 'smooth functioning' of law in practice.[16]

If jurisdictional rearrangements cannot be easily observed, then perhaps they might be evidenced in written documentation? While Valverde shares doubts about the value of pure doctrinal analysis,[17] this may not amount to a dismissal of legal documents. When studying urban governance in Toronto, she describes working with 'a legally trained colleague [...] to study the formal law'.[18] She adds a caveat that the results of such research ought to be detailed in an 'accessible' manner.[19] But still, it is only once she has undertaken this doctrinal legal research that she even begins devising her own empirical study.[20] Before travelling to Denmark, I analysed various legal documents addressing the 2014 reforms, and had transcripts of the parliamentary debates which led to the enactment of the self-declaration translated to provide contextual background of the intentions of legislators. While undertaking fieldwork, I expanded this sample of resources to include less doctrinal documentation, including the medical guidelines which shape clinical practice in Denmark, and the interview questionnaires given to trans people when they present themselves at the Sexological Clinic.

The documentary materials which this thesis draws upon thus range from those that could be considered as representative of abstract legal doctrine to those more likely to be implemented in practice. Researchers analysing how a document 'works' in practice are advised to consider its purposive function; that is, the fact that it was created to formalise, or assist, the activities of an institutional organisation.[21] The institutional life of a document will be dynamic and context-dependent, rather than static or self-evident. Merely analysing its contents, or interviewing its authors, will thus prove insufficient for under-

14 In an earlier plan for my doctoral studies, I myself had a research request to observe the decision-making processes of the Gender Recognition Panel rejected by the UK Ministry of Justice, in March 2014.

15 M Valverde, *Chronotopes of Law: Jurisdiction, Scale and Governance* (Routledge 2015) 56.

16 ibid. 84.

17 Valverde (n 2) 387.

18 M Valverde, *Everyday Law on the Street: City Governance in an Age of Diversity* (University of Chicago Press 2012) 4.

19 ibid. 20–21.

20 ibid. 5.

21 J Scott, *A Matter of Record: Documentary Sources in Social Research* (Polity Press 1990) 11, citing S Webb and B Webb, *Methods of Social Study* (Cambridge University Press 1975) 100.

standing how it is being used in practice. Lindsay Prior notes: 'A study of what the author(s) of a given document (text) "meant" or intended can only ever add up to limited examination of what a document "is".'[22] To acknowledge this, I advocate supplementing documentary analysis with other methods, as I did by interviewing regulators and activists to glean their impressions of how the Danish reforms had played out. These interviews sought to uncover the intentions that motivated these actors and their organisations, and the effects that they had had in practice. Interviews with regulators and activists were then supplemented by interviews with the trans people subjected to regulation, to see how (if at all) their actions and behaviour had been affected.

Conducting interviews to explore how jurisdictional arrangements have been affected by a reform process could be considered as a departure from the more orthodox governmentality literature. The reason for this is that 'it is the world of beliefs and meanings, not of actions, that is clarified by interview research.'[23] These are slightly removed from the concrete observable behaviours and actions favoured within governmentality research. Yet Valverde's work evidences an element of ambiguity here. At no point does she endorse one empirical method as more useful than any other, aside from noting that it can be problematic for scholarship 'to proceed without a clear awareness of the pros and cons of the particular scale we happen to be using'.[24] Yet while she comprehensively outlines the various 'pros' of working at the 'concrete and empirically driven' scale favoured in her own research,[25] she also fails to acknowledge one potential 'con' regarding the question of whether this scale is suited to the investigation of the various aesthetic and affective 'human' dimensions of a governance project.[26] While she is keen that researchers do not ignore aesthetic and human dimensions of governance, there is little guidance as to how they should be measured – particularly in the 'concrete' sense that Valverde advocates.[27]

My solution to this dilemma is to suggest that, for all their limitations, interview techniques can generate useful insights into the arrangement of jurisdiction in a governance project. This is particularly the case where the 'beliefs and meanings' that they reveal can be interrogated reflexively, and to some extent 'triangulated' with insights gleaned through other interviews or from another form of analysis (doctrinal or documentary).[28] Rather than seeking to visually 'observe' how jurisdiction is arranged, I suggest that being attentive to

22 L Prior, 'Repositioning Documents in Social Research' (2008) 42(5) Sociology 821, 824.
23 H Arksey and P Knight, *Interviewing for Social Scientists* (Sage 1999) 15.
24 Valverde (n 2) 386.
25 ibid. 380.
26 ibid. 382.
27 I have noted this previously; C Dietz, 'Book Review: Mariana Valverde, *Chronotopes of Law: Jurisdiction, Scale and Governance*' (2016) 25(1) Social & Legal Studies 126, 128.
28 Mason (n 11) 190–191.

affective and human dimensions of a governance project requires researchers to go beyond conventional participant observation methods. To do so, I utilised legal consciousness, supplementing and augmenting jurisdictional analysis by offering a methodological solution to the question of how the embodied effects of a reform project ought to be uncovered.

Legal consciousness

Early studies of legal consciousness focused upon working class people's perceptions of law in the US.[29] This has since diversified to include, for example, investigations into local government actors,[30] and more recently gay and lesbian lives,[31] in the UK. Davina Cooper describes legal consciousness researchers charting a route between the liberal idea of consciousness as individually held belief and the Marxist understanding of consciousness as determined by social structures. Consciousness is 'formed within and by social action' instead.[32] Law is experienced 'in ways shaped by class, education, geography, and occupational positioning.'[33] Legal consciousness research thus explores experiences of law, questioning how and why people decide to turn to the legal system for assistance (or not). The creation of legal consciousness is hereby understood as 'a situated *practice*' involving both collective and individual agency.[34]

Legal consciousness research has since moved from tracking the 'causal' relationship between law and society to tracing 'the presence of law in society' instead.[35] This constitutes a shift from 'instrumentalist' to 'constitutive' studies.[36] Rather than attempting to quantify the effects of 'law' on 'society',[37] constitutive studies acknowledge law as 'a part of society'.[38] They understand that 'society (and the part of society known as everyday life) creates effects on law as much as law impacts upon society.'[39] Constitutive approaches focus on

29 A Sarat, '" ... The Law Is All Over": Power, Resistance and the Legal Consciousness of the Welfare Poor' (1990) 2 Yale Journal of Law and the Humanities 378.

30 D Cooper, 'Local Government Legal Consciousness in the Shadow of Juridification' (1995) 22(4) Journal of Law and Society 506.

31 R Harding, *Regulating Sexuality: Legal Consciousness in Lesbian and Gay Lives* (Routledge 2011).

32 P Ewick and S Silbey, 'Conformity, Contestation, and Resistance: An Account of Legal Consciousness' (1992) 26 New England Law Review 731, 742.

33 Cooper (n 30) 510.

34 ibid.

35 P Ewick and S Silbey, *The Common Place of Law: Stories from Everyday Life* (University of Chicago Press 1998) 35.

36 A Sarat and TR Kearns, 'Beyond the Great Divide: Forms of Legal Scholarship and Everyday Life' in A Sarat and TR Kearns (eds), *Law in Everyday Life* (University of Michigan Press 1995) 21.

37 Harding (n 31) 18.

38 ibid. 8.

39 ibid.

the wider (potentially non-legal) impact of legal developments.[40] They thus exhibit an influence of the literature on legal pluralism, which 'challenges the idea that state law is the only form of law'.[41] As Rosie Harding notes, 'there are many normative orders of various descriptions that are not attached to the state', but which can be considered 'legal' nonetheless.'[42]

De-centring formal law avoids mythologising legislators as sovereign powers; which again indicates a Foucauldian influence on the legal consciousness literature. Dave Cowan goes as far as to suggest that it was Foucault's theoretical interventions which made the shift to constitutive studies of law and society possible.[43] Beyond reflecting a fear that scholars were 'asking the wrong set of questions', Cowan considers the decision to de-centre law as a social phenomenon a riposte to concerns that socio-legal research had hitherto failed to meet its objective of 'penetrating into everyday life'.[44] Legal pluralists have been criticised for undermining the precision of their favoured concept by neglecting to construct a clear definition of law. Without this definition, legal pluralists may fail to distinguish the legal (even in the broad pluralist sense) from the non-legal ('those normative orders even legal pluralists would not want to call law').[45] But legal consciousness researchers are able to circumvent this problem; developing what Brian Tamanaha calls a 'non-essentialist' version of legal pluralism, which centres the action of legal subjects.[46] As Harding explains, 'The problematic of whether or not 'law' is actually salient in everyday life becomes a moot point if 'law' is anything that people, in their social practices, treat as law.'[47]

Concern with the subjective impact of regulation coincides with Valverde's attention towards the 'human effects' and 'bodily habits' which constitute everyday techniques of governance.[48] Orthodox governmentality studies concern themselves with 'the actual daily practices which constitute a given field of interest',[49] at the 'concrete and empirically driven' scale where the key object of study consists of governing mechanisms and the tools we have to analyse them.[50] Legal consciousness proceeds from a distinct premise. Harding describes a governmentality perspective as 'useful' for thinking about power

40 ibid. 9.
41 ibid. 29.
42 ibid. 30.
43 D Cowan, 'Legal Consciousness: Some Observations' (2004) 67(6) Modern Law Review 928, 930.
44 ibid. 929–930.
45 BZ Tamanaha, 'The Folly of the 'Social Scientific' Concept of Legal Pluralism' (1993) 20(2) Journal of Law and Society 192, 193–194.
46 BZ Tamanaha, 'A Non-Essentialist Version of Legal Pluralism' (2000) 27(2) Journal of Law and Society 296, 316.
47 Harding (n 31) 31.
48 Valverde (n 2) 388.
49 Flyvbjerg (n 6) 134.
50 Valverde (n 2) 380.

in legal consciousness research 'as it helps to draw links between the ways that individuals express their views of law and the ways in which governmental rationality attempts to control the population.'[51] But from here, an alternative conception of ontology is developed, where subjective experience meets governmentality studies' conventional ontological properties of 'rationalities' and 'practices'. This accords with the work on ontology and epistemology I conducted in Chapter 2. It also constitutes the methodology I employed to explore interviewees' experiences of the 2014 reforms. This enabled me to ascertain the extent to which these reforms registered in their consciousness, and what effect they had on their embodied engagement with the law (if any).

So where Valverde leaves the question of how these effects could be investigated open, the legal consciousness literature is clear: take '"ordinary" people's accounts of their everyday experiences as the starting point for thinking about law in everyday life, and the way that law works in society.'[52] This reflects the understanding that 'law' and 'everyday life' are not distinct spheres but are rather 'interlinked'; scholars must examine both if they are to understand one or the other.[53] The aim is not to construct an objective theory of law and its instrumental effects but to focus 'above all' on subjective experience of legalism.[54] The question of exactly how 'concrete' a perspective centred upon the exploration of subjectivity is can be negated with the more humanistic imperative of taking interest in how legality is experienced.[55]

Since regulations play a constitutive role in our embodied experience – shaping our engagement with other bodies and institutions – the question of how conscious (if at all) legal subjects are of such processes offers clear insight into how they are working in practice. On one hand, a gender recognition law could enable subjects to act in straightforward ways, without having to dwell too much on the various complexities of their embodiment. In this case, law would appear to have constructed the 'stable platform for pursuing one's plans' discussed in Chapter 2.[56] On the other hand, if such regulations left interviewees feeling 'consumed' by their physicality almost constantly, the opposite may be inferred.[57] By offering ways to contextualise subjectivity in relation to intersubjective, material, symbolic, and institutional factors, legal embodiment is not only compatible with, but can also offer new directions for, legal consciousness studies.

51 Harding (n 31) 39.
52 ibid. 9.
53 ibid.
54 Cowan (n 43) 929.
55 Harding (n 31) 9, citing Ewick and Silbey (n 35).
56 N Priaulx, 'Rethinking Progenitive Conflict: Why Reproductive Autonomy *Matters*' (2008) 16 Medical Law Review 169, 183.
57 ibid.

Methodological framework

Implementing legal consciousness

Legal consciousness researchers should allow interviewees' understandings of law to emerge organically from their experiences of regulation and legality. If they were to lead with questions about law and legality, interviewers might unwittingly 'steer' interviewees onto these topics. This risks undermining findings and preventing assessment of how highly legal issues would otherwise have featured in their everyday consciousness. To heed this advice when designing my research, I took care not to use terms such as 'law' and 'legal' on my call for participants – on the understanding that such terms might unduly influence both responses to the call, and the eventual interview itself.[58] To guide potential respondents as to what sort of topics would be discussed in the interview, I initially only alluded to 'gender recognition' more broadly instead. Yet maintaining this strategy throughout the recruitment and interview process proved difficult. My strategy of 'snowball' sampling involved me asking interviewees to share my call for participants among their networks in order to recruit subsequent ones. One activist shared my flyer on her website with the following message: 'Have you received legal gender recognition? Would you like to be interviewed, in English, about how legal gender recognition has affected your life?' As well as precluding emerging understandings of legality, this also indicated that I was not interested in hearing from those who had not sought legal gender recognition. When, on the contrary, I was actively seeking the testimony of those who had not felt able to seek recognition in Denmark as avidly as those that had.[59] This highlights a difficulty in maintaining orthodox legal consciousness methods alongside a snowball sampling strategy.

When it came to obtaining respondents' informed consent before interviews, my attempt to allow experiences of legality to emerge organically without unnecessary prompting developed an ethical dimension. I realised that omitting any mention of law and legality in the interview materials would require me to obfuscate both the specific objectives of the research project and my contact information. Though it is accepted that researchers rarely explain '*everything* about the research' to '*all* the people they are studying',[60] I felt that omitting so much information could easily constitute a breach of respondents' trust. In their legal consciousness research, Patricia Ewick and Susan Silbey asked respondents to reflect upon 'community, neighbourhood, work, and family issues'.[61] Interviewees were only informed of the project's actual research objectives

58 Ewick and Silbey (n 35) 25.

59 When I wrote to the activist to explain this, they amended the advertisement as follows: 'Would you like to be interviewed, in English, about how trans people are recognised in Denmark?'

60 M Hammersley and P Atkinson, *Ethnography: Principles in Practice* (3rd edn, Routledge 2009) 210.

61 Ewick and Silbey (n 35) 25, 27.

once each interview had been completed. Arguably this was an inevitable consequence of the framing of their study, which sought to 'locate the place of law in American culture' by testing exactly how and when legality arose in their respondents' legal consciousness.[62] In contrast, in my research, legal consciousness only constituted a methodology for considering how jurisdictional practices have affected trans people's legal embodiment. It offered a way to explore experiences of the regulation of gender rather than constituting the central focus of the study. So, I decided to include my full address (including reference to the 'School of Law') and the objectives of the research project (as concerning 'recent changes in the law, and how these have affected people's everyday lives') on the consent forms that would be completed at the beginning of each interview.

The decision to be open with interviewees was also important due to my research's feminist perspective. The issue of whether certain methods – such as qualitative interviews – are better suited to the production of feminist research has been long-debated within feminist epistemology.[63] Yet it is now widely accepted that there is no one distinct feminist method, or aspect of feminist methods, as 'any method can be used in a pro-feminist or non-feminist way.'[64] But even those who advocate interviewing stress caveats. The conditions of 'proper' qualitative interviewing carry clear marks of gender stereotyping. This is particularly apparent in the demand that interviewers maintain 'distance' between themselves and their interviewees; which reproduces masculinist stereotypes around the desirability of objectivity, rationality, and self-restraint.[65] Feminist researchers ought to debunk these stereotypes and acknowledge what Ann Oakley describes as 'a sociology of feelings and emotion' instead:[66]

> A feminist methodology of social science […] requires […] that the mythology of 'hygienic' research with its accompanying mystification of the researcher and the researched as objective instruments of data production be replaced by the recognition that personal involvement is more than dangerous bias – it is the condition under which people come to know each other and to admit others into their lives.[67]

One of the best-known critiques of the quest for objectivity has come from feminist standpoint theory. Standpoint theorists argue that beginning with experience of discrimination does not risk bias but rather gives marginalised

62 ibid. xii.

63 A Oakley, 'Interviewing Women: A Contradiction in Terms' in H Roberts (ed), *Doing Feminist Research* (Routledge 1981).

64 G Letherby, *Feminist Research in Theory and Practice* (Open University Press 2003) 5.

65 Oakley (n 63) 38.

66 ibid. 40.

67 ibid. 58.

populations 'epistemic privilege' instead.[68] As all attempts to generate knowledge are socially situated, those located 'on the margins' of society might be better placed to account for what goes on there than the privileged few who view such phenomena from the untroubled 'centre'.[69] The key insights of standpoint theory have been developed over subsequent decades, notably in Donna Haraway's idea of 'situated knowledges'.[70] As she is wary of reifying marginal subject positions, Haraway argues that the knowledges produced from such positions should not be 'exempt from critical re-examination' – as there are no '"innocent" positions'.[71] Yet this need not undermine standpoint completely. Situated knowledges and standpoint theory retain common objectives: of challenging those who suggest that hygienic research is possible (let alone desirable) and developing an epistemology which does not advocate simple 'relativism':

> the alternative to relativism is not totalization and single vision [...] The alternative to relativism is partial, locatable, critical knowledges sustaining the possibility of webs of connections called solidarity in politics and shared conversations in epistemology.[72]

The idea that partial, locatable, knowledge should be accorded greater epistemological value than that which purports to offer objectivity accords with Caroline Ramazanoğlu and Janet Holland's suggestion that what distinguishes feminist from non-feminist research is 'the particular political positioning of theory, epistemology and ethics that enables the feminist researcher to question existing 'truths' and explore relations between knowledge and power.'[73] Others would argue that *all* qualitative research should involve 'critical self-scrutiny' or '*active reflexivity*'.[74] In any case, reflexivity allows the researcher to hold themselves to account, to take responsibility for decisions made in the research process, and by implication to increase the validity of their research.

Whether in pursuit of maintaining feminist ethical standards or those of qualitative research generally, I sought to balance being attentive to power dynamics with being transparent about how my research was conducted. On occasion, this was straightforward; for example, recounting my findings in the

68 BA Bar On, 'Marginality and Epistemic Privilege' in L Alcoff and E Potter (eds), *Feminist Epistemologies* (Routledge 1993).

69 S Harding, 'Rethinking Standpoint Epistemology: What Is "Strong Objectivity"?' in L Alcoff and E Potter (eds), *Feminist Epistemologies* (Routledge 1993) 52.

70 D Haraway, 'Situated Knowledges: The Science Question in Feminism and the Privilege of Partial Perspective' (1988) 14(3) Feminist Studies 575.

71 ibid. 584.

72 ibid.

73 Ramazanoğlu with Holland (n 12) 16.

74 Mason (n 11) 7.

first person to challenge traditionally disembodied academic 'authority'.[75] Yet on others, as in accounting for how my own identity position affected interviews, this has been more complicated. As a white, English, middle-class, and able-bodied cis man, I have tried to reflect upon how my experience, appearance, and background affected the research process (particularly in the second part of this chapter). But these categories are also fluid and dynamic, and it has not always been easy to account for them in writing. Even where power relations can be accounted for, it is questionable if they can ever be adequately ameliorated. Sceptics suggest that researchers can merely account for the impact they have had on their work.[76] Others are more optimistic. Suggesting that the problem of unequal power relations is, at least in part, dialectical (i.e. problem and solution are one and the same), Karen O'Reilly notes that awareness of the potential for exploitation and the role of representation 'is the first step in trying to avoid it'.[77]

Irrespective of whether the problems it causes can be answered or not, the question of how I *identify* is arguably of lesser importance than how I *am identified* within the research project. Even where interviewer and respondent share common experiences, the fact that they have assumed these roles for the purposes of the interview could be enough to emphasise differences over similarities.[78] Interestingly, this can also be taken as a positive. For Haraway:

> The knowing self is partial in all its guises, never finished, whole, simply there and original; it is always constructed and stitched together imperfectly, and *therefore* able to join with another, to see together without claiming to be another.[79]

In this formulation, the identity problem is inverted. Rather than seeking to account, individually, for power and resistance – and bemoaning the inevitable difficulty in doing so – scholars are reminded that there are benefits that come with being relationally, and partially, constructed. One is that by seeking to account for how I am identified within interviews I am, in the process, acknowledging the 'embodied experience of the speaking subject'.[80] The trans studies literature considers this an essential step for a cis researcher, like myself, who seeks to conduct research with 'respectful curiosity'.[81] A relational

75 Letherby (n 64) 7.
76 B Matthews and L Ross, *Research Methods: A Practical Guide for the Social Sciences* (Pearson 2010) 77.
77 K O'Reilly, *Key Concepts in Ethnography* (Sage 2009) 60.
78 J Wallbank, 'Returning the Subject to the Subject of Women's Poverty: An Essay on the Importance of Subjectivity for the Feminist Research Project' (1995) 3(2) Feminist Legal Studies 207, 219.
79 Haraway (n 70) 586.
80 S Stryker, '(De)Subjugated Knowledges: An Introduction to Transgender Studies' in S Stryker and S Whittle (eds), *The Transgender Studies Reader* (Routledge 2006) 12.
81 T Raun, 'Trans as Contested Intelligibility: Interrogating how to Conduct Trans Analysis with Respectful Curiosity' [2014] (1) Lambda Nordica 13.

understanding of subjectivity also lays the foundations for an epistemology which is developed and negotiated on a collective, or at least inter-personal, level. Expectations will only ever be provisional, and stereotypes should be avoided as far as possible. In practice, this involves spending less time constructing individualised reflections on identity and more focusing upon how identities are negotiated within a research project instead.

Negotiating outsider status

Researchers utilising legal consciousness methods must take as much care when negotiating their position as they would when using other methods. Research conducted with specific social groups will be affected when the researcher is perceived to be an 'insider' or 'outsider' of the group in question. Yet such are the vagaries of social positioning that this may have an ambiguous or even incalculable effect.[82] This was borne out in the interviews conducted with trans people about how they had been personally affected by the 2014 reforms in Denmark. After deciding to be transparent about my legal background during the consent process, in several online and face-to-face interviews I got the impression that I was being read as a naïve cis law student from England. While it was accepted that I was interested in investigating trans issues in Denmark, I was assumed to be doing so without much prior knowledge. In these cases, respondents engaged quite openly with the questions about the meanings of gender and sexuality which I asked early on in interviews in order to get conversation flowing. Yet this engagement came with a tendency to answer with impersonal definitions ("gender is *x*, sexuality is *y*"), despite me specifying that interviewees should reflect upon what these terms meant to them personally. Although this helped interviewees to bed-in to their interviews, it also delayed the emergence of more complex and personal disclosures until after more strategic representations of trans experience. Being perceived as an 'outsider' may, in these cases, have compromised the richness and diversity of the responses I was able to solicit.

Other face-to-face interviews proceeded differently. Respondents have their own expectations of the interview process, which may involve them attempting to place the researcher 'within the social landscape'.[83] Early on in most face-to-face meetings, particularly in the conversations that preceded the consent process, it seemed on occasion as though the questions I was being asked may have amounted to my being 'tested out' by respondents as to how naïve I actually was.[84] In some, I got the impression that I was read as an 'ally' – and perhaps even as a(nother) queer person. Some of the more unexpected

82 Even where identities are shared, insider/outsider status will never be guaranteed; Wallbank (n 78).
83 Hammersley and Atkinson (n 60) 63.
84 ibid. 46.

and challenging responses to my later questions about topics such as the most important needs of trans people arose out of these situations. Yet some of these interviewees were also taken aback by the same earlier questions about trans and gender which were pounced upon by online interviewees. Straightforward questions came across as too 'basic' once I was understood not to be a complete 'outsider'.[85] Irrespective of how I felt I was being read, I took care not to make any assumptions about this, or to let this affect my interview manner – particularly where I felt that the lines might be being blurred. Drawing attention to commonalities can be viewed as patronising and misguided – as they might be taken as inferring that the interviewer is in some way 'like' the interviewee, or vice versa.[86]

I experienced being designated 'outsider' status most early on in interviews with those involved in designing and implementing the new regulations. In the interviews I conducted with professional regulators, being able to present myself as a relatively naïve legal scholar from abroad may have helped gain access to conduct the interview in the first place rather than undermining the objectivity of the research.[87] In such circumstances, the insights of feminist standpoint theory could be re-construed as practical advantages in terms of access; as the 'problem' of me not being a trans person or activist enabled me to gain access to interview those who I may not have otherwise have had access to. Yet just as Zowie Davy's experienced 'insider' status as proving 'slippery',[88] I found that 'outsider' status is also prone to suspicion. During one interview with a regulator I was asked: "You're not an activist, are you?" I am not, and so felt comfortable answering this question: "No." Yet as a researcher who seeks to illuminate embodied effects of governing practices in a way which might offer useful insights to activists and campaigners, this constituted another ethical challenge in terms negotiating insider/outsider status.

Managing expectations and consent

Being transparent about my legal background did have at least one unexpected consequence in my research. When I asked respondents why they had responded to my advert (as I did at the beginning of each interview), several cited the legal focus of the study as the reason they decided to participate.

85 This impression was particularly marked in an interview conducted with a respondent I met in an activist context.

86 V Waller, K Farquharson, and D Dempsey, *Qualitative Social Research: Contemporary Methods for the Digital Age* (Sage 2016) 89–90.

87 It was suggested to me by different activists and researchers that I would have been less likely to gain access to these 'elite' interviewees had I been a Danish researcher with established links to trans communities.

88 Z Davy, 'Transsexual recognition: embodiment, bodily aesthetics and the medicolegal system' (PhD thesis, University of Leeds 2008) 93.

One drew a comparison with the more intimate and potentially sensationalised focus of calls for participants from "sociologists" or "journalists" that had been circulating with greater frequency over recent years. Trans people are increasingly asked to give up their time – often uncompensated – to respond to researchers. This amounts to a request for 'intellectual and emotional labour', which is best met with financial compensation.[89] Without this, Ben Vincent suggests researchers ensure that they 'have a clear goal of what they wish to achieve and how, to the benefit of (at least part of) the trans population.'[90] Having decided to maximise transparency, I gave each respondent a summary of the aims and objectives of my research on a written consent form at the beginning of every interview. When another interviewee indicated that the 'legal' nature of my research could increase its potential impact, I also sought to manage their expectations as to how unlikely it was that the findings would contribute to any tangible legal change (at least in the short and medium term). Where legal consciousness researchers are open about the legal focus of their research, in a politicised area such as trans rights, managing expectations of potential impact may be more necessary than it would were experiences of legality to be allowed to emerge more organically.

The use of consent forms also indicated the perils of examining the presence of law in a society which is foreign to the researcher studying it. My forms indicated that interviews would be based upon the principle of informed consent. This would be ongoing, and interviewees were entitled to withdraw their responses up until the point that the thesis, or any materials related to it, had been published.[91] The main drawback in seeking to obtain consent in this manner is that being required to sign such a form might prompt rather than alleviate possible concerns.[92] Yet within this project the consent process was viewed by most respondents as quite formulaic. State bureaucracy is more sophisticated in Denmark than it is in the UK – ironically, in no small part due to the wealth of information attached to the CPR number. Danish residents therefore tend to engage less frequently with visible examples of paperwork than their UK counterparts.

Litigation culture is also less pronounced. Hence being asked to sign documentation confirming that you agree to certain terms and conditions is more unusual. Not all interviews were affected by the consent process in the same way. In most, consent was negotiated without much comment. Yet where

89 BW Vincent, 'Studying Trans: Recommendations for Ethical Recruitment and Collaboration with Transgender Participants in Academic Research' (2018) 9(2) Psychology & Sexuality 102, 104, citing S Ahmed, *The Cultural Politics of Emotion* (Edinburgh University Press 2014) and AR Hochschild, *The Managed Heart: Commercialization of Human Feeling* (University of California Press 2012).

90 ibid. 105.

91 Matthews and Ross (n 76) 12.

92 A Bryman, *Social Research Methods* (4th edn, OUP 2012) 140.

it was noted by respondents, it affected the atmosphere of the interview in one of two ways. Either the effect was detrimental, as consent forms gave the impression that the process was more serious than it had previously seemed (or needed to be). Or, the novelty of the consent process served as an ice-breaker, inviting jokes about the formality of my approach (with one interviewee informing me that "No-one sues anyone in Denmark, you know."). In any case, the impression that written consent appeared more about protecting myself, and my university, appeared to have been registered – even though this should never become the primary goal of the consent process.[93] Documenting consent placed a more formal slant on proceedings in Denmark than it might have done had they been conducted in the UK instead. That I had not anticipated this highlights the difficulty of studying law in a culture which one is not entirely familiar with.

Confidentiality and security

Before interviewing, I decided that confidentiality should be negotiated rather than assumed in my research. Assuming the need or desire for anonymity risked perpetuating what Tobias Raun has described as the 'transphobic myth' that being trans is something that one should hide, or which trans people ought to be ashamed of.[94] This principle still had to be applied on a case-by-case basis; to balance the risks of being identifiable in research publications against potential benefits with each interview respondent. Following Sally Hines, I asked interviewees who decided to take up this offer of anonymity to come up with a pseudonym of their own choosing.[95] Some respondents welcomed this as an amusing activity on which to end the process of interviewing. For others, it was off-putting, with one stating: "I had enough trouble settling upon this name!" With hindsight, this process would have passed more smoothly had I prepared a list of potential pseudonyms that I could suggest in the eventuality that the respondent did not have one in mind.

For some interviewees, including those currently undergoing assessment at the Sexological Clinic, I had assumed that confidentiality could allow them to be more candid in their responses – reducing any anxieties about potentially negative consequences for the progress of their treatment. What I had not anticipated was one interviewee's repeated insistence against anonymity. This suggested that this interviewee had inverted the logic of this argument

93 S Webster, J Lewis, and A Brown, 'Ethical Considerations in Qualitative Research' in J Ritchie, J Lewis, C McNaughton Nicholls, and R Ormston (eds), *Qualitative Research Practice: A Guide for Social Science Students and Researchers* (2nd edn, Sage 2014) 92.

94 T Raun, 'Screen-Births: Exploring the Transformative Potential in Trans Video Blogs on YouTube' (2010) 7(2) Graduate Journal of Social Science 113, 116–117.

95 S Hines, 'Transgender Identities, Intimate Relationships and Practices of Care' (PhD thesis, University of Leeds 2004) 102.

– deducing that a positive testimony could also affect the progress of their case through the Sexological Clinic. If I am right that this respondent had developed such a strategy, this would add emphasis to Davy's argument that trans people have developed a 'reflexive agency' (discussed in more detail in Chapter 2); where they disclose information strategically to those whom they assume have the authority to affect their treatment.[96]

Beyond strategic benefits, confidentiality was also rejected by some interviewees on the assumption that it might undermine prospective advantages in terms of political organising. The one intersex person that I interviewed even went beyond rejecting anonymity to demand greater identifiability – requesting that I refer to her by her full name, rather than merely her forename, to increase her profile as an intersex activist in a country with no official intersex policy. I might have anticipated this had I been more attuned to the political dynamics on the ground amongst intersex communities and medical authorities in Denmark. It again raises questions about how appropriate it is to conduct legal consciousness research as an outsider (both as a cis person conducting trans studies research, and as an English person who is not a permanent Danish resident).

The information sheet sent to prospective interviewees sought to elicit personal information about the respondent that could be supplemented by, and expanded upon, during interviews. In the spirit of self-identification, this included a text box after biographical characteristics (including gender, sexuality, and ethnicity) which could be filled in as the respondent saw fit. This led to a variety of responses. Some referred to themselves as a 'transman' or 'transwoman'; a 'trans man' or 'trans woman'; 'male' or 'female'; 'man' or 'woman', etc. There was little consistency, and yet I will reproduce this as faithfully as possible when quoting from these respondents in subsequent chapters. This might appear 'messy', but is still preferable to imposing my own categories on people in accordance with my own ideas or preferences. This open text box was followed by a tick box after the more impersonal question of employment status (including an option to tick 'other', followed by a text box to expand, if necessary).

The information sheet also asked participants to select a preferred name, rather than soliciting their legal (or even birth) name. To insist on 'proper' names would have betrayed an ignorance of the complexities surrounding processes of naming in the formulation of trans identities.[97] Yet one oversight, which put the information sheet at odds with non-binary inclusive practice,[98]

96 Z Davy, 'Transsexual Agents: Negotiating Authenticity and Embodiment within the UK's Medicolegal System', in S Hines and T Sanger (eds), *Transgender Identities: Towards a Social Analysis of Gender Diversity* (Routledge 2010) 108.

97 W Wilkinson, 'Cultural Competency' (2014) 1(1–2) Transgender Studies Quarterly 68, 70.

98 W Anderson, 'Pronoun Round Etiquette' (*The Body is not an Apology*, 22 December 2015) <https://thebodyisnotanapology.com/magazine/pronoun-round-etiquette> accessed 27 September 2016.

was that a requirement to select preferred pronouns was not included. This required me to contact respondents after interviews had been completed to ask what their preferred pronouns would be for publications reporting my findings (including this book). That this request generated some unexpected responses (with one non-binary interviewee stating a preference for "no pronouns", as opposed to gender-neutral ones such as 'they') confirmed that not including a space to self-define preferred pronouns constituted an omission from the information sheet.

Interviews with stakeholders – including representatives from the main campaigning organisations, and the regulators who I interviewees from institutional authorities – were predominantly conducted in their offices. Yet most interviews exploring trans people's personal experiences of the 2014 reforms were conducted in public spaces.[99] Relying upon public space did not always work as well as intended. One interviewee deemed a public meeting place inappropriate on the insistence that this would not allow them to "speak freely". While I was aware of the importance of agreeing upon a space where participants would feel comfortable,[100] I had not anticipated public space being vetoed completely. In response, I sought clearance to depart from the risk assessment I had submitted to my university. This was granted on the condition that this was a one-off, and that I was sure to 'check-in' and 'check-out' with a reliable person who would be sure to take immediate action if I had not 'checked-out' at a time pre-agreed before the interview. The decision not to include the possibility of conducting interviews in private spaces in the original risk assessment was partly motivated by the understanding that public spaces are better suited to mitigating against risks to the researcher's personal safety, as well as shielding them from accusations of impropriety.[101] In the Danish context, where personal litigation is much less common than in the UK, risks to the researcher were deemed less significant than those to the interviewee – whose anonymity in this case seemed more at risk in a public space. This factor ought to be considered by future researchers on trans and other sensitive political issues.

Another unanticipated cultural factor related to the possibility of conducting interviews on campus, in space provided by the Center for Gender Studies at the Faculty of Humanities, University of Copenhagen. The importance of the interviewee feeling comfortable with the interview location led me to assume that the university campus should be avoided, where possible, for fear that this formal setting could seem intimidating.[102] Yet in Denmark, where class-consciousness and elitism appear to register as less of a problem than in higher

99 Waller, Farquharson, and Dempsey (n 86) 83.
100 ibid.
101 Arksey and Knight (n 23) 138.
102 Waller, Farquharson, and Dempsey (n 86) 83.

education institutions in the UK,[103] two respondents overcame my concerns by giving me the impression that they felt that the university was a public space which they had a right to enter – either as a student or interviewee. When I agreed to meet these respondents on campus, I asked them why they had preferred to meet there (rather than in a café in the centre of Copenhagen). Both mentioned that it was easier to find parking spaces on Amager (the island upon which the Faculty of Humanities is located) than in the city centre. This made my concern for how they might perceive the campus buildings seem at best impractical – and at worst patronising. It again highlighted the difficulties which may be faced by researchers who are studying the legal consciousness of residents of a society that the researcher isn't immersed in.

Conclusion

In this chapter, I advocate the importance of conducting legal consciousness research. Though existing instances of jurisdictional analysis, and studies of legal embodiment, have yet to integrate legal consciousness approaches, I laid out the extent to which these different strands of scholarship can be compatible with one another. While their proponents in the different literatures may at times appear to be at cross-purposes, I consider them to be reconcilable. I have sought to bring them together in interesting and productive ways in this book. For the most part, this has been framed in relation to my specific aim of ascertaining the embodied effects of the implementation of self-declaration of legal gender status in Denmark in this chapter. But I hope that the benefit of using legal consciousness approaches to illuminate the embodied effects of jurisdictional arrangements will be apparent enough for other researchers engaged in trans legal studies, feminist legal scholarship, as well as socio-legal studies more widely.

I began the chapter describing my methodological approach and explaining how legal consciousness can be used to uncover the embodied effects of jurisdictional arrangements. This is possible even where legal consciousness does not appear to share the ontological and epistemological priorities of a given research area (including orthodox governmentality studies). Rather than taking this as insurmountable, I suggest that it is precisely because of its subjective focus that legal consciousness might trace the affective and human effects of a governing project which would otherwise go unnoticed. To assess the impact of the implementation of self-declaration of legal gender status in Denmark, I combined qualitative interviews with doctrinal and documentary analysis, and

103 The proportion of Danish citizens from disadvantaged socio-economic backgrounds in tertiary education is higher than the international average; Organisation for Economic Co-operation and Development, *Education at a Glance 2012: OECD Indicators* (OECD 2012) <www.oecd.org/edu/EAG 2012_e-book_EN_200912.pdf> 106.

used the theoretical framework developed in Chapter 2 to situate subjective experiences of regulation in relation to their intersubjective, material, symbolic, and institutional contexts. Other researchers might find it possible, or even preferable, to study legal consciousness by combining qualitative interviews with methods including participant observation.

Having laid out my methodological approach, I described how I implemented legal consciousness methods to interview trans people and regulators in Denmark following the 2014 reforms. I shied away from attempting to allow experiences of legality to emerge, without prompting, from interviewees. This was motivated by methodological and ethical reasons. Methodologically, I found it practically impossible to avoid mentioning law when recruiting interviewees via snowball sampling. This objection could be met by future researchers who have the benefit of taking this into account in their research design. I found the ethical objection more 'sticky'.[104] My gut feeling was that to avoid mentioning law would inevitably limit the transparency of my research – and potentially any socio-legal research project. It could also undermine the informed consent of interviewees. In specific circumstances, such as Ewick and Silbey's (where the central objective of the research is to ascertain how highly law features in the everyday consciousness of respondents), this could be justified as unavoidable – particularly if the research question could not otherwise be answered. But where this is not absolutely necessary – as in my research – I would suggest prioritising informed consent and increasing transparency.

After discussing these issues, I drew from feminist theory and trans studies to consider some of the key challenges which may be faced by legal consciousness researchers when it comes to negotiating insider/outsider status. This discussion reflected heavily upon my experience as a white, English, middle-class, and able-bodied cis man, who conducted research into trans issues in Denmark despite not living there for a period of more than three months at a time. On certain occasions, I noted that my apparent naïveté had unanticipated benefits – notably when it came to gaining access to some 'elite' interviewees and institutional spaces. On others, it may have limited the depth of interview responses, leading to me soliciting only relatively simplified accounts of what it feels like to be trans in Denmark following the 2014 reforms from some interviewees.

My outsider status also led to me encountering difficulties in managing expectations regarding consent, confidentiality, and security, which might have been easier to anticipate had I been more familiar with Danish cultural norms. In highlighting these issues, I am by no means seeking to put subsequent researchers off conducting legal consciousness research abroad. But such researchers should at least be aware that such forks in the road my present themselves for consideration when considering or conducting legal consciousness research in

104 Raun (n 81) 13, citing S Ahmed (n 89).

this area and in other areas. I will go on to discuss the findings that I generated from taking this approach in the remaining three chapters of this book.

Bibliography

Anderson W, 'Pronoun Round Etiquette' (*The Body is not an Apology*, 22 December 2015) <https://thebodyisnotanapology.com/magazine/pronoun-round-etiquette> accessed 27 September 2016

Arksey H and Knight P, *Interviewing for Social Scientists* (Sage 1999)

Bar On BA, 'Marginality and Epistemic Privilege' in Alcoff L and Potter E (eds), *Feminist Epistemologies* (Routledge 1993)

Bryman A, *Social Research Methods* (4th edn, OUP 2012)

Cooper D, 'Local Government Legal Consciousness in the Shadow of Juridification' (1995) 22(4) Journal of Law and Society 506

Cowan D, 'Legal Consciousness: Some Observations' (2004) 67(6) Modern Law Review 928

Davy Z, 'Transsexual Recognition: Embodiment, Bodily Aesthetics and the Medicolegal System' (PhD thesis, University of Leeds 2008)

——— 'Transsexual Agents: Negotiating Authenticity and Embodiment within the UK's Medicolegal System' in Hines S and Sanger T (eds), *Transgender Identities: Towards a Social Analysis of Gender Diversity* (Routledge 2010)

Dietz C, 'Book Review: Mariana Valverde, *Chronotopes of Law: Jurisdiction, Scale and Governance*' (2016) 25(1) Social & Legal Studies 126

Dunne P, 'Rethinking Legal Gender Recognition: Recent Reforms in Argentina, Denmark and the Netherlands' (2015) 1 International Family Law 41

Ewick P and Silbey S, 'Conformity, Contestation, and Resistance: An Account of Legal Consciousness' (1992) 26 New England Law Review 731

——— *The Common Place of Law: Stories from Everyday Life* (University of Chicago Press 1998)

Flyvbjerg B, *Making Social Science Matter: Why Social Inquiry Fails and How It Can Succeed Again* (Sampson S tr, Cambridge University Press 2002)

——— 'Case Study' in Denzin NK and Lincoln YS (eds), *The Sage Handbook of Qualitative Research* (4th edn, Sage 2011)

Hammersley M and Atkinson P, *Ethnography: Principles in Practice* (3rd edn, Routledge 2009)

Haraway D, 'Situated Knowledges: The Science Question in Feminism and the Privilege of Partial Perspective' (1988) 14(3) Feminist Studies 575

Harding R, *Regulating Sexuality: Legal Consciousness in Lesbian and Gay Lives* (Routledge 2011)

Harding S, 'Rethinking Standpoint Epistemology: What Is 'Strong Objectivity'?' in Alcoff L and Potter E (eds), *Feminist Epistemologies* (Routledge 1993)

Hines S, 'Transgender Identities, Intimate Relationships and Practices of Care' (PhD thesis, University of Leeds 2004)

Letherby G, *Feminist Research in Theory and Practice* (Open University Press 2003)

Mason J, *Qualitative Researching* (2nd edn, Sage 2002)

Matthews B and Ross L, *Research Methods: A Practical Guide for the Social Sciences* (Pearson 2010)

O'Reilly K, *Key Concepts in Ethnography* (Sage 2009)

Oakley A, 'Interviewing Women: A Contradiction in Terms' in H Roberts (ed), *Doing Feminist Research* (Routledge 1981)

Organisation for Economic Co-operation and Development, *Education at a Glance 2012: OECD Indicators* (OECD 2012) <http://www.oecd.org/edu/EAG 2012_e-book_EN _200912.pdf>

Priaulx N, 'Rethinking Progenitive Conflict: Why Reproductive Autonomy *Matters*' (2008) 16 Medical Law Review 169

Prior L, 'Repositioning Documents in Social Research' (2008) 42(5) Sociology 821

Ramazanoğlu C with Holland J, *Feminist Methodology: Challenges and Choices* (Sage 2002)

Raun T, 'Screen-Births: Exploring the Transformative Potential in Trans Video Blogs on YouTube' (2010) 7(2) Graduate Journal of Social Science 113

——— 'Trans as Contested Intelligibility: Interrogating How to Conduct Trans Analysis with Respectful Curiosity' (2014) 1 Lambda Nordica 13

Sarat A, '"...The Law is All Over": Power, Resistance and the Legal Consciousness of the Welfare Poor' (1990) 2 Yale Journal of Law and the Humanities 378

——— and Kearns TR, 'Beyond the Great Divide: Forms of Legal Scholarship and Everyday Life' in Sarat A and Kearns TR (eds), *Law in Everyday Life* (University of Michigan Press 1995)

Scott J, *A Matter of Record: Documentary Sources in Social Research* (Polity Press 1990) 11

Stryker S, '(De)Subjugated Knowledges: An Introduction to Transgender Studies' in Stryker S and Whittle S (eds), *The Transgender Studies Reader* (Routledge 2006)

Tamanaha BZ, 'The Folly of the "Social Scientific" Concept of Legal Pluralism' (1993) 20(2) Journal of Law and Society 192

——— 'A Non-Essentialist Version of Legal Pluralism' (2000) 27(2) Journal of Law and Society 296

Valverde M, 'Genealogies of European States: Foucauldian Reflections' (2007) 36(1) Economy and Society 159

——— 'Jurisdiction and Scale: Legal 'Technicalities' as Resources for Theory' (2009) 18 Social & Legal Studies 139

——— *Everyday Law on the Street: City Governance in an Age of Diversity* (University of Chicago Press 2012)

——— 'Studying the Governance of Crime and Security: Space, Time and Jurisdiction' (2014) 14(4) Criminology & Criminal Justice 379

——— *Chronotopes of Law: Jurisdiction, Scale and Governance* (Routledge 2015)

Vincent BW, 'Studying Trans: Recommendations for Ethical Recruitment and Collaboration with Transgender Participants in Academic Research' (2018) 9(2) Psychology & Sexuality 102

Wallbank J, 'Returning the Subject to the Subject of Women's Poverty: An Essay on the Importance of Subjectivity for the Feminist Research Project' (1995) 3(2) Feminist Legal Studies 207

Waller V, Farquharson K, and Dempsey D, *Qualitative Social Research: Contemporary Methods for the Digital Age* (Sage 2016)

Webster S, Lewis J, and Brown A, 'Ethical Considerations in Qualitative Research' in Ritchie J, Lewis J, McNaughton Nicholls C, and Ormston R (eds), *Qualitative Research Practice: A Guide for Social Science Students and Researchers* (2nd edn, Sage 2014)

Wilkinson W, 'Cultural Competency' (2014) 1(1–2) Transgender Studies Quarterly 68

Chapter 4

Visibility and progress in trans rights

Introduction

In this chapter, I challenge the idea that visibility is a necessary precursor to progress in the context of gender recognition law reform. I discuss the imperative, established in the early trans studies literature, for trans people to make themselves 'visible' in the first part of the chapter. I note that uneven visibility did not preclude the enactment of self-declaration of legal gender status in Denmark in 2014. This stands in contrast with the current situation in the US or in England and Wales, where trans people have never been more visible, and yet the enactment of similar reforms has not seemed less likely since the beginning of the 21st century.[1] My argument comes with the caveat that while the research I conducted in Denmark has made me question any straightforward equation of visibility and progress, I would not go as far as to suggest that invisibility offers a more direct route to gender recognition law reform. I am merely suggesting that the fact that self-declaration could be enacted in Denmark via a depoliticised administrative jurisdiction challenges the assumption that visibility is a necessary precursor to progress in trans rights.

In the second part of the chapter, I turn to the idea of 'progress' itself. Drawing upon analysis of the legislative debates in the Danish Parliament, and interviews conducted with stakeholders involved in the reform process, I suggest that this process was largely depoliticised. Policy makers and regulators sought to avoid creating or sustaining moral panic around trans issues (as seen in the US and UK).[2] Danish reforms were considered 'technical' legal amendments, which were subject to the sole jurisdiction of civil administrators. This

1 The Scottish Gender Recognition Reform (Scotland) Bill 2022 provides an exception here. (Though see B Collier and S Cowan, 'Queer Conflicts, Concept Capture and Category Co-Option: The Importance of Context in the State Collection and Recording of Sex/Gender Data' (2022) Social & Legal Studies <https://doi.org/10.1177%2F09646639211061409> for a discussion of ongoing issues in the Scottish context.)

2 Again, the Scottish context – where backlash to the Gender Recognition Reform (Scotland) Bill 2022 continues at the time of writing – provides a useful point of contrast.

DOI: 10.4324/9780429288203-4

had certain advantages, in terms of enabling the law to pass through the parliamentary process without generating heated public debate. It also had limitations, particularly when it came to more holistic issues, including access to health care. Drawing upon political theory, I argue that the administrative jurisdiction that was created was limited in scope, with legal gender recognition separated out from other issues of material significance to trans people.

The result is that trans people in Denmark are offered the right to declare and experience of belonging to 'the other sex/gender', and have this recognised by the Danish Central Person Registry (CPR). But nothing more. They become individually responsible for dealing with any negative consequences that result from changing legal gender status; including when accessing public services or in an employment context. Non-binary people are also excluded from recognition. The Danish government was so keen to avoid creating any novel state responsibilities that it rejected the opportunity to 'de-certify' legal gender status (by removing it from the CPR system).[3] In the third section of the chapter, I draw upon affect theory to conclude that the Danish reforms do not support a unilinear or teleological understanding of progress in trans rights. I suggest that the non-linear, caveated, narrative that characterises the 2014 reforms in Denmark offers a better point of departure for researchers of gender recognition law reform. This argument against straightforward conceptions of progress has significance for those working on trans legal scholarship and activism, and in feminist and socio-legal scholarship more broadly.

Visibility

In the early 1990s, at the inception of what is now known as 'trans studies', Sandy Stone published her 'posttranssexual manifesto'.[4] Amongst other provocations was a challenge to trans people not to always seek to 'pass' as cis people. Instead trans people were encouraged to 'come out' as trans – to affect general understandings about transition, and 'to write oneself into the discourses by which one has been written'.[5] Stone's essay exerts an ongoing influence on trans scholars and activists today. And while this is only implicit in her argument, it is often taken for granted that as the visibility of trans people increases, so will the demand for, and enactment of, trans rights. Visibility and progress are assumed to increase in proportion relative to one another – with increasing visibility constituting a form of progress in itself. Invisibility – or at least a lack of visibility – is by the same token understood to constitute an obstacle to progress.

3 D Cooper and F Renz, 'If the State Decertified Gender, What Might Happen to its Meaning and Value?' (2016) 43(4) Journal of Law and Society 483.

4 S Stone, '*The* Empire *Strikes Back*: A Posttranssexual Manifesto' in S Stryker and S Whittle (eds), *Transgender Studies Reader* (Routledge 2006) 232.

5 ibid.

How will the availability and accessibility of trans rights improve if trans people are not seen and understood by the general public? What chance is there that gender recognition laws will be reformed if trans people do not feature highly in the public imagination? These arguments have merits, at least on the practical level, considering how (some) governments develop their legislative agendas. But a teleological understanding of visibility and progress as unilinear (or even inevitable) is open to challenge; not least when trans people struggle to be anything but visible in difficult public spaces (as Stone noted).[6] Trans people have reported experiencing both hypervisibility and stark invisibility, as their gender status comes under constant scrutiny as they struggle to gain access to various rights.[7] A unilinear understanding of visibility and progress can also be challenged on an empirical level, when states with low trans visibility (such as Denmark) reform gender recognition laws, while others in which trans people are relatively more visible (including in the US and in England and Wales) shy away from reform for fear of actual or perceived backlash.

Trans people have, historically, enjoyed relatively high visibility on domestic and international scales in Denmark. This is in no small part down to the Danish artist Lili Elbe famously travelling to Germany to undergo a series of surgical procedures in the 1920s and 1930s.[8] Former US soldier Christine Jorgensen also underwent two widely reported operations while visiting relatives in Denmark in 1951 and 1952.[9] Yet since Elbe and Jorgensen, the visibility of trans people in Denmark reduced, at least in comparison with their international peers. But this did not stop the Danish government promising – in its 2011 coalition agreement – to review 'the rules concerning sex/gender modification treatment, including opportunities to have a legal sex/gender change without the need for surgical intervention'.[10] Trans visibility did briefly increase in Denmark when a 15-year-old trans person named Caspian Drumm publicly announced that he had undergone a mastectomy at a private hospital in Denmark's third-largest city of Odense, in May 2011. This became known in the Danish media as 'the Caspian case',[11] even though, as I noted in Chapter 1, no formal legal proceedings followed. Yet a period of media con-

6 ibid.

7 S Lamble, 'Unknowable Bodies, Unthinkable Sexualities: Lesbian and Transgender Legal Invisibility in the Toronto Women's Bathhouse Raid' (2009) 18(1) Social & Legal Studies 111, 116, citing S Whittle, 'Introduction' in K More and S Whittle (eds), *Reclaiming Genders: Transsexual Grammars at the Fin de Siecle* (Cassell 1999) 6–11.

8 T Raun, 'The "Caspian Case" and Its Aftermath: Transgender People's Use of Facebook to Engage Discriminatory Mainstream News Coverage in Denmark' in J Björklund and U Lindqvist (eds), *New Dimensions of Diversity in Nordic Culture and Society* (Cambridge Scholars Publishing 2016) 79.

9 ibid.

10 This was included in the 2011 coalition government's policy agreement, introduced in Chapter 1; Prime Minister's Office, 'Et Danmark, Der Står Sammen' (October 2011) <www.stm.dk/publikationer/Et_Danmark_der_staar_sammen_11/Regeringsgrundlag_okt_2011.pdf> accessed 20 August 2015.

11 T Raun (n 8).

troversy did.[12] And as I have noted, in response, the then Minister of Health, Astrid Krag, called upon the Danish Health and Medicines Authority (DHMA) to investigate the existing health care regulations and practices concerning trans people's access to body modification technologies, and to determine whether the private hospital had 'acted responsibly'.[13] The surgeon who performed the mastectomy was reprimanded in November 2012 for failing to subject Caspian to sustained psychiatric assessment beforehand.[14]

The DHMA then issued interim guidelines for all medical practitioners in Denmark, which closed the legal loophole through which trans people could access body modification technologies through private-sector practitioners, and established a *de jure* treatment monopoly at the Sexological Clinic in Copenhagen.[15] This monopoly was maintained even after the CPR law had been enacted; as the DHMA published a new set of formal guidelines 'on the evaluation and treatment of transgender [people]' in December 2014.[16] These codified that 'sex/gender modification' treatments (such as hormone replacement treatment and various surgical operations) could only be administered by a 'multidisciplinary team of collaborating specialists in psychiatry, obstetrics/gynaecology and plastic surgery, who have special knowledge of transgender patients'.[17] As I noted in Chapter 1, this abolished the *de jure* monopoly established by the interim guidelines, as no explicit reference was made to the Sexological Clinic. Yet a *de facto* monopoly was temporarily retained as the Sexological Clinic was, until September 2017, the only clinic with sufficient capacity to put together this multidisciplinary team and meet these requirements.[18]

While the visibility of trans issues within mainstream media in the US and England and Wales has never seemed higher, trans people remain largely invisible in Anglo-American courts.[19] Progress in terms of trans rights seems

12 ibid.

13 T Raun (n 8), citing 'Minister går nu ind i Caspian-sag' (*TV2 Nyhederne*, 15 October 2011) <http://nyhederne.tv2.dk/article.php/id-44674432:minister-går-nu-ind-i-caspiansag.html>.

14 Patients' Ombudsman, 'Kritik for behandling – speciallæge i plastikkirurgi Jens Pilegaard Bjarnesen' (1 November 2012) <www.patientombuddet.dk/Afgoerelser_og_domme/Afgoerelser_fra_Sundhedsvaesenets_Disciplinaernaevn/Afgoerelser_med_navn/2012/1294528.aspx> accessed 16 September 2015.

15 Danish Health and Medicines Authority, 'Behandling af transseksuelle' (23 November 2012) <https://sundhedsstyrelsen.dk/da/nyheder/2012/behandling-af-transseksuelle> accessed 30 November 2015.

16 Guideline no 10353 on the treatment of transgender (19 December 2014) (*Vejledning nr 10353 om udredning og behandling af transkønnede*) (DK).

17 ibid. s 1–2.

18 This monopoly was expanded to a duopoly five years later, when the Danish Health Authority approved treatments at a new Sexological Centre (*Sexologisk Center*) at the Aalborg University Hospital in September 2017. This was authorised by Guideline no 9921 on health care related to gender identity (22 September 2017) (*Vejledning nr 9921 om sundhedsfaglig hjælp ved kønsidentitetsforhold*) (DK); since replaced by Guideline no 9658 on health care related to gender identity (16 August 2018) (*Vejledning nr 9921 om sundhedsfaglig hjælp ved kønsidentitetsforhold*) (DK).

19 S Lamble (n 7) 112.

increasingly unlikely in both (at least beyond a reinstatement of the right to serve in the military).[20] While the historical visibility of trans people has been relatively high in Denmark, trans issues have not drawn much attention in the media aside from the brief moral panic which blew up around Caspian in 2012. Though this had a significant impact upon the Danish reforms of 2014, the timeline established above confirms that it did not spark the government's interest in gender recognition law reform (which pre-dated the media furore). It undoubtedly influenced the reform process, and in particular the creation of the monopoly at the Sexological Clinic. But qualitative interviews conducted with various stakeholders in 2015 suggest that attention to trans issues peaked, and soon dissipated, after Caspian's surgeon was disciplined and the interim medical guidelines had been issued. Interviewees involved in designing the legislative reforms of 2014 indicated that they were passed without garnering much in terms of attention from the Danish public.

While the Danish government had promised to review both civil and medical regulations of trans people in 2011, after Caspian the two were disentangled. This is evidenced by the mandate issued to the working group in 2013; which requested a description of medical *and* legal regulations of trans embodiment in Denmark, but invited international comparisons and reform proposals only in respect of legal recognition.[21] Once the working group was tasked with covering only civil administrative issues, so the scope of its objectives was restricted to technical bureaucratic questions about how the Danish population could be better managed. This followed the introduction of restrictive medical guidelines, and the reduction of visibility of trans people as public attention shifted away from Caspian. After being forced to respond to the moral panic raised by the Caspian furore, interviewees noted the reticence of the Danish government to draw too much attention to the reforms of 2014 once this panic had died down. A representative of the Danish Institute for Human Rights explained:

> [T]his was [...] technical legislation; it was all about name registration, and a change of the CPR legislation, so there was not a big heated discussion about whether it's right or wrong – with declaring your own gender. It was very much a technical issue.
>
> (Peter Ussing, Danish Institute for Human Rights)

That the technical appearance of the CPR law precluded debate "about whether it's right or wrong" indicates that depoliticising this issue allowed the government to limit political opposition to reform. The history of the CPR

20 'Biden Overturns Trump Transgender Military Ban' (*BBC News*, 25 January 2021) <https://bbc.co.uk/news/world-us-canada-55799913> accessed 25 February 2021.

21 Ministry of Justice, 'Kommissorium for tværministeriel arbejdsgruppe om udmøntning af regeringsgrundlagets afsnit om kønsskifte' (17 May 2013) <https://panbloggen.files.wordpress.com/2013/05/kc3b8nsskifte-kommissorium-jm.pdf&usg=ALkJrhjLszn-4IJPOaQMon8NdRzCGtYKSA> accessed 10 September 2015.

generally also indicates that this was not the first occasion such advantages have been gained by framing the CPR as purely administrative. Historical analysis of the process of its inception has put the successful introduction of the CPR down, in part, to the 'close cooperation' between civil servants and technicians and 'a lack of political interference' from politicians.[22] That this was accomplished through a careful mobilisation of jurisdiction on both occasions – initially between politics and public administration, and subsequently, medicine – supports Mariana Valverde's characterisation of jurisdiction as 'the true "anti-politics machine"'.[23] On both occasions, jurisdiction served to preempt potential conflicts between different political constituencies and governing institutions, ensuring the 'smooth functioning of law'.[24]

Activists interpreted this as a deliberate strategy. The centre-left minority government of the time stood to gain little from politicising trans issues. Inviting public debate about sex/gender would only goad social conservatives.[25] Still, the government could be confident that the *prima facie* liberalness of the CPR law would ensure that it was well received by domestic and international interest groups:

> [N]one of the parties – even the ones in the Government – were advertising the new law in any way. I mean, we notice it [...] but I think the broader Danish society had no idea that this law was passing.
>
> (Elvin Pedersen-Nielsen, Trans Political Forum)

> No, not at all. But LGBT Denmark knew it, and Amnesty, and all these organisations had a big part in it, and the international world.
>
> (Elias Magnild, Trans Political Forum)

> To all them it was: "We are working with trans politics." But to the rest of society ... I think no-one noticed in any way [...] I think they tried to slip it [by] as quietly as possible.
>
> (Elvin Pedersen-Nielsen, Trans Political Forum)

As I noted in Chapter 1, the reception that the CPR law received attests to the fact that the involvement of national and international human rights organisations

22 AV Ebbesen, 'The Creation of the Central Person Registry in Denmark' in C Gram, P Rasmussen, and SD Østergaard (eds), *History of Nordic Computing 4* (Springer 2015) 56.

23 M Valverde, *Chronotopes of Law: Jurisdiction, Scale and Governance* (Routledge 2015) 84, citing James Ferguson, *The Anti-Politics Machine: Development, Depoliticization and Bureaucratic Power in Lesotho* (University of Minnesota Press 1994).

24 ibid.

25 Social conservatives comprise a political constituency whose influence is reflected in the rise of the Danish People's Party; which became the second largest in the Parliament in 2015, after tripling the 7% vote-share it achieved the first time it competed in a general election in 1998. When the ontology of sex/gender did arise in parliamentary debates around the CPR law, it was dismissed as irrelevant by the Minister of the Economy and the Interior; Margrethe Vestager, Folketingstidende 20 May 2014, 91. møde, kl. 19:07.

was enough to ensure that its enactment would be well-publicised among select target constituencies, in Denmark and elsewhere. This even invited the suspicion that a purposeful intention to promulgate 'the myth of liberal Denmark'[26] may have been "the main reason" for enacting the CPR law:

> the CPR number law *only* came because Denmark should look like a liberal, trans[-friendly country] [...] because of the national pressure, but also international – because it's really important for Denmark, apparently, to look like an LGBT-friendly country.
>
> (Elias Magnild, Trans Political Forum)

Though the CPR law has been celebrated for what it appears to do at face value, it is limited when considered from the practical perspective of those whose needs it sought to meet. Evidence garnered through interviews with those personally affected by the 2014 reforms suggests that this purely technical amendment to civil regulations cannot respond to the complexities of trans embodiment in practice.

Progress

Having argued that visibility is not a necessary precursor to progress in the context where law reforms can be depoliticised, I now consider the question of what the results of this form of progress look like. From the reception that the CPR law received in the international press, one might assume that it was a groundbreaking piece of legislation. Yet doctrinal analysis confirms that the scope of the legislation is primarily technical. The CPR law merely extends a pre-existing right (to change one's CPR number) to a wider group of people. While previously limited to those who had undergone surgical castration 'for the purposes of sex/gender change',[27] now any Danish resident who wishes to declare 'an experience of belonging to the other sex/gender' is offered the opportunity to change legal gender.[28] This undoubtedly meant a lot to some interviewees, but it also required no significant re-design of the CPR system – and was enacted by inserting a solitary paragraph into the existing law on the CPR.[29]

Interviewees involved in the legislative process were willing to admit that the CPR law constituted nothing more than a technical amendment of existing

26 T Raun (n 8).

27 Ministry of Justice, *Rapport fra arbejdsgruppen om juridisk kønsskifte* (27 February 2014) <http://justitsministeriet.dk/sites/default/files/media/Pressemeddelelser/pdf/2014/Rapport%20om%20juridisk%20k%C3%B8nsskifte.pdf> accessed 21 July 2016, 20.

28 L 182 Law amending the Act on the Central Person Registry (11 June 2014) (*L 182 Lov om ændring af lov om Det Centrale Personregister*) (DK) s 1; Order regarding the Act on the Central Person Registry (9 January 2013) (*Bekendtgørelse af lov om Det Centrale Personregister*) (DK) s 3 para 6.

29 Hence the CPR law's full title: 'L 182 Law amending the Act on the Central Person Registry.'

administrative law. Though LGBT Denmark had lobbied to ensure reforms would pass before the 2015 general election,[30] their Chair was under no illusion as to the scope of the result:

> [W]e were very satisfied with the Gender Recognition Act last year, [but] we actually wanted something a little different, or a little more! Because if you look at that Bill, that Act, it is not a 'Gender Recognition Act' – it is an Act on the CPR system.
>
> (Søren Laursen, LGBT Denmark)

In comparison with UK legislation (which, for all its faults, discusses the various implications of amending legal gender status in some detail),[31] the Danish CPR law only specifies one new right that is offered to trans people – to self-declare legal gender status.

In interviews with trans people who had done this, it emerged that while this was valued, it did also create several potentially unforeseen consequences. Interviewees described assuming additional responsibilities for making sure that the process of changing legal status went smoothly. Some preceded the 2014 reforms, but others can be directly linked to the new CPR law. The former includes the responsibility to explain to various authorities that, and why, their CPR number changed. These conversations proved difficult for interviewees that were not 'out' about their trans history in sensitive spheres – including the workplace. One interviewee described how his CPR number probably had the effect of 'outing' him to his employer (that is, unless it already had done on the day he was hired):

> [W]hen I told my boss that my CPR is not right […] he didn't care – I was really lucky. And now, after I changed it, I actually had to go and talk to him about my contract, because I needed a new copy with my new CPR on it […] I haven't told him why, but I'm pretty sure he did the math […] [H]e can see that it has gone from an even to an odd number – so I suppose he figured it out.
>
> (Peter, Male/FtM, 27)

The implication is that drafters did not consider the (in)accessibility of the CPR law for employed people,[32] who are assumed to be 'out' (open about their legal gender status) to their employers. Prospective applicants are also

30 Which the incumbent Red Bloc government, as anticipated, narrowly lost.

31 Gender Recognition Act 2004, ss 9–21.

32 Research undertaken at the Sexological Clinic found that unemployment rates were, on average, higher among individuals approved for surgical castration than among the Danish population in general; R Simonsen and others, 'Sociodemographic Study of Danish Individuals Diagnosed with Transsexualism' [2015] 3 Sexual Medicine 109, 114.

assumed to have access to disposable income. One interviewee referred to the processing fees required to amend personal documentation:

> A new social security number means that every place where your social security number is registered is going to fuck up [...] I think the passport costs around five hundred kroner [circa £50], I think driver's licence was four hundred kroner [circa £40] [...] I had to go to Copenhagen to hand in my old diplomas, and pick up my new ones – that's time and money. But everything is difficult and nothing's automatic.
>
> (Mark, Transman, 38)

The additional practical and financial responsibilities that come with the right to self-declare legal gender status reflect a neoliberal logic that rights ought not to be granted without corresponding responsibilities.[33] Trans people in Denmark are required to pay – literally – to access their newly granted rights. Wendy Brown defines neoliberalism 'as an order of normative reason that, when it becomes ascendant, takes shape as a governing rationality extending a specific formulation of economic values, practices, and metrics to every dimension of human life.'[34] Here we see the areas of gender recognition and civil registration being 'economised' despite appearing to be largely 'noneconomic',[35] as gender recognition becomes an administrative process which nevertheless comes with private financial consequences.

Recognising gender in a neoliberal manner fails to address the complexity of trans embodiment, which is not experienced individually but in relation to other bodies and institutions. Seeking recognition in a gender other than that which was assigned at birth involves having one's gender status regulated by a range of institutional authorities.[36] This will include civil registration systems, but will not be limited to them. Other institutions – including the family, the workplace, and the clinical setting – must also be negotiated. Yet when trans people are challenged in any of these non-state institutional settings, the CPR law offers little clarification of what rights – beyond the right to make the declaration itself – trans people have, or have not, been granted. When the question of whether they are permitted to access gender-segregated spaces was raised in parliamentary debates,[37] the Minister of the Economy and the Interior would not be drawn into offering concrete guidance; stating only as follows:

33 C Stychin, *A Nation by Rights: National Cultures, Sexual Identity Politics and the Discourse of Rights* (Temple University Press 1998).

34 W Brown, *Undoing the Demos: Neoliberalism's Stealth Revolution* (Zone Books 2015) 30.

35 ibid. 50.

36 D Spade, *Normal Life: Administrative Violence, Critical Trans Politics, and the Limits of Law* (South End Press 2011).

37 JB Olsen, Folketingstidende 20 May 2014, 91. møde, kl. 19:09; Charlotte Dyremose, Folketingstidende 20 May 2014, 91. møde, kl. 19:24.

> [W]e are finding solutions to [challenges such as] that, and we will continue to find solutions to [challenges such as] that. I do not think that that should be the barrier in this case.[38]

The idea that it could be a governmental responsibility to posit clearly defined rights is brushed aside, in a 'hands-off' approach to governance criticised by Natalie Videbæk Munkholm:

> The issue of access to participate in sports on the basis of legal gender or biological gender is not mentioned, neither are practical everyday challenges relating to the use of changing rooms in public sports facilities, or sleeping quarters when in the military, in hospital or in prison [...] Likewise, the amendments have not touched on subjects such as existing employment on the basis of a certain gender (where legitimate).[39]

Ultimately, the question of whether trans people are expected to avoid gender-segregated spaces, or whether the managers of such spaces are expected to accommodate them, has been left unanswered.[40] So the responsibility to negotiate this lack of clarity will in practice be borne by trans people. If they are expected to use spaces reserved for members of their newly assigned gender only when this is unlikely to cause offence, it is up to their individual judgement to determine when this is the case. If the responsibility for accommodating trans people falls upon a business or public service provider, the failure of the Danish government to specify this ensures that this will only become clear if a trans person is able to mount a successful legal challenge against an instance of discrimination. In both instances, trans people must manage the consequences of governmental unwillingness to delineate clear boundaries between what constitutes (un)acceptable discrimination on the basis of sex/gender. They are left to negotiate the legal vacuum created by this poorly drafted legislation – avoiding contention when using toilets or changing facilities in everyday spaces such as leisure centres.

Being merely inserted into the existing CPR system also led to difficulties for those seeking to access 'gender-specific' services. These include those offered by the public health care system, which generates automated calls to undergo certain treatments only to those whose CPR number indicates a certain gender. A ten-digit person number is allocated in accordance with the so-called 'odd/even rule'; which states that the final digit determines the person's legal sex/gender. Before they are granted a new CPR number, these calls will

38 Margrethe Vestager, Folketingstidende 20 May 2014, 91. møde, kl. 19:11.

39 NV Munkholm, 'Legal Status of Transsexual and Transgender Persons in Denmark' in JM Scherpe (ed), *The Legal Status of Transsexual and Transgender Persons* (Intersentia 2015) 174.

40 ibid. 175.

accord with a trans person's assigned gender status. Once they have a new CPR number, they will correspond to the new legal gender status. As they follow a binary format, such calls may or may not correspond to the health care needs of the person in question. The explanatory comments which accompany the amendment to the Health Act state that while recipients of a new CPR number will no longer receive automated calls for 'gender-specific' procedures (including breast examinations, smear tests, and the human papillomavirus vaccine) they do 'of course retain the right to access these treatments'.[41] Yet it falls to the individual patient to make use of such screenings.[42] The experience of one interviewee suggests that this may not prove so simple:

> [T]he last doctor I saw [...] did not understand trans people [...] [B]ecause I'm recognised as male here, when I asked them to do a smear test for me, she was like "I think I can, but you have to pay a lot of money for it. It's not covered, because you're male."
>
> (Steve, Trans man, 28)

In this case, the doctor's advice is factually incorrect. But even with the benefit of this knowledge, Steve is individually responsible for asserting his rights within the doctor–patient relationship. As I noted in Chapter 2, the historical relationship between doctors and trans patients has been particularly complex; and the clinical setting remains a highly sensitive space for trans people.[43] By neglecting to delineate exactly which rights arise out of the CPR law, jurisdiction beyond civil registration is effectively dispersed.

Formal gender status is held to be distinct from the question of what actions and behaviours are legally permissible, and when. Valverde notes that one effect of drawing such jurisdictional divisions is that more general rights may not be 'coordinated or harmonized' with more specific 'low-level' regulations governing particular spheres.[44] Dorsett and McVeigh add that jurisdiction operates in different 'modes'; attaching to a person's status ('being a minor, a soldier or a refugee, for instance') or activities.[45] Both offer insight into the Danish context,

41 Bill for amending the Health Act and the Act on Assisted Reproduction in connection with treatment, diagnosis, and research, etc. (30 April 2014) (*Forslag til Lov om ændring af sundhedsloven og lov om assisteret reproduktion i forbindelse med behandling, diagnostik og forskning m.v.*) (DK), para 2.1.2.

42 ibid.

43 Z Davy, 'Transsexual Agents: Negotiating Authenticity and Embodiment within the UK's Medicolegal System', in S Hines and T Sanger (eds), *Transgender Identities: Towards a Social Analysis of Gender Diversity* (Routledge 2010) 107–110; E Grabham, 'Governing Permanence: Trans Subjects, Time, and the Gender Recognition Act' (2010) 19(1) Social & Legal Studies 107; and SJ Ellis, L Bailey, and J McNeil, 'Trans People's Experiences of Mental Health and Gender Identity Services: A UK Study' (2015) 19 Journal of Gay & Lesbian Mental Health 4.

44 M Valverde, 'Jurisdiction and Scale: Legal "Technicalities" as Resources for Theory' (2009) 18 Social & Legal Studies 139, 141.

45 S Dorsett and S McVeigh, *Jurisdiction* (Routledge 2012) 24.

as the question of what trans people can be (in civil registration) is distinguished from what they can do (in retaining employment, or accessing certain spaces or medical technologies). The logic of the 2014 reforms in Denmark suggests that the two can be sorted, separated, and then governed by different jurisdictions. Yet trans people's embodied experience of these regulations suggests this logic is misguided.

I have discussed respondents' difficulty in accessing body modification technologies in Denmark in previous work,[46] and will go on to examine the medical logic behind this in Chapter 5. But it is worth noting here that trans people who wish to self-declare their legal gender status must also be willing and able to be diagnosed with 'transsexualism' at one of two clinics approved by the Danish public health care system. If not, they become individually responsible for funding their own body modifications (or deal with the consequences of not doing so). Within trans studies, and wider critical literature, the process of psychiatric diagnosis has been criticised for being based upon out-dated,[47] middle-class, and white,[48] gender norms.[49] It is also difficult to be diagnosed with transsexualism if you are in receipt of another psychiatric diagnosis.[50] The accessibility of the Danish reforms hereby depends upon an individual trans person's privilege in terms of age, class, disability, ethnicity, and sexuality. The possibility of going outside the formal health care system is not open to all trans people, with one interviewee citing the costs involved:

> Of course it's easier to get your operation when you pay for it yourself. You can still do that. I can still travel to Thailand or Canada, wherever, if I pay for it myself. It's no problem. Nobody can stop me. I just need the money, and I don't have it – so I have to go through the Danish system.
>
> (Anita, Female, 46)

The effect of the decision to close off existing routes to body modification technologies will therefore have a disproportionate impact upon trans people

46 C Dietz, 'Governing Legal Embodiment: On the Limits of Self-Declaration' (2018) 26(2) Feminist Legal Studies 185.

47 MJ Hird, 'A Typical Gender Identity Conference? Some Disturbing Reports from the Therapeutic Front Lines' (2003) 13 Feminism & Psychology 181.

48 M de Young, *Madness: An American History of Mental Illness and Its Treatment* (McFarland 2010); DE Roberts, 'Race, Gender, and the Political Conflation of Biological and Social Issues' (2012) 9(1) Du Bois Review 235; JM Metzl and H Hansen, 'Structural Competency: Theorizing a New Medical Engagement with Stigma and Inequality' (2014) 103 Social Science & Medicine 126.

49 Z Davy, 'The DSM-5 and the Politics of Diagnosing Transpeople' (2015) 44 Archives of Sexual Behavior 1165.

50 One justification for requiring psychiatric evaluation is to clarify whether the patient is suffering from 'any concurrent physical or mental disorders (comorbidity) [...] that may contraindicate treatment'; Guideline no 10353 on the treatment of transgender (19 December 2014) (*Vejledning nr 10353 om udredning og behandling af transkønnede*) (DK) s 1.

who do not have the resources to travel abroad or turn to the black market.[51] Jurisdictional division again privatises responsibilities, on this occasion in a manner which has class-related consequences.

Again, it appears that the 2014 reforms have led to the 'responsibilisation' of trans people in Denmark. Responsibilisation is defined by Brown as the process of 'forcing the subject to become a responsible self-investor and self-provider'; by reconfiguring them 'from one naturally driven by satisfying interests to one forced to engage in a particular form of self-sustenance that meshes with the morality of the state and the health of the economy.'[52] This results in a 'burdening of the entity at the end of the pipeline.'[53] Beyond requiring individual subjects to provide for themselves, neoliberalism also establishes this as the status quo. By normalising individualism, neoliberal responsibilitisation ensures that trans people's effort can sometimes focus on individual goals; such as, for example, raising money to fund their own surgeries privately rather than campaigning for free and accessible health care for all.[54] This relies upon trans people's different levels of social capital, and could increase inequalities between trans communities. As Brown notes: 'As it discursively denigrates dependency and practically negates collective provisioning for existence, responsibilisation solicits the individual as the only relevant and wholly accountable actor.'[55] Even for those who possess sufficient resources to access body modification technologies through informal or illicit means, the consequences are hardly ideal. Any side-effects or complications associated with accessing technologies in this way could go undetected as restrictive guidelines push trans people outside the formal medical system (as I will discuss in Chapter 5). And yet again, in both instances, the responsibility to facilitate one's own well-being falls upon individual trans people, in the face of 'powers and contingencies radically limiting their ability to do so.'[56] From this perspective, the CPR law fits neoliberal trends including privatisation of responsibilities in health care, limiting state responsibility, and exacerbating inequalities.

Affect

While the depoliticised technical reform of the CPR law may have enabled trans people to self-declare their legal gender status without the need to meet

51 It has been noted in the trans studies literature that the 'vast majority' of trans people will not undergo genital surgeries, with one reason being many do not have access to medical care; AF Enke, 'Introduction' in AF Enke (ed), *Transfeminist Perspectives: In and Beyond Transgender and Gender Studies* (Temple University Press 2012) 6.

52 W Brown (n 34) 84.

53 ibid. 132.

54 I am grateful to the editors of the Routledge Social Justice Book Series for raising this point and example.

55 W Brown (n 34) 133.

56 ibid. 134.

significant pre-requisites, being granted the responsibility to determine their own legal gender status also came with several other responsibilities. It is tempting to assume that the additional responsibilities placed on trans people might have been avoided had trans people been more visible within reform debates, giving legislators a clearer understanding of the issues that they faced. Yet to do so would be to identify a lack of knowledge of trans issues among regulators as the primary cause of the limitations of the Danish reforms. Ignorance was by no means the only factor at play (if indeed it was at all). The CPR law was purposefully limited and depoliticised so that it could pass through the Danish Parliament without generating a public backlash.

The reform focused on amending the existing CPR system, rather than offering a new comprehensive form of gender recognition law. Though consolidation of the existing CPR system weighed heavily on the minds of interviewees professionally involved in the legislative process, it was valued much less by the trans and non-binary people personally affected by the reforms. Most of these interviewees were critical of the fact that the CPR law only permitted amendment of legal status within the binary constraints of 'male' and 'female'. In addition to the various administrative consequences that this had created for binary-identified trans people, it also led to the formal exclusion of non-binary people. This included Roi, who responded to my question as to whether they had considered changing their CPR number as follows:

> No, because that would give me a male social security number – but I'm not a male, and I don't identify as a male. If they had made one that was unisex or non-gendered, I could have applied for that, definitely.
>
> (Roi, Non-binary transgender, 26)

A preference for removing binary classification was shared by a majority of interviewees:[57]

> it would be easier if the system had our ID number, but with the last number not depending on whether I was male or female.
>
> (Jakob, Male, 31)

> I fail to see the good thing about a system that divides people into odd and even numbers, when the diversity of sex is broader than two sets.
>
> (Stephanie Stine Skaaning, Intersex woman, 29)

> The whole problem could be solved by not having these social security numbers gender-specific; that would make everything easier [...] I still

57 Some still wanted the option to change CPR number to have been included in this hypothetical reform – so that they could avoid being misrecognised as belonging to the gender they were assigned at birth while assumptions that sex/gender status could be deduced from the final digit of the CPR number were yet to fall away completely.

> don't know why they're doing it this way [...] It'd be a lot easier just to keep my old number, definitely.
>
> (Jon, Male, 40)

> I think that would be ideal, if the whole odd-even number system was just dropped.
>
> (Pippin, Non-binary, 42)

> I think it is very problematic today with the numbers so separated – because it doesn't fit with how gender is. It's binary, in a way that gender is not. I wouldn't have changed it if it wasn't a binary system.
>
> (Adam, Male, 30)

This group included some interviewees who had nevertheless been able to make use of the CPR law even in its binary form, which could indicate that binary-identified trans people feel a sense of solidarity with non-binary people. It might alternatively corroborate Sally Hines's finding that trans people pursue gender recognition for strategic reasons as much as they do to reflect personal identification.[58] Yet fledgling attempts to have the wording of the CPR law re-phrased to allow for the declaration of 'another sex/gender' were publicly dismissed at the consultation stage – on the tautological basis that this would be incompatible with the binary orientation of the CPR itself.[59] At no other point was abolishing the odd/even rule and creating a gender-neutral CPR system discussed in the public documentation of the reform process. Interestingly, though, interviews established that the possibility was considered by the working group, though only at its very earliest stages. It was then summarily dismissed, before being omitted from their report:

> we [the working group] knew that there wasn't any political agreement on that – so we didn't go that much into it – but of course we considered it. But changing the CPR system is also very costly [...] [W]e also knew that, in general, it seems that the Parliament is happy with the even and odd numbers.
>
> (Trine Ingemansen, Department for Gender Equality)

58 S Hines, *Gender Diversity, Recognition and Citizenship* (Palgrave Macmillan 2013) 56, 62.

59 The government received an unsolicited recommendation from the Danish AIDS Foundation (*AIDS-Fondet*) during the consultation process, which suggested replacing the phrase 'the other sex/gender' with 'another sex/gender'; see AIDS Foundation, *Letter to the CPR Office* (28 March 2014) <www.ft.dk/samling/20131/lovforslag/l182/bilag/1/1364174/index.htm> accessed 18 October 2015. Yet the proposal was dismissed by the Minister of the Economy and the Interior: 'Sex/gender is currently recorded in the CPR as either male or female. For this reason, it is deemed inappropriate to amend the Bill as proposed'; Consultation Note regarding the Bill for amending the Act on the Central Person Registry (*Kommenteret høringsnotat over forslag til lov om ændring af lov om Det Centrale Personregister*), para 2.6 (30 April 2014) <www.ft.dk/samling/20131/lovforslag/l182/bilag/1/1364173/index.htm> accessed 18 October 2015.

This message was also communicated to campaigners and other interest groups:

> we had a meeting with the Minister of [the Economy and] Internal Affairs [...] and she said "No! We don't want to do that – it is too expensive!" Because [...] if we got rid of that rule you would have to change all these systems.
>
> (Søren Laursen, LGBT Denmark)

Many administrative systems do not record gender in any way other than by the final digit of the CPR number. Abolishing the odd/even rule would have meant that numerous institutions would have had to develop a new registration system, or give up the possibility of registering this 'certified' form of gender altogether.[60] For this reason, abolishing the odd/even rule did not align with governmental interests. This is reflected by the limited mandate handed to the working group, which precluded consideration of abolishing the odd/even rule by requiring that proposals 'should not result in additional public expenditure.'[61] As in the previous section, the possibility of extending state responsibilities is avidly avoided, with individual trans people made responsible for dealing with the consequences of neoliberal reforms.

With possibilities of 'decertifying' gender,[62] or registering it differently, dismissed from the outset of the reform process, the jurisdiction of the working group was limited to maintaining – and arguably even augmenting – the binary orientation of the Danish CPR system. The CPR law was drafted with a view to avoiding potential conflict, and to ensure it was cheap and easy to implement. It contained no substantive rights beyond the right to self-declare legal gender status, and failed to address contemporaneous reforms of access to body modification technologies – at the same time as being given the air of being more inclusive. Divisions between civil and medical institutions were established and maintained, along with the consolidation of the existing CPR system. Jurisdiction was mobilised in a way that limited the effectiveness of self-declaration from the outset, individualising trans subjects, and privatising concerns that might – at another time, or in another political context – have been considered collective or state responsibilities. Even if trans people had been more visible within reform debates, the goal of trans inclusion would have still had to compete with the priorities or limiting state responsibilities and expenditure, and maintaining existing civil registration systems.

In this section of the chapter, I draw upon affect theory to suggest that the question of how far regulators misunderstood the extent to which limitations

60 For a 'speculative' theoretical analysis of the potential regulatory consequences of 'decertifying' gender identity at state level, see D Cooper and F Renz (n 3).

61 Ministry of Justice, 'Kommissorium' (n 21).

62 D Cooper and F Renz (n 3).

would affect the accessibility of self-declaration in practice, or merely accepted them as inevitable in maintaining other government imperatives, is a moot point. I argue that trans legal scholars ought to be generally wary of adopting unilinear or teleological understandings of progress, as these tend to underestimate the complex power dynamics at play within any legislative reform project. I suggest that a non-linear, caveated progress narrative might be a better starting point for those analysing the effect of gender recognition laws such as the Danish reforms of 2014.

Affect theory has admittedly been utilised less extensively in legal studies than in literary studies, queer theory, and the wider humanities. While affect does at first seem primarily to concern subjectivity, Lauren Berlant notes that its activity 'saturates the corporeal, intimate, and political performances of adjustment that make a shared atmosphere something palpable'.[63] In its patterning, affect reveals a 'theory-in-practice of how a world works.'[64] Berlant's own work on optimism and citizenship resists being dichotomised into consideration of the 'juridical object' and the 'intimate object' (the usual points of focus of legal and queer theory, respectively).[65] While juridical matters might appear to be distinct from the intimate realm, the embodied desire of the legal subject could just as easily be seen as holding the two together. The subject of trans legal studies exemplifies this better than most. Trans people across the world have demanded juridical recognition for decades. Recognition has, in some cases, been demanded for its own sake. But just as often it has been desired for the associated 'intimate' rights that this could enable them access to (including rights to marry or adopt, for example). What appears at first glance 'like a conflict between institutional attachment to the world and intimate models of attachment' can be misleading, as these are not necessarily in conflict at all, but are both, as Berlant puts it, 'part of the problem of imagining and living attachments to lifeworlds.'[66]

In the first part of this chapter, I demonstrated that trans visibility wasn't integral to the adoption of self-declaration of legal gender status in Denmark. In the second, I discussed the drawbacks of the resulting legislation. Affect theory offers clear insight into the thinking behind the question of whether greater visibility of trans people would have helped overcome these drawbacks. I have already contrasted the visibility of trans people in Denmark during the period of the reforms of 2014 with the current high visibility of trans people in England and Wales, at a time when gender recognition law reforms seem increasingly unlikely. In a US context, Eric Stanley argues that with 'increased

63 L Berlant, *Cruel Optimism* (Duke University Press 2011) 16.

64 ibid. 16.

65 D Seitz, Interview with L Berlant, 'On Citizenship And Optimism' (*Society & Space*, 23 March 2013) <https://societyandspace.org/articles/on-citizenship-and-optimism> accessed 19 November 2020.

66 ibid.

representation comes heightened, or at least sustained, instances of violence' against trans people, citing the fact that after 2014 was named the 'Trans Tipping Point' by Time magazine, 2016 saw the highest number of violent murders of black trans women in the US.[67] The conceptual tools offered by affect theory can help explain this apparent conundrum. In *Epistemology of the Closet*, Eve Sedgwick characterises progress as taking the shape of 'a sort of pincers movement'.[68] Berlant adds that this amounts in practice to 'one step forward, one step back' (or, 'how a crab walks').[69] At a time when trans people in the US have more role models than ever before appearing in the public eye, they are also just as, if not more, likely to be the victims of violence. To explain this, Sedgwick notes:

> Knowledge, after all, is not itself power, although it is the magnetic field of power. Ignorance and opacity collude or compete with knowledge in mobilizing the flows of energy, desire, goods, meaning, persons.[70]

This offers an interesting point of contrast with unilinear or teleological understandings of progress, which assume that as visibility equals progress, knowledge equals power. Yet the relation is more complex. The capacity to 'not see' or 'not know' queer bodies is not inadvertent but rather involves 'wilful acts of ignorance.'[71] Ignorance of and opacity around trans people thus colludes or competes with knowledge of trans issues to shape, for example, a gender recognition law reform process.

To a greater or lesser extent, such conflicts will be at play within any law reform project. For this reason, I argue that trans legal scholars, and legal scholars more broadly, ought to begin their analysis with the awareness that progress – where apparent – is more likely to be non-linear and caveated. As Sarah Lamble has noted, visibility can be a double-edged sword, ushering in new forms of political freedom *and* more intensive modes of surveillance and regulation.[72] Evelynn Hammonds adds that 'visibility in and of itself does not erase a history of silence'.[73] Experiences in England and Wales, the US, and Denmark demonstrate that trans people are unlikely to have significant levels of control over gender recognition law processes – regardless of how visible or invisible they are. The same is likely to be true for most marginalised groups.

67 EA Stanley, 'Anti-Trans Optics: Recognition, Opacity, and the Image of Force' (2017) 116(3) The South Atlantic Quarterly 612, 617.
68 EK Sedgwick, *Epistemology of the Closet* (University of California Press 1990) 50.
69 D Seitz and L Berlant (n 65).
70 EK Sedgwick (n 68) 4.
71 S Lamble (n 7) 112.
72 ibid. 126.
73 ibid. 125, citing E Hammonds 'Black (W)holes and the Geometry of Black Female Sexuality' (1994) 6(2/3) Differences: A Journal of Feminist Cultural Studies 126, 141.

Questioning the apparent optimism behind feminist scholars' desire to label forms of oppression as cultural rather than biological, Sedgwick raises doubts as to how far culture can be manipulated by one campaign group (irrespective of how pressing the ethical imperative to do so might have seemed).[74] In the context of feminist activism within literary studies, she describes adopting her own two-pronged pincers movement; of both naming the straight, male, literary canon as such, and of forming a feminist or gay canon to challenge it.[75] We have already established that adopting apparently conflicting strategies is not an uncommon governmental strategy, but Sedgwick indicates that a similar method can be adopted by activists.

The insight that apparently divergent tactics can, and perhaps should, be pursued within scholarship and campaigning offers important lessons for trans legal studies. I would advise researchers and activists involved in gender recognition law reform debates to continue criticising existing and ongoing exclusions from legal protections while also fighting for material gains in the instances where inclusion looks achievable (as some undoubtedly already are). Trans visibility may prove achievable and useful, in which case it should be pursued and even embraced. But only if this is with the knowledge that it can have unpredictable and even contradictory outcomes.[76] Alternatively, activists might seek to embrace 'opacity', and what Vika Kirchenbauer, drawing upon Édouard Glissant,[77] calls 'the right not to be understood'.[78] Demands – including for accessible health care provision – could be made without the accompanying attempt to increase trans visibility (and therefore without the need to present a 'Trans 101' which defines what it is to be trans). Both approaches acknowledge the state as 'a resource' and 'a site of domination.'[79] Bearing this in mind raises greater possibility of working in and against the state in the context of trans rights, all the while tempering optimism as to what the results of this engagement will be.

Conclusion

This chapter drew upon my research into the 2014 reforms of legal gender recognition in Denmark to dispute the assumption that visibility will necessarily promote progress in trans rights. It demonstrates that trans people were not particularly visible in Denmark during the reform process, at least not once the

74 EK Sedgwick (n 68) 41–42.

75 ibid. 50, 58.

76 S Lamble (n 7) 126.

77 É Glissant, *Poetics of Relation* (B Wing tr, University of Michigan Press 1997) 189.

78 G Kunak, 'Body//Opacity Politics: An Interview with Vika Kirchenbauer' (*BerlinArtLink*, 22 April 2016) <www.berlinartlink.com/2016/04/22/body-an-interview-with-vika-kirchenbauer> accessed 29 June 2021.

79 D Seitz and L Berlant (n 65).

media panic around Caspian Drumm died down. This stands in contrast to the relatively high visibility of trans issues in the US and in England and Wales. While reform in those states seems increasingly unlikely, self-declaration of legal gender status was enacted in Denmark without much controversy. Yet the depoliticised process through which this reform was enacted had knock-on effects in terms of the final product of the legislative process. As I noted, with the benefit of insights from political theory, the type of progress that the Danish reforms of 2014 represent is significantly limited. Unlike its UK predecessor, the Danish CPR law is not a comprehensive gender recognition act. For while it does grant trans people in Denmark the right to self-declare their legal gender status, and to have this recognised without further pre-requisites in the national CPR system, it offers no substantive rights beyond this basic minimum.

As a result, the 2014 reforms can be understood as bringing about a responsibilisation of trans people in Denmark. This is not only in the desired way of making them arbiters of their own gender status, but also in dealing with the consequences of doing so in challenging spheres. They are expected to bear the cost of changing legal gender status, and to negotiate using public facilities and health services without sufficiently accessible and clearly defined rights to do so. If they are not able to be diagnosed with transsexualism at one of the two state-approved psychiatric institutions, then they must also foot the bill for accessing body modification technologies such as hormones and surgeries either abroad or on the black market. This increases the likelihood that trans people's energies will be spent on private fundraising rather than collective campaigning, which could in turn increase inequalities between different trans communities. A distinctly neoliberal form of legislation, this plays into wider trends including privatisation of responsibilities in health care, which limits state responsibilities, and exacerbates existing inequalities (an idea that I will return to in Chapter 5).

While some may be tempted to wonder if the limitations of the 2014 reforms could be explained by the low visibility and involvement of trans people in the legislative process at the time, my argument is that this would only serve to underestimate the significant weight of other factors and demands upon the legislative agenda. The second part of this chapter demonstrated that these included the neoliberal imperatives to limit state expenditure and responsibility, and the third focused upon the demand to maintain the existing binary infrastructure of the CPR system as far as possible. To analyse these findings, I turned to affect theory. This helped support my argument that trans, feminist, and socio-legal scholars more broadly ought to pay close attention to competing objectives when assessing the impact of a law reform. When they do, I suggest that they would be better advised to begin with the hypothesis that 'progress' – if it is apparent at all – will be non-linear and subject to important caveats in most reform projects. I conclude by arguing that ambivalence about visibility demands a more tactical approach to law reform. The pincers form that such reforms often end up adopting could be re-purposed as a tactic for activists to challenge norms in and against the state. The outcome of this engagement will be difficult to anticipate. But it will be interesting to see the results, and to analyse them from a perspective that accepts that visibility doesn't always lead to progress, and understands that progress is not inevitably on the way.

Bibliography

AIDS Foundation, 'Letter to the CPR Office' (28 March 2014) <http://www.ft.dk/samling/20131/lovforslag/l182/bilag/1/1364174/index.htm> accessed 18 October 2015

Berlant L, *Cruel Optimism* (Duke University Press 2011)

Brown W, *Undoing the Demos: Neoliberalism's Stealth Revolution* (Zone Books 2015)

Collier B and Cowan S, 'Queer Conflicts, Concept Capture and Category Co-Option: The Importance of Context in the State Collection and Recording of Sex/Gender Data' (2022) Social & Legal Studies <https://doi.org/10.1177%2F09646639211061409>

'Consultation Note Regarding the Bill for Amending the Act on the Central Person Registry' (Kommenteret høringsnotat over forslag til lov om ændring af lov om Det Centrale Personregister), para 2.6 (30 April 2014) <http://www.ft.dk/samling/20131/lovforslag/l182/bilag/1/1364173/index.htm> accessed 18 October 2015

Cooper D and Renz F, 'If the State Decertified Gender, What Might Happen to its Meaning and Value?' (2016) 43(4) Journal of Law and Society 483

Danish Health and Medicines Authority, 'Behandling af Transseksuelle' (23 November 2012) <https://sundhedsstyrelsen.dk/da/nyheder/2012/behandling-af-transseksuelle> accessed 30 November 2015

Davy Z, 'Transsexual Agents: Negotiating Authenticity and Embodiment within the UK's Medicolegal System' in Hines S and Sanger T (eds), *Transgender Identities: Towards a Social Analysis of Gender Diversity* (Routledge 2010)

——— 'The DSM-5 and the Politics of Diagnosing Transpeople' (2015) 44 Archives of Sexual Behavior 1165

de Young M, *Madness: An American History of Mental Illness and Its Treatment* (McFarland 2010)

Dietz C, 'Governing Legal Embodiment: On the Limits of Self-Declaration' (2018) 26(2) Feminist Legal Studies 185

Dorsett S and McVeigh S, *Jurisdiction* (Routledge 2012)

Ebbesen AV, 'The Creation of the Central Person Registry in Denmark' in Gram C, Rasmussen P, and Østergaard SD (eds), *History of Nordic Computing 4* (Springer 2015)

Ellis SJ, Bailey L, and McNeil J, 'Trans People's Experiences of Mental Health and Gender Identity Services: A UK Study' (2015) 19 Journal of Gay & Lesbian Mental Health 4

Enke AF, 'Introduction' in Enke AF (ed), *Transfeminist Perspectives: In and Beyond Transgender and Gender Studies* (Temple University Press 2012) 6

Glissant É, *Poetics of Relation* (Wing B tr, University of Michigan Press 1997)

Grabham E, 'Governing Permanence: Trans Subjects, Time, and the Gender Recognition Act' (2010) 19(1) Social & Legal Studies 107

Hines S, *Gender Diversity, Recognition and Citizenship* (Palgrave Macmillan 2013)

Hird MJ, 'A Typical Gender Identity Conference? Some Disturbing Reports from the Therapeutic Front Lines' (2003) 13 Feminism & Psychology 181

Kunak G, 'Body//Opacity Politics: An Interview with Vika Kirchenbauer' (*BerlinArtLink*, 22 April 2016) <http://www.berlinartlink.com/2016/04/22/body-an-interview-with-vika-kirchenbauer> accessed 29 June 2021

Lamble S, 'Unknowable Bodies, Unthinkable Sexualities: Lesbian and Transgender Legal Invisibility in the Toronto Women's Bathhouse Raid' (2009) 18(1) Social & Legal Studies 111

Metzl JM and Hansen H, 'Structural Competency: Theorizing a New Medical Engagement with Stigma and Inequality' (2014) 103 Social Science & Medicine 126

Ministry of Justice, 'Kommissorium for tværministeriel arbejdsgruppe om udmøntning af regeringsgrundlagets afsnit om kønsskifte' (17 May 2013) <https://panbloggen.files.wordpress.com/2013/05/kc3b8nsskifte-kommissorium-jm.pdf&usg=ALkJrhjLszn-4IJPOaQMon8NdRzCGtYKSA> accessed 10 September 2015

——— 'Rapport fra arbejdsgruppen om juridisk kønsskifte' (27 February 2014) <http://justitsministeriet.dk/sites/default/files/media/Pressemeddelelser/pdf/2014/Rapport%20om%20juridisk%20k%C3%B8nsskifte.pdf> accessed 21 July 2016

Munkholm NV, 'Legal Status of Transsexual and Transgender Persons in Denmark' in Scherpe JM (ed), *The Legal Status of Transsexual and Transgender Persons* (Intersentia 2015)

Patients' Ombudsman, 'Kritik for behandling – speciallæge i plastikkirurgi Jens Pilegaard Bjarnesen' (1 November 2012) <https://www.patientombuddet.dk/Afgoerelser_og_domme/Afgoerelser_fra_Sundhedsvaesenets_Disciplinaernaevn/Afgoerelser_med_navn/2012/1294528.aspx> accessed 16 September 2015

Prime Minister's Office, 'Et Danmark, Der Står Sammen' (October 2011) <http://www.stm.dk/publikationer/Et_Danmark_der_staar_sammen_11/Regeringsgrundlag_okt_2011.pdf> accessed 20 August 2015

Raun T, 'The 'Caspian Case' and Its Aftermath: Transgender People's Use of Facebook to Engage Discriminatory Mainstream News Coverage in Denmark' in Björklund J and Lindqvist U (eds), *New Dimensions of Diversity in Nordic Culture and Society* (Cambridge Scholars Publishing 2016)

Roberts DE, 'Race, Gender, and the Political Conflation of Biological and Social Issues' (2012) 9(1) Du Bois Review 235

Sedgwick EK, *Epistemology of the Closet* (University of California Press 1990)

Seitz D, Interview with Berlant L, 'On Citizenship and Optimism' (*Society & Space*, 23 March 2013) <https://societyandspace.org/articles/on-citizenship-and-optimism> accessed 19 November 2020

Simonsen R, Hald GM, Giraldi A, and Kristensen E, 'Sociodemographic Study of Danish Individuals Diagnosed with Transsexualism' (2015) 3 Sexual Medicine 109

Spade D, *Normal Life: Administrative Violence, Critical Trans Politics, and the Limits of Law* (South End Press 2011)

Stanley EA, 'Anti-Trans Optics: Recognition, Opacity, and the Image of Force' (2017) 116(3) The South Atlantic Quarterly 612

Stone S, 'The *Empire* Strikes Back: A Posttranssexual Manifesto' in Stryker S and Whittle S (eds), *Transgender Studies Reader* (Routledge 2006)

Stychin C, *A Nation by Rights: National Cultures, Sexual Identity Politics and the Discourse of Rights* (Temple University Press 1998)

Valverde M, 'Jurisdiction and Scale: Legal 'Technicalities' as Resources for Theory' (2009) 18 Social & Legal Studies 139

——— *Chronotopes of Law: Jurisdiction, Scale and Governance* (Routledge 2015)

Chapter 5

Vulnerability in medical institutions

Introduction

In this chapter, I contest the idea that the gatekeeping of access to body modification technologies including hormones and surgeries indicates a concentration of power in medical institutions. I argue that medical guidelines which determine gatekeeping practices can be better understood as specific responses to a more general problem of institutional vulnerability instead. Though gatekeeping practices vary between and within public and private health care providers, both sets of institution can be conceived of as vulnerable. Real terms austerity cuts to budgets have affected public health care institutions in the UK, for instance, for decades; despite rising demand from patients generally, and trans patients specifically. In this context, they have had to develop gatekeeping practices which can both withstand the public scrutiny and fit within budgetary requirements. Private clinics are generally understood to provide more straightforward access to body modification technologies in most jurisdictions. Trans people who can afford to finance their own body modification treatments often prefer this route. Yet this does not make private-sector health care providers invulnerable. Like their public-sector counterparts, they face internal and external pressures, and are also vulnerable to regulatory and economic pressures.

By exploring the vulnerability of health care providers in their management of trans patients, I contribute to an undeveloped strand of vulnerability theory – concerning the vulnerability of institutions. I take as a point of departure Martha Fineman's idea that societal institutions can, like the people that depend upon them, be understood as essentially and inevitably vulnerable.[1] The regulations and practices which limit trans people's access to body modification technologies such as hormones and surgeries tend to be justified with some reference to human vulnerability. Yet it is my contention that such

1 MA Fineman, 'The Vulnerable Subject: Anchoring Equality in the Human Condition' (2008) 20(1) Yale Journal of Law and Feminism 1, 12; MA Fineman, 'Vulnerability and Inevitable Inequality' (2017) 4(3) Oslo Law Review 133.

DOI: 10.4324/9780429288203-5

restrictions are equally as reflective of the perceived and actual vulnerability of medical institutions. To evidence this claim, I draw again upon research I conducted in Denmark in 2015, at a time when access to public and private health care became difficult for trans people. Since institutional vulnerability is apparent within both public- and private-sector health care institutions, this argument has broader relevance within trans legal studies and the wider literature on access to health care. Public regulators and clinics in national health care systems across Europe and beyond will experience institutional vulnerability whenever financial resources are limited, and treatment decisions must be justified to tax-payers as well as the wider public.[2] Institutional vulnerability will also be present in fully privatised and mixed economy health care systems, whenever private providers compete for the custom of patients.

To date, researchers who have considered institutional vulnerability have not tended to draw upon new public management literatures, even though these offer useful insights into why institutions that are under-funded are nevertheless expected to meet certain targets that quantify things like efficiency. Nor have vulnerability scholars fully explored the potential in engaging with literatures on the neoliberal management of risk.[3] This is something I will remedy in this chapter, by explaining how Danish medical regulators responded to their institutional vulnerability by developing risk-averse policies. It is impossible to say whether these policies are designed to promote trans people's health, or merely to minimise the chances of institutional reputational damage. But my research demonstrates that either way, they are in some cases putting trans people at even greater risk – and thus undermining the stated institutional objectives of these same regulators. This finding will not surprise those that are familiar with the new public management and risk literatures; which have detailed in numerous contexts how, in the shadow of neoliberal austerity, institutions become increasingly risk-averse in managing prospective costs – be they financial, reputational, or otherwise.[4] But what the literature on institutional vulnerability adds to this descriptive analysis is a normative element justifying why state institutions must both be better funded, and focused upon mitigating human vulnerability. It is not enough for them to deflect criticism and maximise 'efficiency' in a way which undermines their entire *raison d'être*.

The chapter is made up of three parts. The first introduces vulnerability theory; describing how this has been used to better understand the human condition, before moving on to advocate exploring the comparatively underdeveloped idea of institutional vulnerability. The second part puts this into practice, as my

2 This is certainly the case in the UK, as exemplified by the recent case of *Quincy Bell & Mrs A v The Tavistock and Portman NHS Foundation Trust and Ors* [2021] EWCA Civ 1363.

3 Though for an exception that I will consider later in the chapter, see B Reiss, 'Madness after Virginia Tech: From Psychiatric Risk to Institutional Vulnerability' (2010) 28(4) Social Text 25.

4 I am grateful to the editors of the Routledge Social Justice Book Series editors for highlighting this.

analysis shifts onto the vulnerability of the health care institutions tasked with managing trans patients in Denmark. I chart how medical competences have expanded in Danish trans health care law, in response to internal and external pressures on medical institutions. In the third part of the chapter, I turn my attention to the embodied effects of the expansion of medical regulation in this area, from the perspective of the trans people who are affected by them. I conclude by returning to vulnerability theory, echoing Fineman's call for a more responsive state which, in this context, seeks to develop and fund institutions which can actively meet, rather than withdrawing from, people's health care needs.

Vulnerability theory

Vulnerability theory has gained precedence in recent years as an approach to conceptualising the operation of law in society. But its potential has yet to be realised within the area of trans legal studies. To address this, Ruth Pearce and I explored vulnerability theory's potential to inform strategies which seek to depathologise trans phenomena.[5] We expressed two concerns about how the activists and scholars currently seeking to establish a human right to depathologisation risk undermining key objectives of 'the trans depathologisation movement'.[6] First, adopting human rights languages – which centre individual freedom and autonomy over relationality and vulnerability – could unwittingly motivate states to becoming more 'withdrawn' from the issue of trans health.[7] This would increase the expectation that trans people self-fund body modification treatments – working against demands for accessible, publicly funded, health care. Second, we cautioned against labelling trans people as 'a particularly vulnerable group'.[8] Classifying trans people as 'particularly vulnerable' could inadvertently justify existing practices of 'trans exceptionalism' (whereby trans people must overcome additional hurdles to access health treatments because of their trans status) in the trans health context.[9] Instead, if vulnerability were understood to be particular and universal,[10] trans health could be re-framed as a specific area of health care that is nonetheless commensurate with the diverse needs of the wider population.[11] This could encourage a

5 C Dietz and R Pearce, 'Depathologising Gender: Vulnerability in Trans Health Law' in C Dietz, M Travis, and M Thomson (eds), *A Jurisprudence of the Body* (Palgrave Macmillan 2020).
6 Z Davy, A Sørlie, AS Schwend, 'Democratising Diagnoses? The Role of the Depathologisation Perspective in Constructing Corporeal Trans Citizenship' (2018) 38(1) Critical Social Policy 13, 15.
7 Fineman, 'The Vulnerable Subject' (n 1) 6.
8 As in recent ECtHR jurisprudence; P Cannoot, 'The Pathologisation of Trans∗ Persons in the ECtHR's Case Law on Legal Gender Recognition' (2019) 37(1) Netherlands Quarterly of Human Rights 14, 33–34.
9 CJ Heyes and JR Latham, 'Trans Surgeries and Cosmetic Surgeries: The Politics of Analogy' (2018) 5(2) TSQ: Transgender Studies Quarterly 174.
10 Fineman, 'The Vulnerable Subject' (n 1) 10.
11 Dietz and Pearce (n 5) 194.

move towards 'just and equitable treatment',[12] and 'secure access to competent, legal, respectfully provided medical services for a nonpathological need'.[13]

Towards the end of our piece, Pearce and I moved beyond addressing the idea of human vulnerability – the most obvious starting point for any vulnerability analysis of trans issues – to consider the corresponding vulnerability of medical institutions, including clinics and regulators.[14] To date, institutional vulnerability is a concept which remains underdeveloped, even within the vulnerability literature. Vulnerability theory identifies interactions with institutions as one of the main ways through which human can increase their resilience. Institutions thus play an important role in mitigating (or not) people's inherent embedded and embodied vulnerability. Yet institutions are themselves vulnerable to various 'corruptions and disruptions' which they could ultimately fail to adequately respond to.[15] These include (but are not limited to): market fluctuations, changing international policies, institutional and political compromises, and human prejudices.[16] Institutions are therefore susceptible to challenges from both internal and external agents and forces.

Many would baulk at the idea that the institutions which exert significant influence over their lives are themselves vulnerable. I suspect most of the trans people that I interviewed in Denmark would, given the expanding jurisdiction of medical regulators and clinics that they have witnessed over recent decades there. I too acknowledge concerns that vulnerability theory's clearest insights could be limited by shifting its analysis from humans to institutions.[17] Foremost among these are the conceptual, political, and ethical implications of the fact that institutions are not vulnerable in the embodied sense that trans people are.[18] When institutional bodies fail, they do not break a bone, and their skin cannot be pierced in the same way that a human's can. Yet history tells us that even the most established institutions are 'potentially unstable'.[19] This has been identified in multiple areas vulnerability scholarship; including in the context of US colleges and universities,[20] marriage,[21] the criminal justice

12 Heyes and Latham (n 9) 186.

13 S Stryker, *Transgender History* (Seal Press 2008) 98.

14 Dietz and Pearce (n 5) 195-197.

15 MA Fineman, 'The Vulnerable Subject and the Responsive State' (2010) 60 Emory Law Journal 251, 256.

16 Fineman, 'The Vulnerable Subject' (n 1) 12.

17 I am grateful to the editors of the Routledge Social Justice Book Series for pushing me to emphasise this point.

18 Like employers in Jonathan Fineman's vulnerability analysis of the employment relationship, regulators and clinics are not human. This means that they are vulnerable in a different way to their patients; J Fineman, 'The Vulnerable Subject at Work: A New Perspective on the Employment At-Will Debate' (2013) 43(2) Southwestern Law Review 275, 299 fn 125.

19 Fineman (n 15) 273.

20 Reiss (n 3).

21 S Marvel, 'The Evolution of Plural Parentage: Applying Vulnerability Theory to Polygamy and Same-Sex Marriage' (2015) 64 Emory Law Journal 2047.

system,[22] and even heterosexuality.[23] Medical institutions play a decisive role in determining how easily and safely trans people are able to access hormones and surgeries. And while, again, they are not vulnerable in the embodied sense that the trans people that attend them are, this does not make them invulnerable. Organisational, political, and financial concerns can and do place regulators and clinics under significant pressures which will invariably affect how regulatory decisions are made.

The insight that medical regulators and clinics experience institutional vulnerability constitutes the starting point for my analysis of how claims to expertise over trans phenomena have led to significant expansions of medical jurisdiction in Denmark over recent years. I consider the effect of this jurisdictional expansion on the accessibility of health care to trans people. Since public-sector health care has become the only permitted route to body modification technologies for trans people in Denmark, my critique focuses on public health care providers. Publicly funded clinics are generally subjected to greater public scrutiny than their private-sector counterparts – and to the extent that such institutions distribute social goods, it is appropriate that they are closely monitored. State involvement in the creation and maintenance of institutions should be enough to ensure that it remains vigilant in ensuring that the distribution of assets is accomplished 'with attention to public values, including equality or justice, or objectives beyond private or profit motivation.'[24] Fineman adds:

> One implication of recognizing institutional vulnerability should be acceptance of the need for monitoring, evaluating, updating, and reforming our societal institutions when necessary. These processes should be undertaken consistent with the mandate of equality of access and opportunity and the obligation of the state to act with equal regard for the vulnerability of all.[25]

In seeking to ensure equitable access of trans people to health care including body modification technologies such as hormones and surgeries, this chapter proceeds in this spirit.

Expanding jurisdictions

The jurisdictional expansion that medical regulators and public clinics have successfully overseen in Denmark over recent decades is notable. When

22 R Dehaghani and D Newman, '"We're Vulnerable Too": An (Alternative) Analysis of Vulnerability within English Criminal Legal Aid and Police Custody' (2017) 7(6) Oñati Socio-legal Series 1199.

23 M Travis, 'The Vulnerability of Heterosexuality: Consent, Gender Deception and Embodiment' (2019) 28(3) Social & Legal Studies 303.

24 Fineman (n 15) 272.

25 ibid. 273.

Christine Jorgensen became the first trans person to publicly undergo surgical castration in Denmark in 1951,[26] she had to seek permission to do so not from a medical institution but from the Danish Ministry of Justice.[27] This remained the case for all those seeking to undergo this procedure until 2005, when joint responsibility to determine access to this procedure was taken on by the Ministry of Health and the Ministry of the Interior.[28] This responsibility was only formally granted in statute to a medical institution – the Danish Health and Medicines Authority (DHMA) – only when the Health Act was reformed in 2014.[29] Yet the DHMA had in fact began governing access to surgical castration almost a decade earlier, when they published official medical guidelines concerning 'surgical castration for the purposes of sex/gender modification' in 2006 ('the 2006 guidelines').[30] These require an applicant for castration to have been diagnosed with 'transsexualism';[31] a diagnosis which can only be made by certain 'highly specialised' clinics.[32] Such clearance has only, to date, been granted to the Sexological Clinic of the National Hospital in Copenhagen,[33] and more recently (in September 2017) at the new Sexological Centre at the Aalborg University Hospital.[34] If a patient's desire for castration is deemed to have remained 'stable and persistent' for the duration of a programme of psychiatric observation,[35] then they may be authorised to seek permission to undergo this procedure from the DHMA and the Danish Medico-Legal Council.[36]

26 Denmark's eugenics programme saw 5,940 sterilisations performed between 1929 and 1950, so it is possible Jorgensen was not the first trans person to undergo surgical castration there; BS Hansen, 'Something Rotten in the State of Denmark: Eugenics and the Ascent of the Welfare State' in G Broberg and N Roll-Hansen (eds), *Eugenics and the Welfare State: Sterilization Policy in Denmark, Sweden, Norway and Finland* (East Lansing 1996) 60.

27 Order on sterilisation and castration (12 July 1994) (*Bekendtgørelse af lov om sterilisation og kastration*) (DK), s 14. The Ministry of Justice would base their decision upon evidence provided by the Danish Medico-Legal Council (*Retslægerådet*); T Sørensen and P Hertoft, 'Sexmodifying Operations on Transsexuals in Denmark in the Period 1950–1977' (1980) 61 Acta Psychiatrica Scandinavica 56.

28 L 546 Health Act (24 June 2005) (*Sundhedsloven*) (DK), s 116.

29 Health Act (19 November 2014) (*Bekendtgørelse af sundhedsloven*) (DK), s 116.

30 Guideline no 10077 on surgical castration for the purposes of sex/gender modification (27 November 2006) (*Vejledning nr 10077 om kastration med henblik på kønsskifte*) (DK).

31 ibid. s 1. The definition of 'transsexualism' can be found in the WHO ICD-10, 'F64.0 Transsexualism' <http://apps.who.int/classifications/icd10/browse/2015/en#/F64> accessed 22 May 2015.

32 ibid. s 3.

33 Ministry of Justice, *Rapport fra arbejdsgruppen om juridisk kønsskifte* (27 February 2014) <http://justitsministeriet.dk/sites/default/files/media/Pressemeddelelser/pdf/2014/Rapport%20om%20juridisk%20k%C3%B8nsskifte.pdf> accessed 21 July 2016, 8.

34 Guideline no 9658 on health care related to gender identity (16 August 2018) (*Vejledning nr 9921 om sundhedsfaglig hjælp ved kønsidentitetsforhold*) (DK).

35 Ministry of Justice (n 33) 13.

36 Guideline no 10353 on the treatment of transgender (19 December 2014) (*Vejledning nr 10353 om udredning og behandling af transkønnede*) (DK), s 4.1.

The jurisdiction of the DHMA significantly expanded in 2006, then, as it assumed responsibility for prescribing the conditions under which access to surgical castration for the purposes of sex/gender modification (and, at the time, the possibility of legal gender recognition) would be determined. In an interview, the author of these guidelines described how this occurred:

> we took that over in 2006 [...] That meant that we had a more medical focus on what happened. So, the first thing we did was to make a guideline on what you had to have to get a sex change, because before that it was a black box. Anybody – the people, or the patients – who applied for a sex change wouldn't know what criteria they had to meet. They were either just accepted or not accepted; and we thought that was a very bad situation – for people not to know what they actually had to go through. So, we made the first guideline saying what it was that they schematically had to go through [...] that was the first point where there was a little more transparency.
>
> (Anne Mette Dons, (formerly) DHMA)

In the sociological literature on the professions, Andrew Abbott argues that professional groupings are defined by the boundaries that they draw between themselves and other groups.[37] These boundaries are practically useful in that they help create and then delimit professional jurisdiction.[38] They are also under perpetual dispute.[39] In response, regulators engage in 'boundary-work';[40] a term coined by Thomas Gieryn to conceptualise the processes whereby expert bodies seek to claim or expand jurisdiction over contested domains.[41] The 2006 guidelines offer one example of this, as the DHMA claimed a jurisdiction to govern access to surgical castration in medical guidelines which was not formally allocated to them on a statutory basis until 2014. The literature on the professions adds that such displays of professional autonomy are often justified by '*claims* to special expertise and 'ethicality'.'[42] Both are apparent in Dons's testimony; expertise, in the "more medical focus" that the DHMA's guidelines could provide; and ethicality, in that they would increase "transparency" by doing so.

The 2006 guidelines state that the DHMA, the Sexological Clinic, and other, related, institutions (including the Medico-Legal Council) determine access to

37 A Abbott, 'Things of Boundaries: Defining the Boundaries of Social Inquiry' (1995) 62 Social Research 857, 860.

38 S McGuinness and M Thomson, 'Medicine and Abortion Law: Complicating the Reforming Profession' (2015) 23(2) Medical Law Review 177, 180.

39 A Abbott, *The System of Professions: An Essay on the Division of Expert Labor* (University of Chicago Press 1988) 2.

40 TF Gieryn, 'Boundary-Work and the Demarcation of Science from Non-science: Strains and Interests in the Professional Interests of Scientists' (1983) 48 American Sociological Review 781.

41 McGuinness and Thomson (n 38) 177.

42 ibid. 180, citing E Friedson, *Profession of Medicine: A Study of the Sociology of Applied Knowledge* (University of Chicago Press 1988).

surgical castration within Danish borders. But in being so specific with regard to the object that they govern, the guidelines unwittingly neglected a regulatory grey area whereby medical professionals practising outside the Sexological Clinic were not formally prohibited from performing body modifications other than surgical castration. A small number of private-sector gynaecologists and endocrinologists had been willing to exploit this loophole, authorising and administering hormone replacement treatment on an informed consent basis. These practitioners became well-known among trans communities, ensuring that many trans people could access hormones in this way. From a vulnerability perspective, those operating within this loophole could be said to have exerted an internal and external pressure upon medical institutions: internal to the DHMA, as this alternative route to body modification came from within the Danish medical profession; but external to the Sexological Clinic, as the medical professionals willing to provide access to hormones on an informed consent basis did so from outside of the primary institution intending to gate keep trans people's access to such treatments. Either way it evidenced institutional vulnerability, which the DHMA and Sexological Clinic would go on to address in subsequent jurisdictional expansions.

Within the loophole, it was legally possible to perform surgeries other than surgical castration, including 'top surgeries' such as mastectomies and breast augmentation procedures. Interviews indicate that this practice was not as widespread as hormone provision – none of the 15 interviewees personally affected by the 2014 reforms had undergone such procedures in a Danish clinic (though several had done so abroad). Yet the Caspian case – which I discussed in Chapters 1 and 4 – saw a surgeon reprimanded for performing a mastectomy on a trans person.[43] This confirms that such procedures took place. The institutional response to the Caspian case marks a turning point away from the previously existing informal system of treatment based on informed consent, towards the more tightly regulated jurisdictional settlement that governs trans embodiment in Denmark today.

From an institutional vulnerability perspective, the Caspian case constituted an external pressure on Danish medical institutions, as emphasised by the context in which the story was initially reported in Danish media in October 2011.[44] Tobias Raun notes that print media focused on the more 'sensational' aspects of Caspian's mastectomy; asking whether body modification ought to be available for trans people under the age of 18 without contextualising this in

43 Patients' Ombudsman, 'Kritik for behandling – speciallæge i plastikkirurgi Jens Pilegaard Bjarnesen' (1 November 2012) <www.patientombuddet.dk/Afgoerelser_og_domme/Afgoerelser_fra_Sundhedsvaesenets_Disciplinaernaevn/Afgoerelser_med_navn/2012/1294528.aspx> accessed 16 September 2015.

44 T Raun, 'The "Caspian Case" and Its Aftermath: Transgender People's Use of Facebook to Engage Discriminatory Mainstream News Coverage in Denmark' in J Björklund and U Lindqvist (eds), *New Dimensions of Diversity in Nordic Culture and Society* (Cambridge Scholars Publishing 2016).

relation to the health care needs of trans people more generally.[45] The issue was also framed in a polarising way – readers of the online version of one reputable newspaper (*Politiken*) were asked to position themselves either 'for' or 'against' the possibility of trans minors accessing body modification technologies – in a manner which discouraged nuanced discussion.[46]

The DHMA's response was to restrict access to body modification technologies for all trans people, irrespective of their age.[47] Interim guidelines, issued in the immediate aftermath of the Disciplinary Committee's decision to reprimand Caspian's surgeon, stated that while the DHMA conducted a comprehensive review of how trans people ought to be treated, private practitioners were to refer all new patients, and all existing patients below the age of 18, to the Sexological Clinic.[48] The only concession to the importance of Caspian's age in media debates was that private practitioners would be permitted to continue treating existing adult patients provided they met the minimum standards of the seventh edition of the World Professional Association for Transgender Health 'Standards of Care'.[49] All other trans people would have to be assessed at the Sexological Clinic. This established a *de jure* monopoly on treatment at the Sexological Clinic, closing off the only route that trans people had to *both* hormone *and* surgical treatment on an informed consent basis, irrespective of their age.[50]

An external (media) threat to Danish medical regulators thus instigated a response which led to the expansion of their 'objects of governance';[51] from surgical castration to *any* technology that could be understood as constitutive of sex/gender modification treatment. Danish law moved from a position where procedures conducted upon specific body parts had to be authorised by the DHMA, to a point where sex/gender modification in general (and anything deemed to be relating to it) became exceptional. It demanded the authoritative oversight of the DHMA, and the specific clinics that it authorised. In their discussion of professional boundaries in abortion law, Sheelagh McGuinness and Michael Thomson note:

> Professions need to be able to define the borders of their professional jurisdiction with 'utmost clarity', leaving no ambiguity regarding their 'claimed universe of tasks'. In pursuing this, professions are policing the boundaries

45 ibid.
46 ibid.
47 ibid.
48 Danish Health and Medicines Authority, 'Behandling af transseksuelle' (23 November 2012) <https://sundhedsstyrelsen.dk/da/nyheder/2012/behandling-af-transseksuelle> accessed 30 November 2015.
49 ibid.
50 Raun (n 44).
51 M Valverde, 'Jurisdiction and Scale: Legal "Technicalities" as Resources for Theory' (2009) 18 Social & Legal Studies 139, 144.

> between themselves and the public as well as defending their 'task areas' from encroachment by other professions. Crucially, a lack of clarity here creates jurisdictional vulnerability.[52]

The institutional response to the Caspian case constitutes an example of boundary-work between different professional medical specialists. Before 2012, a lack of formal clarity on how access to body modification technologies other than surgical castration ought to be authorised and administered created a jurisdictional vulnerability. This was exploited by the gynaecologists, endocrinologists, and surgeons willing to offer trans people access to such technologies on an informed consent basis without the authorisation of the Sexological Clinic. In response to the institutional vulnerability exposed by the Caspian case, this loophole was closed. New boundaries were established between medical regulators, clinics, different professionals, and the Danish public, expanding the medical jurisdiction of the DHMA and its preferred clinics – with a view, I suggest, to insulating them from future threats and institutional vulnerability.

In its 2011 coalition policy agreement, the Danish government promised to review 'the rules concerning sex/gender modification treatment, including opportunities to have a legal sex/gender change without the need for surgical intervention'.[53] Yet nothing came of this until after the Caspian controversy. In the original formulation, medical and legal reform were positioned alongside one another – indicating that they should be reviewed together. Again, this could be read as an example of institutional vulnerability, as medical jurisdiction over trans phenomena was at risk from legal reform. Yet after Caspian, the two were disentangled. In December 2014 – only months after the CPR law introduced the possibility of self-declaring legal gender status – the DHMA replaced its interim guidelines with substantive medical guidelines. These codified that 'sex/gender modification' treatments could only be administered by a 'multidisciplinary team of collaborating specialists in psychiatry, obstetrics/gynaecology and plastic surgery, who have special knowledge of transgender patients'.[54] While the *de jure* monopoly established by the interim guidelines was formally abolished, a *de facto* state monopoly was effectively retained – at least until the Sexological Centre in Aalborg joined the Sexological Clinic in Copenhagen as the only clinics with the capacity to meet these requirements in 2017.

The immediate result of this jurisdictional settlement is that barriers to legal gender recognition were reduced, as the need to seek approval from the

52 McGuinness and Thomson (n 38) 191, citing Abbott, *The System of Professions* (n 39) 56.

53 Prime Minister's Office, 'Et Danmark, Der Står Sammen' (October 2011) <www.stm.dk/publikationer/Et_Danmark_der_staar_sammen_11/Regeringsgrundlag_okt_2011.pdf> accessed 20 August 2015.

54 Guideline no 10353 (n 36), s 2.

DHMA before being assigned new legal gender status has been removed. But the *de facto* centralisation of access to body modification technologies at the DHMA's authorised clinics had the effect of closing off the only route to such technologies that did not involve a sustained process of psychiatric assessment. As I noted in previous chapters, the process of psychiatric diagnosis is not accessible to all trans people. This saw the constituent parts of the 2014 reforms being interpreted as working in different directions by interviewees:

> you need recognition by the health authorities to get access to the treatment and that is also today way too restrictive in our opinion – way too restrictive. Whereas we got this wonderful, great access to the legal gender change, the physical, the health, part of it has really gone the wrong way. And that's really a calamity – that's annoying – and I'm sad that this Government don't put down their foot and say: "Stop, we have to do something better than this."
>
> (Søren Laursen, LGBT Denmark)

As Chair of LGBT Denmark, Laursen campaigned for accessible civil and medical regulations. His complaint – that the Government did not "put down their foot" to stop the DHMA's jurisdictional expansion in the aftermath of Caspian – implies that they might have done so. This is corroborated by Natalie Videbæk Munkholm's doctrinal analysis of the structure of Danish law. Munkholm notes that rules around accessing body modification technologies are covered by the Health Act, and through orders and guidelines issued in accordance with that Act.[55] When it establishes statutory laws via Acts of Parliament (*lov*) such as this, the Danish Parliament delegates jurisdiction to the relevant ministries.[56] Ministries issue administrative orders (*bekendtgørelser*), in accordance with the delegated mandate, which are legally binding on both citizens and institutions.[57] Ministries also develop administrative guidelines (*cirkulærer* or *vejledning*) – such as the 2014 guidelines – in accordance with the administrative orders, which are binding only upon public institutions.[58] In this hierarchical regulatory system, lower level rules – such as the 2006 and 2014 guidelines – cannot expand upon or derogate from upper level rules – including statutory Acts of Parliament such as the Health Act or CPR law.[59] In terms of legal doctrine, then, the 2014 guidelines must be authorised by, and thus subject to the will of, the Danish Government in Parliament. Medical

55 NV Munkholm, 'Legal Status of Transsexual and Transgender Persons in Denmark' in JM Scherpe (ed), *The Legal Status of Transsexual and Transgender Persons* (Intersentia 2015) 151.

56 ibid. 149.

57 ibid.

58 ibid.

59 ibid.

institutions such as the DHMA are therefore vulnerable to political pressures that emanate from government.

Though medical institutions avoided legislative control when drafting the 2014 guidelines, they did not for long. For, at the time it disciplined Caspian's surgeon, the DHMA was simultaneously embroiled in several apparently unrelated scandals which put them under pressure to demonstrate that they were in control of the medical practitioners that they were charged with regulating. One concerned the cases of two psychiatrists implicated in the deaths of several patients, even after the DHMA had been aware that they had been subject to numerous complaints.[60] Another involved the unauthorised use of the drug Misoprostol to induce births in hospitals, which resulted in a number of tragic deaths.[61] Both controversies highlight the strain that the DHMA was under at the time of drafting the 2014 guidelines.

Fineman notes that 'institutional vulnerability is almost always obscured, and those in control of institutions have a powerful interest in disclaiming the appearance of any vulnerability.'[62] So even though vulnerability is not apparent in the expansion of the jurisdiction of medical institutions in Denmark over recent decades, it was still there at this time. External pressure from the media and politics was enough to ensure the resignation of three senior managers in DHMA between September 2014 and March 2015.[63] It would eventually lead to the DHMA itself being broken up into three smaller institutions in August 2015.[64] Acknowledging these forces could offer significant insight into what motivated the DHMA to stand by their immediate response to the Caspian case, despite its apparently disproportionate effect on trans people and

60 One psychiatrist had been allowed to continue practising despite being reprimanded by the DHMA Disciplinary Committee on 11 separate occasions in a three year period; L Damløv, 'Overblik: Disse sager førte til kulegravning af Sundhedsstyrelsen' *DR* (11 June 2014) <www.dr.dk/nyheder/indland/overblik-disse-sager-foerte-til-kulegravning-af-sundhedsstyrelsen> accessed 7 December 2016. Another, who – having suffered brain damage in a car accident in 2002 – continued to practise for 9 years before his certification was revoked by the DHMA in May 2013 following 20 serious complaints; A Fischer, L Gertsen, and LM Sørensen, 'Tidslinje få overblik over sagen om den hjerneskadede psykiater' *DR* (1 February 2015) <www.dr.dk/nyheder/indland/tidslinje-faa-overblik-over-sagen-om-den-hjerneskadede-psykiater> accessed 7 December 2016.

61 Misoprostol causes frequent contractions during childbirth; 41 different cases saw cases of severe pain and heavy blood-loss, including 7 ruptured wombs and 5 stillbirths; Ritzau, 'Sundhedsstyrelsen skal sørge for sikre fødsler' *Politiken* (18 May 2013) <http://pol.dk/5447315> accessed 7 December 2016.

62 Fineman (n 15) 273.

63 Including Anne Mette Dons, who headed the Department of Supervision and Patient Safety, and two consecutive Directors of the DHMA; JM Fejerskov, 'Portræt: Skandaleramt Sundhedstyrelse bløder tillid' *Politiken* (12 March 2015) <http://pol.dk/5574126> accessed 7 December 2016.

64 The work of the DHMA is now shared between the Danish Health Authority, the Danish Medicines Authority, and the Danish Patient Safety Authority; LI Rasmussen, 'Sundhedsstyrelsen splittes i tre – lægemidler og patientsikkerhed får egen styrelse' *Politiken* (10 August 2015) <http://pol.dk/5585037> accessed 7 December 2016.

the medical professionals that had granted them access to body modification technologies on an informed consent basis. Whether these scandals directly motivated the development of the DHMA's strict policy of centralisation of approval for access to body modification technologies, or the Caspian case merely presented an opportunity to expand medical jurisdiction over trans phenomena, is a moot point.[65] Either way, the Caspian case was the vehicle which made the eventual jurisdictional settlement possible. It therefore amounts to an important trigger – or 'nodal point'[66] – for the expansion of medical jurisdiction over body modification technologies in Denmark. The most prosaic effect of this example of intra-professional boundary-work was to expand the jurisdiction of the DHMA in 2012, and construct a prospective defence of this jurisdictional competence from future encroachment by other institutions.[67] Medical jurisdictions could thus be expanded before and maintained throughout the 2014 reform process, enabling civil and medical reforms to develop contrasting results. The effects of this will be considered next.

Effects of governance

While the DHMA was responsible for developing medical guidelines and ensuring that these are put into practice by individual clinicians, it has never directly determined whether an individual patient is to be granted access to hormones and surgeries. It merely authorised and policed the institutions that were permitted to perform this function. The main result of its 2012 decision to standardise access to body modification technologies understood as constitutive of sex/gender modification treatments is that access to such technologies is now centralised at authorised clinics in Copenhagen and Aalborg. It is these clinics that are tasked with doing the practical work of regulating access to such body modification technologies. Vulnerability theory has a descriptive function, in that it can explain why medical institutions pursued the course of jurisdictional expansion that they did. But unlike some theoretical approaches, vulnerability also has a normative dimension. As I acknowledged in the first part of this chapter, social institutions including medical regulators and clinics play an important role in determining access to resources – including trans

65 That the DHMA's centralisation policy with wider tendencies in health care across the Nordic states cautions against over-stating the importance of the Caspian case. While health care policy and finance have now been largely centralised in Denmark and Norway, in Sweden and Finland a 'similar if somewhat slower process' is now underway; RB Saltman and others, 'Consolidating National Authority in Nordic Health Systems' (2012) 18(3) Eurohealth 21.

66 A 'nodal point' marks a 'momentary frame of joint reference', wherein 'several different trends' in contemporary thought or policy might 'converge'; N Lykke, 'The Timeliness of Post-Constructionism' (2010) 18(2) NORA – Nordic Journal of Feminist and Gender Research 131, 132, 135.

67 McGuinness and Thomson (n 38) 181.

health care. The practices which they enact are therefore ripe for 'monitoring, evaluating, updating, and reforming' in line with principles including equity and justice.[68] In this section of the chapter, I present my own evaluation of the practices of Danish medical institutions, with a view to starting a conversation about how they could be updated and reformed to better meet the health needs of trans people.

In the interviews I conducted with representatives of various medical authorities – including the DHMA, the Ministry of Health, the Sexological Clinic, and the Sexological Centre – the health care regulators' policy of centralisation of governance and access to body modification technologies was consistently justified in relation to the medical ethical principle of non-maleficence. The understanding was that centralising access to treatments constituted a risk-averse strategy which was intended to reduce harm to prospective patients. The Sexological Clinic was, at the time, the only clinic understood to have the capacity to undertake a sustained psychiatric assessment of a patient before deciding whether to grant access to body modification technologies.[69] It was therefore the sole clinic capable of mitigating against two risks which were said to have arisen in relation to the practices of some of the private-sector practitioners that had been authorising and administering access to body modification technologies on an informed consent basis.

The first risk concerned how straightforwardly people had been granted access to body modification technologies that could lead to 'irreversible' changes to the patient's body. In contrast with the private-sector alternatives, the Sexological Clinic was understood to minimise the risk of a trans person 'regretting' body modification by developing a cautious analysis of their patient's mental health before deciding upon whether to authorise their access to body modification. Though such concerns might be assumed to relate to the aesthetic dimensions of transition, the functionality of different organs was also emphasised in interviews (including organs linked to a patient's sexual or reproductive capability). The same concern arose when Caspian's surgeon sought to justify performing the mastectomy without considering the gendered aspect of this treatment on the basis that this type of procedure was akin to the breast reductions he had performed on cis women. This was rejected by the DHMA Disciplinary Committee, who decided that 'a breast reduction operation is clearly different from the total removal of the mammary gland' as breast reduction is reversible, mastectomy is not.[70] A patient who underwent a mastectomy would no longer be able to have 'a physiologically functioning breast,

68 Fineman (n 15) 273.

69 The length of these assessments varies in practice. In our interview, Annamaria Giraldi, Senior Registrar at the Sexological Clinic, noted that trans people who wish to access hormones but not undergo surgeries may not be required to undergo the assessment programme (provided they can be diagnosed with 'unspecified transsexualism').

70 Patients' Ombudsman (n 43).

but only a certain prominence in the chest', in contrast to one who had undergone a breast reduction.[71] The implication was that if Caspian had undergone sustained psychiatric assessment, the risk of him subsequently regretting his mastectomy – and not being able to breastfeed any potential offspring – would have been lessened.

The second risk identified by regulators related to the way in which certain body modification treatments had been administered by some private-sector practitioners. Concern was expressed that the monitoring of the effects of these treatments was not conducted with sufficient diligence to mitigate the risk of patients suffering side-effects (including those associated with hormone replacement treatment). Though this charge was not aimed at *all* private-sector practitioners (with the practices of those that had been permitted to retain their existing adult patients deemed adequate), the assumption was that endocrinologists formally affiliated with the Sexological Clinic would offer greater guarantees that patients would receive quality health care:

> we also did supervision at my old department, and we saw a lot of back-street gynaecologists or psychiatrists that offered treatment for gender-specific purposes but didn't do it properly. They didn't do the proper blood tests; they didn't make sure that they didn't have any other illnesses, or psychiatric issues; and there were a lot of problems with their work. In my opinion, these patients didn't deserve such bad treatment.
>
> (Anne Mette Dons, (formerly) DHMA)

Referring to practitioners willing to prescribe hormones on an informed consent basis as "back-street" gynaecologists alludes to doctors that conduct life-threatening illegal abortions. And just as some see the actions of these doctors as a justifiable response to unjust limitations on abortion, so many of the trans people interviewed expressed gratitude towards these doctors. Dons's analogy amounts to a paradigmatic form of boundary-work, as she distinguishes the formal 'above-board' scientific practice of the Sexological Clinic from the illicit and 'less authoritative, residual non-science'[72] of the gynaecologists and endocrinologists favoured by some trans interviewees.

When the concept of 'risk' arises, Ulrich Beck argues that we begin 'calculating the incalculable, colonizing the future.'[73] I have considered the risk of 'regret' in previous work; noting that this is marked by a future-orientated temporality which contrasts with the immediate concerns of the CPR law – and that different temporalities correspond with the different jurisdictions'

71 ibid.

72 Gieryn (n 40) 783.

73 U Beck, 'The Terrorist Threat: World Risk Society Revisited' (2002) 19(4) Theory, Culture & Society 39, 40.

distinctive governing rationalities.[74] I will now critique the governing rationality employed within the medical jurisdiction on its own terms. For, while I acknowledge that intertemporal struggles are highly political within medical law,[75] both concerns held by medical authorities – about the risk of regret and the intention to improve the quality of treatment – deserve to be scrutinised alongside critical and clinical literature.

Numerous studies have demonstrated that trans people enjoy high rates of satisfaction with different types of body modification procedures.[76] The Royal College of Psychiatrists, in the UK, cites research evidencing dissatisfaction levels as falling below four per cent.[77] It bases its own guidelines on evidence that the most significant factor for regret is a poor outcome after genital reconstruction.[78] Even these studies have come under criticism for the way in which they frame questions of regret, for implying that the minority of patients who are dissatisfied with their new gender status would wish to 'go back' to the previous one (rather than claiming, for example, a non-binary or 'post-transsexual' position).[79] Yet Danish medical authorities did not consider these critiques, favouring a risk-averse policy which restricts access to treatment. Valverde argues that assessment of governing logics ought to include 'the affective and aesthetic dimensions of governance.'[80] And she rejects attempts to construe risk-averse rationalities of governance as 'lacking in passion, affect, and aesthetics', as 'the passion for technocracy and rational risk management is a passion too, and has its own (modernist) aesthetic.'[81] Beck agrees that calculating risk

74 C Dietz, 'Jurisdiction in Trans Health' (2020) 47(1) Journal of Law and Society 60, 78.

75 J Harrington, 'Time as a Dimension of Medical Law' (2012) 20 Medical Law Review 491, 512; F Garland and M Travis, 'Temporal Bodies: Emergencies, Emergence, and Intersex Embodiment' in C Dietz, M Travis, and M Thomson (eds), *A Jurisprudence of the Body* (Palgrave Macmillan 2020).

76 C Klein and BB Gorzalka, 'Sexual Functioning in Transsexuals Following Hormone Therapy and Genital Surgery: A Review' (2009) 6(11) Journal of Sexual Medicine 2922; K Wierckx and others, 'Quality of Life and Sexual Health after Sex Reassignment Surgery in Transsexual Men' (2011) 8(12) Journal of Sexual Medicine 3379.

77 Royal College of Psychiatrists, *Good Practice Guidelines for the Assessment and Treatment of Adults with Gender Dysphoria* (CR181, 2013) 19–20, citing M Landén and others, 'Factors Predictive of Regret in Sex Reassignment' (1998) 97 Acta Psychiatrica Scandinavica, 284; F Pfäfflin and A Junge, 'Sex Reassignment. Thirty Years of International Follow-Up Studies after Sex Reassignment Surgery: A Comprehensive Review, 1961–1991' (1998) International Journal of Transgenderism; and YL Smith and others, 'Sex Reassignment: Outcomes and Predictors of Treatment for Adolescent and Adult Transsexuals' (2005) 35 Psychological Medicine 89–99.

78 ibid. 19, citing AA Lawrence, 'Factors Associated with Satisfaction or Regret Following Male-to-Female Sex Reassignment Surgery' (2003) 32 Archives of Sexual Behavior 299.

79 J St Jacques, 'Retrotranslations of Post-Transsexuality, Notions of Regret' (2007) 6(1) Journal of Visual Culture 77.

80 M Valverde, 'Studying the Governance of Crime and Security: Space, Time and Jurisdiction' (2014) 14(4) Criminology & Criminal Justice 379, 384.

81 M Valverde, *Chronotopes of Law: Jurisdiction, Scale and Governance* (Routledge 2015) 78.

is part of 'the master narrative of first modernity.'[82] But failing to anticipate the unintended consequences of a health care policy belies this modernist aesthetic.

It emerged during my interviews that the DHMA policy of centralisation was not always compatible with its purported governing rationality in practice. All 15 interviewees asked about how they had been affected by the 2014 reforms reported at least considering body modification, yet around half were unwilling or unable to undergo the proscribed process of psychiatric diagnosis.[83] Their reasoning varied. Some felt that gaining such a diagnosis would be impossible for them. For others this was a matter of principle. Several had previously been rejected by the Sexological Clinic or had a negative experience that would prevent them from returning. Non-binary people, and those in receipt of psychiatric diagnoses other than transsexualism, expressed reluctance to undergo psychiatric assessment at the Sexological Clinic as they feared that they would face discrimination and not be approved for treatment. The diagnostic process also exhibits a clear affective dimension. Even interviewees who felt confident that they would be diagnosed with transsexualism reported frustration with the required number of consultations, and long waiting times between appointments.[84] One described attempting to speed up her access to treatment:

> They have great difficulty deciding that it is enough; when they have talked enough about this person. It's very hard for them to say: "This is enough." [...] But I'm giving them a lot of pressure: "Why should we just hold meetings for [the sake of] holding meetings – talking about the weather? Why?! I'm ready, and you know it." [...] I'm giving them a hard time, and putting a lot of pressure on them because it's not okay.
>
> (Anita, Female, 46)

Comparing patient testimonies with those of regulators who seek to justify the policy of centralisation identifies a divergence. The cautious, risk-averse, process of psychiatric authorisation which is understood as a benefit by regulators keen to diminish the risk of regret can just as easily be interpreted as a 'push' factor or 'driver of travel' by those required to undergo it.[85] As Richard

82 Beck (n 73) 41.

83 C Dietz, 'Governing Legal Embodiment: On the Limits of Self-Declaration' (2018) 26(2) Feminist Legal Studies 185, 190.

84 Long waiting times before and between appointments are common in the UK context; SJ Ellis, L Bailey, and J McNeil, 'Trans People's Experiences of Mental Health and Gender Identity Services: A UK Study' (2015) 19 Journal of Gay & Lesbian Mental Health 4. The difference is that, in contrast with Denmark, they are acknowledged as a problem with the diagnostic process; see Women and Equalities Committee, *Transgender Equality* (HC 2015–2016, 390) paras 186–253.

85 R Holliday and others, 'Beautiful Face, Beautiful Place: Relational Geographies and Gender in Cosmetic Surgery Tourism Websites' (2015) 22(1) Gender, Place & Culture 90, 92–93.

V Ericson and Aaron Doyle have noted, there is also risk in inaction.[86] Around two-thirds of interviewees reported having travelled, or planning to travel, abroad to undergo specific surgeries in response to Denmark's risk-averse health policy. A similar proportion admitted having considered turning to the black market to ensure access to hormone treatments (with a minority admitting that they had already begun a process of self-medication). Self-medication is not uncommon among trans communities, as it allows people to initiate their own transition without first having to seek approval from the medical profession.[87] Yet it has unsurprisingly provoked anxieties in the clinical literature. Interviews confirm that such concerns were held by health policymakers in Denmark:

> Yes, we are aware of this [...] but we are convinced by the [Danish] Health and Medicines Authority's argument that the hormone treatment is also irreversible and should be administered with some care – which has not always been the case in the past.
>
> (John Erik Pedersen, Ministry of Health)

> It's always a concern [...] Of course it is. But I think that people know that they're undergoing a great risk if they, for example, go on the internet and buy hormones by postal order from Taiwan or whatever. It is a big risk to take. But you can't do much about that, because a lot of stuff is available on the internet.
>
> (Anne Mette Dons, (formerly) DHMA)

Such concerns were raised in a clinical study published by psychiatrists at the Sexological Clinic.[88] Trans people in Denmark as elsewhere are deterred from seeking alternative sources of treatment. This can either be interpreted generously as representing sincere concern about risks to patients, or more cynically as a strategy concerned with maintaining medical jurisdiction over this area of body modification.[89] Either way, it constitutes a form of boundary-work in the face of institutional vulnerability as regulators seek to gain or maintain control of a disputed domain.[90]

86 RV Ericson and A Doyle, 'Risk and Morality' in RV Ericson and A Doyle (eds), *Risk and Morality* (University of Toronto Press 2003) 4, citing A Giddens, *The Consequences of Modernity* (Polity 1990) 32.

87 Z Davy, 'Transsexual Agents: Negotiating Authenticity and Embodiment within the UK's Medicolegal System', in S Hines and T Sanger (eds), *Transgender Identities: Towards a Social Analysis of Gender Diversity* (Routledge 2010).

88 R Simonsen and others, 'Sociodemographic Study of Danish Individuals Diagnosed with Transsexualism' [2015] 3 Sexual Medicine 109.

89 Davy (n 87).

90 McGuinness and Thomson (n 38) 182.

Concern about the risks of self-medication has pushed UK regulators to the position of recommending that clinicians adopt a contrasting harm reduction strategy – including proscribing 'bridging' hormones before a patient has received a full diagnosis.[91] Yet regulators in Denmark shy away from the possibility that any rise in self-medication might be linked to their own risk-averse policies. This is despite the fact that risk presumes decision-making.[92] Each trans person that I interviewed about how they had been affected by the 2014 reforms interpreted the medical guidelines as evidencing greater restriction by medical authorities (with only one exception). Yet this was not formally acknowledged as a concern by regulators. Irrespective of how quickly hormones were prescribed before 2012, and how well evidence of side-effects was being monitored, it could be argued that this at least took place within a clinical setting. This raises the question as to whether this previous position was actually better suited to minimising harm than risk-averse policies of centralisation which could inadvertently lead to widespread self-medication. By prohibiting practitioners who favoured a process based on informed consent, those who are determined to undertake treatment but unable or unwilling to undergo psychiatric diagnosis are pushed onto the black market, or abroad. Once they begin self-medicating, they become exposed to the very same risks – including the risk of regret, and poor-quality treatment – that are cited to justify the DHMA's policy of centralisation in the first place.

A commonplace understanding of vulnerability might suggest it is good that policymakers harbour concern about the vulnerability of trans patients (even if this only applies before they travel abroad or turn to the black market). But vulnerability theory demands consideration of the vulnerability of all people. So, trans people's needs ought to be understood as diverse and yet also commensurate with other patient groups. In the context of US campus shootings, Benjamin Reiss has noted that 'whereas "risk" rationalizes and objectifies problems, the concept of vulnerability is relational and flexible.'[93] Instead of framing students with mental health issues as risky objects ripe for surveillance, a vulnerability approach considers them as subjects whose vulnerabilities can be compounded by the vulnerability of institutions. Within this shift, Reiss argues:

> Exploring the nature of this relationship might yield campus policies that integrate the thinking of administrators, counselors, students, faculty, and security forces rather than segmenting their fears and liabilities and imposing top-down strategies for controlling them.[94]

91 Royal College of Psychiatrists (n 77) 21–22.
92 Beck (n 73) 40.
93 Reiss (n 3) 39.
94 ibid. 40.

In Denmark, a similarly relational conception of the power dynamics at play – involving regulators, medical professionals, and trans patients – would constitute decent starting point for those who seek to develop supportive and collaborative health care practices. While this might sound utopian in light of current Danish health policy, such practices could constitute a much preferable alternative to the top-down policy of risk-averse centralisation evidenced within recent reforms.

From there, to understand the 'qualitative' aspects of governance (which concern *how* governance is practised) Valverde suggests distinguishing between 'governing rationalities' and 'capacities of governance'.[95] The two clinics approved by the DHMA – in Copenhagen and in Aalborg – are required to perform three interrelated functions. The primary function is that of health care provider. In accordance with their training as medical practitioners, clinicians must seek to improve the health of patients. Their secondary function involves assuming the role of the official state gatekeeper to body modification technologies deemed to be constitutive of sex/gender modification treatments. Here, the main concern is with assessing patient suitability for treatment. The tertiary function is that of academic research institution. Clinicians are also researchers, who are expected to produce accurate, valid, knowledge about patient experiences of treatment.

During interviews with respondents who had undergone, or were in the process of undergoing, the assessment programme at the Sexological Clinic in Copenhagen, it became clear that these three functions might not be compatible. Of the 12 interviewees who had attended the Sexological Clinic, only one described going there with an open mind:

> I wasn't 100 percent sure what I needed when I went there; I was in a process of figuring out [...] I wasn't sure – with feeling non-binary – whether it would be the right thing for me to change my body; I needed to figure some things out. So, I thought: "Well, they're the experts; they must be able to help me."
>
> (Pippin, Non-binary, 42)

All 11 other interviewees reported adopting an instrumental stance, seeing medicine as facilitating their transition. Some admitted approaching the clinic strategically. Sasha – who does not identify within the gender binary – described exaggerating masculine aspects of their aesthetic to maximise the chances of being prescribed testosterone hormones:

> I feel like I'm lying. Well. I am kind of lying when I'm there [...] I've been planning what sort of clothes to wear, not wearing tight pants; and I

95 Valverde (n 81) 84.

> cut my hair short even though I want to have long hair. I don't know if it matters – what sort of hair I have – but, you know, just to be on the safe side I've put myself in this masculine box, or at least tried to.
>
> (Sasha, Non-binary, 23)

Viewing medical clinics as gatekeepers rather than spaces of self-discovery accords with Davy's finding that trans people are accustomed to reproducing the stereotypical narratives to gain authorisation for treatment.[96] Of the three functions of the approved clinics, this suggests that clinicians are perceived primarily within their secondary role – as gatekeepers to hormones and surgeries – rather than as health care providers or academic researchers. This appears to have affected the capacity of the clinic to perform the other functions it has assumed.

In terms of the clinicians' primary function, questions must be asked about how far the quality of health care provision will be reduced once staff are perceived primarily as gatekeepers to material resources. Interviews suggest that this has had more serious repercussions for trans people with specific health care requirements. One interviewee explained how being rejected from the programme at the Sexological Clinic due to suffering from anxiety and depression motivated an (ultimately unsuccessful) attempt to wean herself off her medication:

> I was taking anti-depressants and anxiety medication [...] [Yet] [i]n order to be assessed you have to be cured of all psychological ailments beforehand; which is really weird because any modern gender clinic would take into account that, if you have gender dysphoria then you would, most likely, be slightly depressed, or have anxiety [...] [But] because of my medication I was rejected. I actually went home and talked with my doctor, and started getting off the medication – which was really hard and made me sick [...] I was really, really depressed for a fortnight. I just couldn't get out of bed for two weeks.
>
> (Freyja, Transwoman, 46)

Another interviewee, who also lives with a psychiatric diagnosis for which they undergo therapy, explained how the same requirement for gaining the Sexological Clinic's approval – of being mentally 'stable' – impacted his mental health treatment:

> [E]very single appointment I went to, they asked: "Are you stable?" [...] and what I told myself is that, even if I'm not stable at all [...] I'm going

96 Davy (n 87) 123.

to lie to them. If that's the requirement – to be stable – then of course I'm going to lie, and fake that I'm stable in order for them to be sure.

(Curtis, Male, 25)

Curtis describes being in a situation where being honest about his mental health might jeopardise his access to testosterone. Yet strategically prioritising access to body modifications might require him to cover up any problems he has had with his mental health. This dilemma was compounded by the centralising practice of the Danish health care system, which recorded all patient notes on an online database which are then accessible both to the patient and other medical professionals:

I also have to lie to my psychiatrist, because they can read her notes as well [...] I wouldn't dare say: "I really had a bad week."

(Curtis, Male, 25)

This ensured that Curtis's decision to be strategic about what he disclosed to his caseworker at the Sexological Clinic must be replicated with his other psychiatrist – even if this meant hiding "a bad week" from both clinicians. Evidence that being admitted to the Sexological Clinic could lead to a patient's mental health care being compromised in this ways casts doubt as to how far their secondary, gatekeeping, function is compatible with the clinic's primary function of providing the best possible health care for their patients.

The perception of clinicians as gatekeepers to body modification technologies also affects the Sexological Clinic's capacity to perform the tertiary function of producing empirical academic research on trans phenomena. One interviewee described how he got the impression that the progression of his caseworker's thesis was affecting his treatment:

He was so focused on my sexual behaviour, and my sexuality, [that] we barely even talked about my gender identity. He was really focused on trying to convince me that maybe I was just homosexual, or that maybe something bad happened with my parents, that I thought I had to be a guy to please my father or something like that [...] He was writing this thesis or something, and I really felt like I was a case study to use in his thesis – and that was his focus more than getting me help.

(Peter, Male/FtM, 27)

Peter's caseworker exhibits poor academic and clinical practice. He seems to be trying to force his theory onto the patient, rather than theorising from Peter's experience. Yet even then, epistemological concerns about the validity of his research findings would remain. Evidence that trans people do not admit to the full complexity of their experience of transition within the clinical setting suggests similar questions could be asked of the research produced by clinicians at the Sexological Clinic. While it is generally accepted that overcoming unequal power relations is difficult, researchers are still required to account for the effect that this might have had on their findings (as I discussed in Chapter 3).[97] The ethicality of research conducted on participants keen to gain the researcher's approval – based upon the understanding that that researcher holds the key to resources – is questionable. Such methodological limitations raise questions about the validity of research based on data generated in the Sexological Clinic.

This has consequences for the regulation of embodiment. As the Sexological Clinic has been the only clinic to authorise sex/gender modification treatments, no other institution has historically had access to trans research subjects. The Sexological Clinic's research has therefore been the only empirical clinical research published on trans phenomena in Denmark. It has therefore played a pivotal role in the development of treatment frameworks, as one activist lamented:

> if I went there tomorrow, to get my hormones, I would of course do whatever I could to get the hormones – I would totally buy into their system. I don't think I have any choice [...] because I would be really afraid that if I didn't get in, I would never get any. And that's a really fucking big problem because I know so many people who do exactly the same and just say what they know that the Sexological Clinic wants us to say. And in that way, we will never get any different system, because that works.
>
> (Elias Magnild, Trans Political Forum)

Wider concerns about how clinical stereotypes and psychiatric research practices are used to shape one another barely register.[98] A feedback loop is created; whereby trans people conform to narratives that they think their clinician needs to hear, and that clinician then reports tropes that they assume to be accurate and truthful – and which they keep happening to hear.[99] Advice to be wary that consistency between different testimonies may indicate 'answers that are intended to conceal rather than clarify' either goes unheard or is simply ignored.[100] Stereotypical tropes are used to shape clinical practice, ensuring that they will be learned and repeated by trans people keen to gain access to body modification technologies.

97 B Matthews and L Ross, *Research Methods: A Practical Guide for the Social Sciences* (Pearson 2010) 76–77.

98 Z Davy, 'The DSM-5 and the Politics of Diagnosing Transpeople' (2015) 44 Archives of Sexual Behavior 1165, 1174.

99 Filmmaker Vika Kirchenbauer notes, wryly, that: 'You learn that you are doing well when they tell you: "It's funny but it always sounds like the exact same story. But when you see the people, you just know it's true."' V Kirchenbauer, *Like Rats Leaving a Sinking Ship* (2012) <http://vk0ms.com/like_rats.html> 15:30.

100 CA Davies, *Reflexive Ethnography: A guide to researching selves and others* (Routledge 2005) 86.

Since it was established in 1986, the Sexological Clinic has been the sole institution to publish empirical academic research on trans phenomena in Denmark.[101] This suggests that the epistemological concerns described above are far from novel. Yet, along with the issue of ensuring trans people's mental and physical health, they may have been less pronounced before the DHMA's medical jurisdiction expanded in 2012. Before then, trans people had private-sector clinicians to turn to in order to access body modification technologies in Denmark if they were unable to access treatment via authorised clinics. The removal of this option could reduce the chances of someone presenting themselves at the Sexological Clinic undecided as to what they want but hoping "to figure some things out", and willing to undertake an honest and supported process of self-reflection. Even Pippin noted that the feelings of disappointment experienced upon being rejected from the Sexological Clinic would have been nothing in comparison to the devastation that they would have felt had this happened more recently:

> I was disappointed of course that I'd been going there for two years and nothing came of it. Fortunately, at that point I had got the name of the gynaecologist who could also help, so I was not totally without options – if I'd been that, I would probably have been devastated.
>
> (Pippin, Non-binary, 42)

Danish health policy has exacerbated anxieties that trans people have developed around securing access to body modification technologies. These anxieties produce barriers which prevent trans people from accessing health care services. Those that are unable or unwilling to undergo psychiatric diagnosis at the approved clinics are left with the choice of turning to the black market or foreign clinics to access body modification technologies. They must accept the economic costs and associated health risks that that entails. As well as responsibilising trans people in a neoliberal manner, as discussed in Chapter 4, this jurisdictional arrangement will have a differential impact upon trans people depending upon their circumstances and backgrounds. It risks exacerbating inequalities in access to health which run along intersections of age, class, disability, ethnicity, gender and sexuality.

Since the Sexological Clinic became solely responsible for directly determining an individual's access to body modification technologies, its patient roster greatly increased.[102] Being construed mostly as gatekeepers to these technologies in the eyes of their patients, and having access to these patients' wider medical

101 C Graugaard and others, 'Denmark' in RT Francoeur and RJ Noonan (eds), *The Continuum Complete International Encyclopaedia of Sexuality* (Continuum 2004) 331.

102 Annamaria Giraldi noted in her interview that the Sexological Clinic has seen "more than a 200 or 300 percent increase [in the number of referrals it receives] in the last eight years." This could explain the authorisation of the Sexological Centre at the Aalborg University Hospital.

records, puts staff at these clinics in an undesirable position whereby their clinical practice may become a barrier to their patients' good health. Meanwhile, the research they produce risks being undermined by being based upon information that their patients strategically report. This, in turn, ensures the reproduction of homogenous knowledge about trans phenomena. This has consequences for academic knowledge production, and for those whose embodiment will be measured against these compromised standards at some point in the future.

Conclusion

In this chapter, I utilised institutional vulnerability as a lens through which to analyse the medical and legal management of trans health care in Denmark. A straightforward analysis of medical institutions' expanding jurisdiction over trans phenomena would assume that this would reflect the presence of strong, and even strengthening, clinics and regulators. Yet I have demonstrated that this expansion could also be interpreted as a defensive response to jurisdictional vulnerability, with medical institutions engaging in boundary-work to gain and maintain control over important but contested terrain. As Fineman and others have established, even the most powerful of our social institutions are vulnerable – though this might be hard to capture at face value (especially when people struggling to access the services of those institutions, or indeed those employed to manage them, would have difficulty acknowledging this). Institutions are always subject to internal and external pressures, which put them at a constant risk of critique or even failure. And while the risk of failure that intuitions face is conceptually distinct from the embodied vulnerability of the humans who are governed by, or manage, them, this does not mean that vulnerability is not there.

In the context of the 2014 reforms in Denmark, this is readily apparent. Before 2012, medical regulators and approved clinics which regulated trans people's access to body modification technologies came under pressure from private-sector medical professionals who were willing to prescribe hormones and surgeries on an informed consent basis. In the aftermath of the Caspian controversy, regulators and approved clinics came under pressure from trans patients, the media, politicians, and the wider public – responding by closing the legal loophole that enabled diverse provision of health care in this area. Even if vulnerability is not immediately apparent in this process of jurisdictional expansion and centralisation, it can be found in seemingly unrelated developments which saw the DHMA lose three directors before being disbanded into three separate regulatory institutions in the period after the 2014 reforms.

Existing research on the neoliberal institutional management of risk has charted how institutions have become increasingly risk-averse in managing costs – irrespective of whether those are real or symbolic, financial or reputational.[103] The concept of institutional vulnerability also has this useful descriptive

103 I am again grateful to the Routledge Social Justice Book Series editors for highlighting this point.

dimension, in that it helps explain the expansion of medical jurisdiction over the area of trans health. But, as with vulnerability theory more generally, it also offers normative insights. Institutional practices demand scrutiny, not least in light of their potential to help people become resilient in response to their own, human, vulnerability. In the Danish context, the narrow focus of medical regulators and clinics on their own institutional vulnerability has been shown to have motivated a policy of risk-aversion which has in turn neglected the complex vulnerability of trans people.[104] Risk management is by no means incompatible with public institutional health care provision. The collectivisation of risk was one of the main intentions behind the creation of European welfare states.[105] More recently, risk-based actuarial models have proven themselves to be relatively compatible with welfarism.[106] But when they are '[r]iddled with their own vulnerabilities, society's institutions cannot eradicate, and often operate to exacerbate, our individual vulnerability.'[107]

Again, vulnerability theory normatively cautions against dismissing public-sector regulators and health care providers for failing to overcome their institutional vulnerabilities. To ensure access to health care for the patients that rely upon them, vulnerability theory requires scholars and activists to think carefully about what they should demand from, and for, these institutions. Though it is tempting to criticise the state for investing too much power in medical regulators and clinics, in the long term it would only exacerbate people's vulnerabilities if the state was to become more withdrawn in this area. The criticisms raised of institutions such as the DHMA and its approved clinics in this chapter ought to be read as precursors to demands for something better. This could be a more realistic and responsive management of trans health, which acknowledges the vulnerability of all patients, and is not characterised by self-defeating risk-aversion. Only with adequate funding and governmental support will it be likely that medical institutions can move beyond their risk-aversion, and ideally towards one better placed to encourage supportive and non-judgemental health care practices for trans people, and all other patients.

Bibliography

Abbott A, *The System of Professions: An Essay on the Division of Expert Labor* (University of Chicago Press 1988)

——— 'Things of Boundaries: Defining the Boundaries of Social Inquiry' (1995) 62 Social Research 857

104 I am grateful to Mitch Travis for helping me formulate this point.

105 Beck (n 73) 41.

106 Though it tends to be that 'the principle of universal access [...] gives way to targeted and streamlined interventions' in these situations; K Hannah-Moffat, 'Criminogenic Needs and the Transformative Risk Subject: Hybridizations of Risk/Need in Penality' (2005) 7(1) Punishment and Society 29, 42.

107 Fineman (n 15) 273.

Beck U, 'The Terrorist Threat: World Risk Society Revisited' (2002) 19(4) Theory, Culture & Society 39

Cannoot P, 'The Pathologisation of Trans* Persons in the ECtHR's Case Law on Legal Gender Recognition' (2019) 37(1) Netherlands Quarterly of Human Rights 14

Damløv L, 'Overblik: Disse sager førte til kulegravning af Sundhedsstyrelsen' *DR* (11 June 2014) <https://www.dr.dk/nyheder/indland/overblik-disse-sager-foerte-til-kulegravning-af-sundhedsstyrelsen> accessed 7 December 2016

Danish Health and Medicines Authority, 'Behandling af transseksuelle' (23 November 2012) <https://sundhedsstyrelsen.dk/da/nyheder/2012/behandling-af-transseksuelle> accessed 30 November 2015

Davies CA, *Reflexive Ethnography: A Guide to Researching Selves and Others* (Routledge 2005)

Davy Z, 'Transsexual Agents: Negotiating Authenticity and Embodiment within the UK's Medicolegal System' in Hines S and Sanger T (eds), *Transgender Identities: Towards a Social Analysis of Gender Diversity* (Routledge 2010)

——— 'The DSM-5 and the Politics of Diagnosing Transpeople' (2015) 44 Archives of Sexual Behavior 1165

———, Sørlie A, and Schwend AS, 'Democratising Diagnoses? The Role of the Depathologisation Perspective in Constructing Corporeal Trans Citizenship' (2018) 38(1) Critical Social Policy 13

Dehaghani R and Newman D, "We're Vulnerable Too': An (Alternative) Analysis of Vulnerability within English Criminal Legal Aid and Police Custody' (2017) 7(6) Oñati Socio-legal Series 1199

Dietz C, 'Governing Legal Embodiment: On the Limits of Self-Declaration' (2018) 26(2) Feminist Legal Studies 185

——— and Pearce R, 'Depathologising Gender: Vulnerability in Trans Health Law' in Dietz C, Travis M, and Thomson M (eds), *A Jurisprudence of the Body* (Palgrave Macmillan 2020)

——— 'Jurisdiction in Trans Health' (2020) 47(1) Journal of Law and Society 60

Ellis SJ, Bailey L, and McNeil J, 'Trans People's Experiences of Mental Health and Gender Identity Services: A UK Study' (2015) 19 Journal of Gay & Lesbian Mental Health 4

Ericson RV and Doyle A, 'Risk and Morality' in Ericson RV and Doyle A (eds), *Risk and Morality* (University of Toronto Press 2003)

Fejerskov JM, 'Portræt: Skandaleramt Sundhedstyrelse bløder tillid' *Politiken* (12 March 2015) <http://pol.dk/5574126> accessed 7 December 2016

Fineman J, 'The Vulnerable Subject at Work: A New Perspective on the Employment At-Will Debate' (2013) 43(2) Southwestern Law Review 275

Fineman MA, 'The Vulnerable Subject: Anchoring Equality in the Human Condition' (2008) 20(1) Yale Journal of Law and Feminism 1

——— 'The Vulnerable Subject and the Responsive State' (2010) 60 Emory Law Journal 251

——— 'Vulnerability and Inevitable Inequality' (2017) 4(3) Oslo Law Review 133

Fischer A, Gertsen L, and Sørensen LM, 'Tidslinje få overblik over sagen om den hjerneskadede psykiater' *DR* (1 February 2015) <http://www.dr.dk/nyheder/indland/tidslinje-faa-overblik-over-sagen-om-den-hjerneskadede-psykiater> accessed 7 December 2016

Friedson E, *Profession of Medicine: A Study of the Sociology of Applied Knowledge* (University of Chicago Press 1988)

Garland F and Travis M, 'Temporal Bodies: Emergencies, Emergence, and Intersex Embodiment' in Dietz C, Travis M, and Thomson M (eds), *A Jurisprudence of the Body* (Palgrave Macmillan 2020)

Gieryn TF, 'Boundary-Work and the Demarcation of Science from Non-Science: Strains and Interests in the Professional Interests of Scientists' (1983) 48 American Sociological Review 781

Graugaard C, Eplov LF, Giraldi A, Kristensen E, Munck E, Møhl B, Owens AF, Risør H, and Winther G, 'Denmark' in Francoeur RT and Noonan RJ (eds), *The Continuum Complete International Encyclopaedia of Sexuality* (Continuum 2004)

Hannah-Moffat K, 'Criminogenic Needs and the Transformative Risk Subject: Hybridizations of Risk/Need in Penality' (2005) 7(1) Punishment and Society 29

Hansen BS, 'Something Rotten in the State of Denmark: Eugenics and the Ascent of the Welfare State' in Broberg G and Roll-Hansen N (eds), *Eugenics and the Welfare State: Sterilization Policy in Denmark, Sweden, Norway and Finland* (East Lansing 1996)

Harrington J, 'Time as a Dimension of Medical Law' (2012) 20 Medical Law Review 491

Heyes CJ and Latham JR, 'Trans Surgeries and Cosmetic Surgeries: The Politics of Analogy' (2018) 5(2) TSQ: Transgender Studies Quarterly 174

Holliday R, Bell D, Jones M, Hardy K, Hunter E, Probyn E, and Taylor JS, 'Beautiful Face, Beautiful Place: Relational Geographies and Gender in Cosmetic Surgery Tourism Websites' (2015) 22(1) Gender, Place & Culture 90

Kirchenbauer V, *Like Rats Leaving a Sinking Ship* (2012) <http://vk0ms.com/like_rats.html>

Klein C and Gorzalka BB, 'Sexual Functioning in Transsexuals Following Hormone Therapy and Genital Surgery: A Review' (2009) 6(11) Journal of Sexual Medicine 2922

Lykke N, 'The Timeliness of Post-Constructionism' (2010) 18(2) NORA – Nordic Journal of Feminist and Gender Research 131

Marvel S, 'The Evolution of Plural Parentage: Applying Vulnerability Theory to Polygamy and Same-Sex Marriage' (2015) 64 Emory Law Journal 2047

Matthews B and Ross L, *Research Methods: A Practical Guide for the Social Sciences* (Pearson 2010)

McGuinness S and Thomson M, 'Medicine and Abortion Law: Complicating the Reforming Profession' (2015) 23(2) Medical Law Review 177

Ministry of Justice, 'Rapport fra arbejdsgruppen om juridisk kønsskifte' (27 February 2014) <http://justitsministeriet.dk/sites/default/files/media/Pressemeddelelser/pdf/2014/Rapport%20om%20juridisk%20k%C3%B8nsskifte.pdf> accessed 21 July 2016

Munkholm NV, 'Legal Status of Transsexual and Transgender Persons in Denmark' in Scherpe JM (ed), *The Legal Status of Transsexual and Transgender Persons* (Intersentia 2015)

Patients' Ombudsman, 'Kritik for behandling – speciallæge i plastikkirurgi Jens Pilegaard Bjarnesen' (1 November 2012) <https://www.patientombuddet.dk/Afgoerelser_og_domme/Afgoerelser_fra_Sundhedsvaesenets_Disciplinaernaevn/Afgoerelser_med_navn/2012/1294528.aspx> accessed 16 September 2015

Prime Minister's Office, 'Et Danmark, Der Står Sammen' (October 2011) <http://www.stm.dk/publikationer/Et_Danmark_der_staar_sammen_11/Regeringsgrundlag_okt_2011.pdf> accessed 20 August 2015

Rasmussen LI, 'Sundhedsstyrelsen splittes i tre - lægemidler og patientsikkerhed får egen styrelse' *Politiken* (10 August 2015) <http://pol.dk/5585037> accessed 7 December 2016

Raun T, 'The 'Caspian Case' and Its Aftermath: Transgender People's Use of Facebook to Engage Discriminatory Mainstream News Coverage in Denmark' in Björklund J and Lindqvist U (eds), *New Dimensions of Diversity in Nordic Culture and Society* (Cambridge Scholars Publishing 2016)

Reiss B, 'Madness after Virginia Tech: From Psychiatric Risk to Institutional Vulnerability' (2010) 28(4) Social Text 25

Ritzau, 'Sundhedsstyrelsen skal sørge for sikre fødsler' *Politiken* (18 May 2013) <http://pol.dk/5447315> accessed 7 December 2016

Royal College of Psychiatrists, *Good Practice Guidelines for the Assessment and Treatment of Adults with Gender Dysphoria* (CR181 2013) 19–20

Saltman RB, Vrangbaek K, Lehto J, and Winblad U, 'Consolidating National Authority in Nordic Health Systems' (2012) 18(3) Eurohealth 21

Simonsen R, Hald GM, Giraldi A, and Kristensen E, 'Sociodemographic Study of Danish Individuals Diagnosed with Transsexualism' (2015) 3 Sexual Medicine 109

Sørensen T and Hertoft P, 'Sexmodifying Operations on Transsexuals in Denmark in the Period 1950–1977' (1980) 61 Acta Psychiatrica Scandinavica 56

St Jacques J, 'Retrotranslations of Post-Transsexuality, Notions of Regret' (2007) 6(1) Journal of Visual Culture 77

Stryker S, *Transgender History* (Seal Press 2008)

Travis M, 'The Vulnerability of Heterosexuality: Consent, Gender Deception and Embodiment' (2019) 28(3) Social & Legal Studies 303

Valverde M, 'Jurisdiction and Scale: Legal 'Technicalities' as Resources for Theory' (2009) 18 Social & Legal Studies 139

——— 'Studying the Governance of Crime and Security: Space, Time and Jurisdiction' (2014) 14(4) Criminology & Criminal Justice 379

——— *Chronotopes of Law: Jurisdiction, Scale and Governance* (Routledge 2015)

WHO ICD-10, 'F64.0 Transsexualism' <http://apps.who.int/classifications/icd10/browse/2015/en#/F64> accessed 22 May 2015

Wierckx K, Van Caenegem E, Elaut E, Dedecker D, Van de Peer F, Toye K, Weyers S, Hoebeke P, Monstrey S, De Cuypere G, and T'Sjoen G, 'Quality of Life and Sexual Health after Sex Reassignment Surgery in Transsexual Men' (2011) 8(12) Journal of Sexual Medicine 3379

Women and Equalities Committee, *Transgender Equality* (HC 2015-16, 390)

Chapter 6

Governmentality and managing trans health

Introduction

My main objective in this book has been to examine the impact of self-declaration law in practice. Taking the Danish reforms of 2014 as my case study, I identified gaps between the law as written and its embodied effects on trans and other gender diverse people. Yet my intention in doing so has not strictly been 'reformist'.[1] By highlighting flaws in governing practice, I did not mean to suggest that these problems could easily be resolved. My critique of risk-averse medical regulation in Chapter 5 was not meant to be read, for instance, as a straightforward call for more risk-taking in medical practice. Rather, by considering existing regulations through the lens of institutional vulnerability, I sought to offer pointers as to how health care systems might be put in a better position to mitigate their vulnerabilities, and by consequence, the diverse vulnerabilities of their patients.

Similarly, the critique of visibility and progress narratives that I presented in Chapter 4 was intended to promote scepticism among its target audience of trans scholars and activists, rather than being addressed towards policymakers and regulators. Yet even that chapter could be charged with betraying signs of residual 'reformism'. One sub-text of its argument is that if scholars and activists were more sceptical about the possibilities of visibility and progress, they might be better placed to promote reforms which would materially benefit trans people – in health care, employment, and housing, for instance. In Eve Sedgwick's terms, both Chapters 4 and 5 could thus be characterised 'reparative' readings of the 2014 reforms in Denmark. They afford the reader 'room to realize that the future may be different from the present', while entertaining the possibility that 'the past, in turn, could have happened differently from the way it actually did.'[2]

1 For a discussion of feminist perspectives on law reform, see V Munro, *Law and Politics at the Perimeter: Re-Evaluating Key Debates in Feminist Theory* (Hart 2007) ch 3.

2 EK Sedgwick, *Touching Feeling: Affect, Pedagogy, Performativity* (Duke University Press 2003) 146.

DOI: 10.4324/9780429288203-6

This chapter could harbour similarly reparative undercurrents.[3] Yet it precedes from what Sedgwick would consider a more 'paranoid' position; in that it exhibits an 'alertness to the dangers posed' by law reform.[4] Inspired by the work of Michel Foucault, I present a governmentality analysis of the Danish reforms of 2014. Governmentality rests upon the distinction between what Foucault called 'discipline' and 'regulation'. The first part of this chapter focuses upon 'disciplinary' power, which concerns which norms and subject positions are permitted or excluded by a governmental practice such as the Central Person Registry (CPR) law. 'Disciplinary' controls promote norms of good behaviour by positioning them in hierarchies of permissibility. These are then incorporated and reproduced at the level of the individual subject.[5] The exclusion of non-binary people from formal recognition in Denmark exemplifies this, as a risk of criminalisation awaits those non-binary people who seek to self-declare legal gender status. This first section of the chapter also considers political economy, alongside previously discussed theories including progress and institutional vulnerability, as ways to understand the disciplinary effect of the 2014 reforms.

The second part of the chapter addresses 'regulatory' controls. It considers the effect of the 2014 reforms from a bio-political perspective. As regulatory power attempts to secure the health of the nation, it looks beyond norms and subjectivities. The focus of governance thus shifts from the individual subject to the population level. This requires analysis to move from considering the effect of the CPR law on primarily trans and gender diverse people, to the broader function of the CPR as a system for managing the Danish population. In this part of the chapter, I consider the Health Act, which was amended as part of the 2014 reforms to remove the requirement that an applicant for castration must evidence 'suffering of the soul'. I draw links between this requirement and Denmark's eugenics programme – which was active for most of the 20th century – and contemporary anti-migration policies and border controls. From here, bio-political analysis enables me to challenge the nation-state form. This has consequences both for trans and feminist legal scholarship, but also policy-focused socio-legal research more broadly. Governmentality analysis enables me to look beyond the question of how law failed to include all those that it sought to, to consider how various governmental preferences were prioritised over and above the inclusion of trans and gender diverse people. It charts how the 2014 reforms are failing in ways that were expected, and perhaps even intended, to fail.[6]

3 Sedgwick notes that much reparative work is generated from 'paranoid' positions; ibid. 128–129.

4 ibid. 128.

5 M Foucault, *The Will to Knowledge: The History of Sexuality Volume One* (first published 1976, R Hurley tr, Penguin 1998) 48.

6 I am grateful to Dean Spade for helping me formulate this critique of the 2014 reforms in this way.

Discipline

Critiques of flaws in legislative drafting, such as those that I have developed in previous chapters, could be said to address, primarily, the 'disciplinary' effects of the 2014 reforms. As I noted in Chapter 2, disciplinary power is constitutive of normative subject positions, as exemplified by Foucault's analysis of the 19th-century medicalisation of homosexuality.[7] At this time, sodomy was no longer understood as an act that could be committed by anyone, but as one which was would be committed by a 'homosexual' person.[8] Though the 2014 reforms do not name the trans subject that they apparently target, they nevertheless reflect certain norms which could be said to produce a normative trans subject. Namely, they address a trans person who:

i) 'experiences themselves as belonging to the other sex/gender';
ii) is willing to make 'a written declaration that the desire for a new personal identity is based upon an experience of belonging to the other sex/gender'; and
iii) is, at the time of the application, at least 18 years old.[9]

It is widely acknowledged that the principles of self-declaration make it hard for states to guarantee that such conditions are being met.[10] In Denmark, the concern that it would not be possible to conduct 'a proper examination of whether the application is indeed justified by an experience of belonging to the other sex/gender' was raised by the working group tasked with proposing reforms.[11] This was also mentioned in the explanatory comments which accompany the CPR law.[12] In response, a safeguarding provision was explicitly included to protect the new system from misuse:

> it will not, for example, be permitted to change sex/gender 'for fun', as part of an action for greater equality between men and women etc., to obtain gender-related benefits, or in an attempt to disguise one's identity.[13]

7 Foucault (n 5) 42–43.

8 ibid. 48.

9 L 182 Law amending the Act on the Central Person Registry (11 June 2014) (*L 182 Lov om ændring af lov om Det Centrale Personregister*) (DK) s 1; Order regarding the Act on the Central Person Registry (9 January 2013) (*Bekendtgørelse af lov om Det Centrale Personregister*) (DK) s 3 para 6.

10 P Dunne, 'Ten Years of Gender Recognition in the United Kingdom: Still a "Model for Reform"?' [2015] Public Law 530, 538.

11 Ministry of Justice, *Rapport fra arbejdsgruppen om juridisk kønsskifte* (27 February 2014) <http://justitsministeriet.dk/sites/default/files/media/Pressemeddelelser/pdf/2014/Rapport%20om%20juridisk%20k%C3%B8nsskifte.pdf> accessed 21 July 2016.

12 Bill for amending the Act on the Central Person Registry (30 April 2014) (*Forslag til Lov om ændring af lov om Det Centrale Personregister*) (DK).

13 ibid.

From a disciplinary perspective, this provision explicitly excludes the possibility of a legal subject making a declaration of gender status based upon any of these reasons. These normative exclusions are prohibited with reference to this hypothetical scenario:

> if the Ministry of the Economy and the Interior later – for example through publicity in the press – becomes aware that the statement is inaccurate, permission for legal sex/gender change could be revoked by the general rules of administrative law. The consequence of this would be that the person is reassigned their original social security number. Misrepresentation in the declaration of the reasons for the application for change of sex/gender will in these circumstances be punishable by section 163 of the Penal Code.[14]

The relevant section of the Penal Code states that 'Whoever gives false statements to a public authority about matters as to which he is obliged to give evidence, shall be punishable by fine or imprisonment for up to 4 months.'[15]

That the implementation of a model of gender recognition as accessible as self-declaration would require the backing of Danish criminal law would come as no surprise to the scholars researching the coincidence of LGBT rights reforms and the expansion of the 'prison industrial complex' in both US and UK contexts.[16] Though it seems unlikely that a trans person would be criminalised in accordance with this provision in Denmark, it remains a formal possibility nonetheless. The mere threat of criminal sanction may be enough to make trans people take care to 'pass' as quietly and with as little controversy as possible. The explicitly cited example of receiving negative 'publicity in the press' posits one scenario in which a prosecution might be pursued (for example, if a trans person were to seek access to an unwelcoming gender-segregated space). Foucauldian analysis has established that it is not just norms about 'good' behaviour that are relayed by such a prohibition, but also normative (and non-normative) subject positions.[17] Here, the incentive to stick to normative trans embodiment is clearly communicated to trans people in Denmark.

The same logic appears in the Danish Government's decision to avoid responding to the calls, discussed in Chapter 4, to grant trans people the opportunity to declare an experience of belonging to 'another sex/gender', or to be allocated a gender-neutral CPR number. The effect was to formally exclude

14 ibid.

15 Penal Code (4 July 2014) (*Bekendtgørelse af straffeloven*) (DK), s 163.

16 D Spade, *Normal Life: Administrative Violence, Critical Trans Politics, and the Limits of Law* (South End Press 2011); R Conrad (ed), *Against Equality: Prisons Will Not Protect You* (AE Press 2012); S Lamble, 'Queer Necropolitics and the Expanding Carceral State: Interrogating Sexual Investments in Punishment' (2013) 24(3) Law and Critique 229.

17 Foucault (n 5) 42–43.

non-binary trans people from legal recognition. Interviews demonstrate that this had not stopped some non-binary-identified interviewees from accessing recognition for strategic reasons (if, for example, they were often 'read' as 'the other sex/gender' to the one they were assigned at birth). Yet the safeguarding provision – by design or accident – has compounded the formal exclusion of non-binary trans people from the scope of legal gender recognition by making it more likely that they will be prosecuted on the basis of their application having not been justified by an experience of belonging to *the other* sex/gender. Concerns around this risk of criminalisation had registered with interviewees, including one non-binary interviewee who had changed gender status before 2014:

> the way it's phrased criminalises non-binary people if they want to change their legal gender for pragmatic reasons. So I got my number changed before the new law; and of course having to go through surgery, and losing your reproductive system – I was going to do that anyway – but something like that should never be a prerequisite for having gender recognised. But at least I did it legally. If I wanted to do it today, I would have to lie.
>
> (Pippin, Non-binary, 42)

Pippin demonstrates an interesting legal consciousness, celebrating the CPR law abolition of the need to undergo surgical castration, adding: "something like that should never be a prerequisite for having gender recognised." Yet, for all the faults of the previous regulatory regime, that Pippin could acquire a new CPR number "legally" before 2014 – and would have undergone surgical castration "anyway" – makes it difficult to celebrate this change with any enthusiasm. That it is no longer formally possible for a non-binary-identified trans person to amend their legal status without risking criminal prosecution problematises attempt to situate the CPR law within a 'progress' narrative, even when disciplinary critique is limited to its internal dynamics.

In her critique of the UK Gender Recognition Act (GRA) 2004, Sally Hines identifies the production of 'dichotomous frameworks, which reinstate old – and bring into being, new – hierarchies', marked by intersections of age, class, disability, ethnicity, gender, and sexuality.[18] These privilege 'the rights of individuals and social groups who are able and/or willing to conform to normative modes of being', to the detriment of others.[19] A similar critique could be made of the Danish CPR law, as norms about what constitutes an appropriate transition ensure that only some trans people are included. The

18 S Hines, *Gender Diversity, Recognition and Citizenship* (Palgrave Macmillan 2013) 105.
19 ibid.

effect of the safeguarding provision is also relevant to UK-based readers in light of the recent 'gender deception' cases, which have established a precedent for the criminalisation of non-normative gender expression.[20] While reform of the UK Gender Recognition Act 2004 no longer seems imminent,[21] aside from in Scotland,[22] close analysis was demanded even when it was by the assurance of a former chair of the Women and Equalities Committee that 'Any new system that is put into place has to make sure that there are ways to catch abuses.'[23] The desire to stress the need for safeguarding, even among advocates of self-declaration,[24] indicates a concern that self-declaration may be *too* accessible (at least among certain groups). This appears to have been the case in Denmark, as the civil jurisdiction of the CPR law was underscored by a criminal jurisdiction with the capacity to punish non-normative expressions of gender and/or transition.

Safeguarding exhibits a temporal dimension, in that as well as denying the possibility of non-binary transition, it also prohibits more fluid movements across the gender binary. Parallels can thus be drawn with the GRA 2004 'permanence provision'.[25] Though the CPR law does not require the 'acquired' legal gender status to be permanent,[26] applicants are still required to make a formal declaration of gender status to access recognition. Emily Grabham notes that such a declaration

> does very little to hide its conceptual connections with racialized citizenship oaths. Even for race- and class-privileged trans subjects, the requirement of self-declaration (proving one's identity and proving one's gender) form part of a complex governmental terrain in which 'inclusion' begins (and arguably ends) with the assumption that one is an outsider, a potential fraud.[27]

20 A Sharpe, *Sexual Intimacy and Gender Identity Fraud: Reframing the Legal and Ethical Debate* (Routledge 2018).

21 The UK government has decided that 'the current provisions within the [Gender Recognition] Act [2004] allow for those that wish to legally change their sex to do so safely and fairly'; Government Equalities Office, 'Government responds to Gender Recognition Act consultation' (2020) <https://gov.uk/government/news/government-responds-to-gender-recognition-act-consultation> accessed 17 June 2021.

22 Gender Recognition Reform (Scotland) Bill 2022.

23 N Duffy and B Cohen, 'Maria Miller: The Law, The NHS and Public Services Are All Letting Trans People Down' *Pink News* (London, 14 January 2016) <www.pinknews.co.uk/2016/01/14/maria-miller-the-law-the-nhs-and-public-services-are-all-letting-trans-people-down> accessed 20 April 2016.

24 Dunne has admitted that 'Without doubt, self-declaration exacerbates risks of fraud or misuse'; P Dunne (n 10) 538.

25 E Grabham, 'Governing Permanence: Trans Subjects, Time, and the Gender Recognition Act' (2010) 19(1) Social & Legal Studies 107, 110.

26 Changing CPR number numerous times is permitted.

27 Grabham (n 25) 121.

The impression that the state remains suspicious of trans people resonated among interviewees. When asked to reflect upon the safeguarding clause, Mark responded:

> it [...] indicates that probably some people would abuse it in order to gain access to whatever. And it also questions whether people can actually make that decision. Why make it easy, but not easy? [...] [B]ecause you can't trust people with this decision, apparently.
>
> (Mark, Transman, 38)

As a legal mechanism, jurisdiction is mobilised to de-politicise and individualise, pre-empting and containing potential controversy.[28] Here, fear for the integrity of the CPR system inspires new exclusions to be drawn up and enforced with the threat of the criminal law. Even in its own provisions, then, the CPR law fails to take trans people seriously. My examination of trans people's legal consciousness suggests that this has not gone unnoticed.

The notion that the self-declaration model constituted part of a 'progressive' realisation of trans rights in Denmark was challenged by a majority of interviewees. Among these was Freyja, who, when asked to reflect upon her ideal scenario, responded as follows:

> That would be to go back to how the system was two or three years ago; where you could at least go another way if you didn't like the Sexological Clinic. You could choose some other paths – go private. And if your doctor felt up to it, you could get your hormones from your general practitioner, and that's not possible anymore.
>
> (Freyja, Transwoman, 46)

That this was not unrepresentative of the trans people interviewed raises questions as to whether self-declaration, or any model of gender recognition implemented alongside restrictions to health care, constitutes an example for other states to follow. With only some trans people included, and concurrent reforms undermining stated objectives, the CPR law offers no panacea.

By proceeding in this vein, disciplinary critique has inspired a rich body of critical scholarship on the regulation of gendered embodiment. Drawing attention to the groups which are excluded from the scope of law, it constitutes a concerted challenge to such reforms on their own terms. Yet as Dean Spade has noted, disciplinary analysis is not without conceptual limitation. While it is useful for identifying *how* law reforms fail, and for *which* groups they appear to have failed, it offers only limited insight into broader reasons as to *why* they might have failed. Spade notes that research which concentrates solely on

28 M Valverde, *Chronotopes of Law: Jurisdiction, Scale and Governance* (Routledge 2015) 86.

identifying discrimination against behaviours and subject positions is liable to co-optation by reformists who wish to further a specific political agenda centred on law reform.[29] Disciplinary scholars rarely pursue an explicitly reformist agenda. Often they merely seek to identify the limitations of certain legislative strategies (as I have done in previous chapters, and above). But the concern is that by raising instances of discriminatory application and unequal treatment, readers of a more reformist persuasion may be tempted to take such critiques out of their immediate context – responding to them by constructing a blueprint for future reforms.

In Chapter 5, I analysed the stated aims and objectives of the governing rationalities behind the Danish medical authorities' policy of centralisation. To do so, I drew upon interviews conducted with those professionally involved in the 2014 reforms – including clinicians and representatives of medical authorities. I then compared these intentions with the experiences of those governed in accordance with the regulations. This helped ascertain how these regulations are experienced, and what effects they might have in practice. This in turn enabled me to highlight inconsistencies and flaws in the logic of centralisation and risk-aversion (notably where governing capacities appeared to work against its stated aims). This constituted a self-contained critique of health care policy in this area, which could be mobilised by those who might wish to reform and improve these regulations – to better equip the public health care system to meet its stated aims and objectives. As this book does seek to inform debates around reforming gender recognition legislation, it is important to stress that affirmative policy-work can be valuable – particularly where it offers a detailed critique of a system which might otherwise be assumed to be functioning well. Yet trans legal scholars and trans activists alike must be wary of giving the impression that reforming legal and medical systems will be *the* answer to the identified problems.

Where disciplinary scholarship limits itself to a study of the 'implementation gap',[30] it will be ripe for co-optation by reformists. There are, of course, well-intentioned policymakers and regulators (including some who may have the interests of trans people and other patients at heart). But the reformist logic is open to critique for appearing to over-emphasise the influence that such individuals have within governing assemblages. For, this often leads to them taking the supposedly inclusive intentions of law 'at face value',[31] paying less attention to the structural dimensions of inequality and harm. Reformists deploy a logic which is at odds with important strands of Foucault's work. Mariana Valverde suggests that rather than assessing the impact of law reforms

29 D Spade, 'Laws as Tactics' (2011) 21(2) Columbia Journal of Gender and Law 40, 57–58.
30 D Cowan, 'Legal Consciousness: Some Observations' (2004) 67(6) Modern Law Review 928, 931.
31 Spade (n 29) 54.

against their purported intentions, an alternative Foucauldian conception is to understand governing practices as

> pragmatically put together collections of governing techniques whose success or failure depends upon their usefulness not to 'society' but rather to contenders in particular battles or struggles.[32]

Attention turns from legislative intentions and towards other, potentially unspoken, advantages that might be gained through the process of law reform. Spade adopts a similarly Foucauldian understanding of laws as 'tactics' or 'devices' which can re-arrange power relations in such a way to achieve certain ends.[33] Unlike critiques which castigate law for failing to meet purported intentions, Spade notes that viewing laws as tactics

> allows us to suspend expectations of a certain kind of rationality or consistency and suspend a belief that irrationality or incoherence are terribly helpful charges to make in opposition to various legal regimes, which are of course decentralized and full of contradiction. Instead, we might look for the broader patterns, beyond what law says it is doing, to see how it contributes to certain arrangements that concern us.[34]

When governing practices are read as an accumulation or assemblage of devices arranged to suit immediate governmental interests, the reformist understanding that a well-drafted piece of more formally inclusive legislation will significantly transform the lives of trans people and other marginalised groups appears misguided. Rather than simply highlighting governmental irrationality or inconsistency in the Danish reform project, and dwelling on the ways in which a governing rationality fails to meet its purported intentions, researchers should instead look beyond these stated aims to see what other interests a governing rationality might have furthered.

For instance, an important factor shaping governing rationalities is that of political economy. When viewed as a device or tactic in pursuit of governmental interests, the self-defeating and risk-averse strategy of centralisation pursued by medical authorities should be considered in relation to broader trends in the governance of health care. As I noted in Chapter 5, these include maintaining public health funding deficits, and pressure from increasing private health care provision. Such tendencies may not be stark in Denmark, but they are

32 M Valverde, 'Genealogies of European states: Foucauldian Reflections' (2007) 36(1) Economy and Society 159, 161.

33 Spade (n 29) 54, citing M Foucault, 'Governmentality' in G Burchell, C Gordon, and P Miller (eds), *The Foucault Effect: Studies in Governmentality: With Two Lectures by and an Interview with Michel Foucault* (University of Chicago Press 1991) 95.

34 ibid.

present; private health insurance has risen from 228,000 instances in 2003 to 1,850,000 in 2013.[35] In response, medical regulators face political questions about resource allocation for treatment and research, as I noted in Chapter 2.[36] This forms a backdrop to the Danish reforms of 2014. Evidence that the restrictions which resulted from this policy of centralisation might be explained as an exercise in cost management was offered by one interviewee. Reflecting upon a discussion he had about his treatment priorities at the Sexological Clinic, Jakob described the impression he came away with as follows:

> I have the feeling that they try to put off the operation as long as they can because they know that many of us will get the money and go to Germany or England [...] At my first conversation, she [the clinician] asked me what was my goal with this, and I told her that the first goal was to get top surgery. I'm just taking the hormones because the top surgery means so much to me. And then she told me [...]: "The top surgery you can get anywhere in the world." So, when I went out of the room I had the feeling that they know [...] the operation is 30 thousand kroner; and that I can get anywhere. It's cost-saving.
>
> (Jakob, Male, 31)

While Jakob's clinician did not spell it out explicitly, that he was being advised to travel abroad is implied in her advice. Another interviewee also reported being advised to consider travelling overseas, but this time explicitly, by a therapist who had previously worked at the Sexological Clinic:

> My therapist [...] says that, in my case, because I'm not public, because I have a[nother] diagnosis, it's going to be really difficult for me to get in there [at the Sexological Clinic]. But even if I got in there, because I'm non-binary transgender, there is a chance that I would get to the level of getting hormones in a couple of years, but that's it [...] I'm a bit undecided about the hormones; my first thing is that I want top surgery, so [the therapist] was like: "They're never going to approve you for top surgery if you're not taking hormones." And I think it's been really real saying: "They're not going to help you. So instead of spending a lot of time and energy trying to make them help you, it's better to do it on your own."
>
> (Roi, Non-binary transgender, 26)

Both interviewees gained the impression that it would be easier to circumvent the restrictive diagnosis programmes in the Danish health care system. As in

35 NV Munkholm, 'Legal Status of Transsexual and Transgender Persons in Denmark' in JM Scherpe (ed), *The Legal Status of Transsexual and Transgender Persons* (Intersentia 2015) 162 fn 101.

36 M Fox and T Murphy, 'The Body, Bodies, Embodiment: Feminist Legal Engagement with Health' in M Davies and VE Munro (eds), *The Ashgate Research Companion to Feminist Legal Theory* (Ashgate 2013) 250.

Chapter 4, we see a responsibilisation of trans people, with the expectation that they should finance their own body modification treatments. World trade law has encouraged 'health tourism' 'as a means of reducing the burden on domestic services and as an invisible export for the receiving nation'.[37] This applies whether the prospective patient is travelling from a relatively rich country to a poorer one (as in Iwo Nord's research into a private hospital in Serbia),[38] or between rich countries, as Jakob describes above. When viewed in this light, the finding that the 2014 reforms maintain regulations which are driving trans people abroad can be re-framed as a benefit more than a criticism – easing medical regulators' concerns about resource allocation and privatising the responsibility for care.

A second way of viewing the 2014 reforms as tactical interventions which might be useful 'to contenders in particular battles or struggles' more than the public as a whole is by viewing them through the lens of institutional vulnerability.[39] As I noted in Chapter 5, this involves looking beyond the intentions of professional regulators and medical practitioners, to assess the embodied effects of the 2014 reforms. Danish medical authorities have been subject to various pressures which have included, but also exceeded, political economy in recent years. Paramount among these pressures are the numerous various scandals in which the Danish Health and Medicines Authority (DHMA) became embroiled (before it was eventually disbanded). Reading the 2014 reforms through a lens of institutional vulnerability allowed me in Chapter 5 to contextualise the risk-averse governing rationalities adopted by medical authorities as a pragmatic reaction to these scandals. The policy of centralising access to body modification technologies may have come under fire from trans communities. But it still had the effect of relieving political pressure that had built up around the DHMA in the aftermath of the Caspian case (discussed in Chapters 1, 4, and 5). That resistance was restricted to trans communities – and not linked to protests around the other scandals discussed in Chapter 5 – suggests that the policy may have had the intended effect on a wider population level. That trans people were not happy may even be construed as a benefit; giving a more general audience the impression that the DHMA had responded decisively, shielding the institution from wider public criticism.

All of these readings offer insight into how institutional regulations like the 2014 reforms can work to further imperatives other than their stated aims.

37 J Harrington, 'Migration and access to Health Care in English Medical Law: A Rhetorical Critique' (2009) 4(4) International Journal of Law in Context 315, citing P Arnold, 'Disciplining Domestic Regulation: The World Trade Organization and the Market for Professional Services' (2005) 30 Accounting, Organizations and Society 299.

38 I Nord, 'Routes to Gender-Affirming Surgery: Navigation and Negotiation in Times of Biomedicalization' in G Griffin and M Jordal (eds) *Body, Migration, Re/Constructive Surgeries: Making the Gendered Body in a Globalized World* (Routledge 2019).

39 Valverde (n 32) 161.

Rather than failing, they could be said to have succeed in terms of how they contribute to broader patterns and arrangements.[40] But Spade also specifies that it may be worth focussing upon another set of 'regulatory' powers which relate to the political management of the population as a whole. Within Foucault's account of power, this would require a shift in focus from that of discipline to the question of bio-political 'regulation'.

Regulation

Regulatory power focuses upon securing the health of the nation, intervening only at the macro-level of 'the population'.[41] Foucault describes this as 'an important substitution' or 'doubling'; 'since the subjects of rights on which political sovereignty is exercised appear as a population that a government must manage.'[42] He distinguished between disciplinary controls as 'an *anatomo-politics of the human body*', and regulatory controls as '*a bio-politics of population*'.[43] The shift from disciplinary to regulatory analysis thus requires critique of the reproduction of norms and subject positions to be contrasted, or at least supplemented, with a population-level perspective.

Valverde understands bio-power literally, as 'the politics of life'.[44] Bio-politics addresses the political methods through which some lives are valued and cared for while others are 'discontinued'.[45] This form of politics can be conducted through waging wars against external enemies or internal threats – provided that the rationale for choosing who lives and who dies is 'a biopolitical one.'[46] Bio-political regulation tends to be mobilised through 'sorting technologies that produce structured security and insecurity for various populations in the distribution of life chances.'[47] Spade offers the example of social welfare and immigration enforcement programmes, which give contrasting impressions as to their benevolence or malevolence.[48] These can be read as constituting examples of 'positive' and 'negative' bio-power, respectively.[49] What unites them is that they both claim to serve a 'care-taking function' for the population at large.[50] As Foucault noted:

40 Spade (n 29) 54.
41 ibid. 45.
42 M Foucault, *The Birth of Biopolitics: Lectures at the Collège de France 1978–1979* (M Senellart [ed], G Burchell tr, Picador 2008) 21 fn.
43 Foucault (n 5) 139.
44 Valverde (n 32) 175.
45 ibid.
46 ibid. 175.
47 Spade (n 29) 46.
48 ibid. 45.
49 Valverde (n 32) 176.
50 Spade (n 29) 45.

> Liberalism must produce freedom, but this very act entails the establishment of limitations, controls, forms of coercion, and obligations relying on threats, etcetera. [...] [S]trategies of security, which are, in a way, both liberalism's other face and its very condition, must correspond to [...] the need to ensure that the mechanism of interests does not give rise to individual or collective dangers.[51]

Foucault describes the 'age of freedoms' offered by liberal government ('freedom of the market, freedom to buy and sell, the free exercise of property rights, freedom of discussion, possible freedom of expression, and so on') as 'exactly contemporaneous' with the development of regulatory controls.[52] These controls utilise administrative technologies that are mobilised 'in the name of promoting the life of the national population against perceived threats and drains and operate through sorting and producing regularities rather than individual targeting.'[53]

Different methods of population management have been developed for the purposes of bio-politics. Susan Stryker describes how gender has been mobilised, as

> an apparatus within which all bodies are taken up, which creates material effects through bureaucratic tracking that begins with birth, ends with death, and traverses all manner of state-issued or state-sanctioned documentation practices in between. It is thus an integral part of the mechanism through which power settles a given population onto a given territory through a given set of administrative structures and practices.[54]

In the context of the Danish reforms, this could easily describe the CPR system – such is the degree of overlap between how gender has tended to be regulated generally and in Denmark specifically. And when read through a bio-political lens, the 2014 reform of the CPR law has greater significance that when it was analysed from an anatomo-political perspective. Interviews indicate that of the governmental interests at stake in the process of civil reform, promoting Denmark's reputation for liberalism was second only to the need to ensure that the CPR system would be retained in something as close as possible to its existing form.

Though the CPR law has been criticised by Danish trans people and activists, the reception it received from international audiences suggests that both of

51 Foucault (n 42) 65.
52 ibid. 63, 67.
53 Spade (n 29) 45.
54 S Stryker, 'Biopolitics' (2014) 1(1–2) Transgender Studies Quarterly 38, 39.

these objectives have largely been met. As one interviewee, who had migrated to Denmark from another European country, explained to me:

> in Denmark I can't really complain, because I'm always surprised because I get everything like the others – Danish people. So the only thing is that. Being a foreigner, only with a residence permit, I get the same – which is pretty amazing, I think.
>
> (Curtis, M, 25)

Curtis could be forgiven for believing in 'the myth of liberal Denmark'.[55] As recognition is not limited to citizens but is also open to registered residents, he can draw a positive comparison between recognition in Denmark and that which was available in his home country. But for undocumented migrants, without formal residency, access to recognition remains as unattainable as it was before 2014. Without a CPR number, accessing numerous other basic services – including health care – remains fraught. By granting gender recognition through the CPR, the Danish Government includes some trans people, while simultaneously consolidating the identity surveillance and population management system that is tasked with excluding others. This population management system is also given the impression of having facilitated equality by becoming more inclusive.[56] The resulting critique exceeds the disciplinary analysis that trans people who are naturalised as Danish are accommodated at the expense of those who are racialised as migrants. Instead, the regulatory critique is that this is achieved through a mechanism which excludes undocumented migrants from basic services – whether they are trans or not.

Bio-political analysis illustrates how 'the nation' is discursively constructed through the production of different populations.[57] Some are positioned as deserving of cultivation, while others are construed as potential dangers, threats, and drains. Valued populations are encouraged to maximise their lives, while surplus populations are 'killed or abandoned'.[58] Which category a person falls into depends upon blunt calculations based around the 'costs and benefits' of managing them 'for state or state-like ends'.[59] At the heart of this calculation is

55 T Raun, 'The "Caspian Case" and Its Aftermath: Transgender People's use of Facebook to Engage Discriminatory Mainstream News Coverage in Denmark' in J Björklund and U Lindqvist (eds), *New Dimensions of Diversity in Nordic Culture and Society* (Cambridge Scholars Publishing 2016).

56 LGBT Denmark awarded their 'Salmon of the Year' (for 'swimming upstream' on LGBT rights) to the CPR Office at the 2015 Copenhagen Pride; R Ingerslev, 'Årets laks går til CPR-kontoret' *Out and About* (Copenhagen, 17 August 2015) <www.out-and-about.dk/visnyhed.asp?id=6270#.Vz3hMvl97IV> accessed 19 May 2016.

57 Spade, 'Laws as Tactics' (n 29) 53.

58 ibid. 58.

59 Stryker (n 54) 38.

a bio-political conception of 'race'.[60] Here, race is not a synonym for 'identity', 'ethnicity', or 'culture'.[61] Instead it refers to blood, descent, and lineage.[62] So while a commonplace understanding of race can explain why black people tend to be rendered more killable by processes of population management, this is not quite in line with its bio-political meaning. By disarticulating race and ethnicity, Foucault understands racialisation as the naturalisation of various social, cultural, linguistic, and economic differences within what is otherwise understood as a unitary population group.[63]

Understanding race-as-racialisation suggests that positions may shift as governmental priorities change over time. Hence the paradox, identified by Stryker, whereby some groups of trans people who have historically been excluded from protection, and thus managed in directions which lead towards death rather than life may now, on occasion, find themselves included within systems targeted towards the cultivation of life.[64] This forms an important reference point when exploring the bio-political impact of the 2014 reforms. As I discussed in Chapter 5, the idea behind subjecting trans people to sustained psychiatric diagnosis is that they will be less likely to 'regret' undergoing one form of treatment or another. And the decision to condemn the removal of 'a physiologically functioning breast' in the Caspian case appeared to be linked to the organ's prospective role in reproduction.[65] It can appear, then, that in some cases trans people's 'natural' reproductive capacities are now valued by the Danish state – at least to the extent that they cannot be permitted to limit these on an informed consent basis.

This contrasts with the historical mobilisation of some of the same body modification technologies to which access is now restricted, as part of a eugenics programme that was in practice through much of the 20th century.[66]

60 ibid. 40, citing M Foucault, *Society Must Be Defended: Lectures at the Collège de France, 1975–1976* (St Martin's 1997) 254.

61 A Lentin, 'Europe and the Silence about Race' (2008) 11(4) European Journal of Social Theory 487, 498.

62 Valverde (n 32) 166. This explains why nascent eugenics movements initially targeted 'degenerate' working classes before embracing welfare nationalism and targeting 'external' threats instead; A Lentin, 'Racial States, Anti-Racist Responses: Picking Holes in 'Culture' and 'Human Rights'' (2004) 7(4) European Journal of Social Theory 427, 431.

63 Stryker (n 54) 40, citing Foucault, *Society Must Be Defended* (n 60) 80.

64 ibid. 40.

65 Patients' Ombudsman, 'Kritik for behandling – speciallæge i plastikkirurgi Jens Pilegaard Bjarnesen' (1 November 2012) <www.patientombuddet.dk/Afgoerelser_og_domme/Afgoerelser_fra_Sundhedsvaesenets_Disciplinaernaevn/Afgoerelser_med_navn/2012/1294528.aspx> accessed 16 September 2015.

66 BS Hansen, 'Something Rotten in the State of Denmark: Eugenics and the Ascent of the Welfare State' in G Broberg and N Roll-Hansen (eds), *Eugenics and the Welfare State: Sterilization Policy in Denmark, Sweden, Norway and Finland* (Michigan State University Press 1996); K Wren, 'Cultural Racism: Something Rotten in the State of Denmark?' (2001) 2(2) Social & Cultural Geography 141, 145.

A direct link to Danish eugenics can be made by analysing the amendment of the Health Act which was passed immediately after the CPR law, in June 2014, to elaborate adjustments resulting from the introduction of the possibility to self-declare legal gender status.[67] These amendments primarily introduced gender-neutral terms into its text (replacing, for instance, references to 'the pregnant woman' with 'the pregnant person', and changing pronouns from 'her' to 'their' as required). Yet the amendment also made a substantive change to section 115 of the Health Act, inserting a new paragraph as follows:

> A person may apply to be allowed to be castrated as part of sex/gender change if the applicant has been diagnosed with transsexualism, has a persistent desire for castration and can foresee the consequences.[68]

Section 115 previously stated that permission to undergo surgical castration could be granted only if an 'applicant's sexual desire caused them significant emotional suffering or social deterioration.'[69] The way in which 'emotional suffering' was formulated – as '*sjælelige lidelser*' –translates directly to 'suffering of the soul'. The decision to update this 'suffering of the soul' requirement was interpreted differently by interviewees. Anne Mette Dons, who represented the DHMA in the working group, described the intention as follows:

> it was really old-fashioned to a degree where [...] it was really difficult to say that that was the case with anybody today [...] it was much too old-fashioned – and it was very hard for the doctors to actually relate to it, or relate their patients to it.
>
> (Anne Mette Dons, (formerly) DHMA)

The idea that the need to identify 'suffering of the soul' hindered medical practice was accepted by Sofie Aviaja Bünger, who drafted the Danish Institute for Human Rights's consultation response:

> it was very old wording before. And I think it's always good to change it so that it's actually more direct, because how do you assess whether or not your gender identity [...] should give you mental pain? [...] But of course if you find a definition of transsexual in the WHO's list, it also has this kind of wording. But still, it's more accurate, I think.
>
> (Sofie Aviaja Bünger, (formerly) Danish Institute for Human Rights)

67 L 189 (n 9).
68 ibid. s 19.
69 Health Act (13 July 2010) (*Bekendtgørelse af sundhedsloven*) (DK) s 115.

While Bünger accepts that the previous wording may have impeded doctors, she admits doubting whether 'transsexualism' is inherently clearer or easier to diagnose. Ole Møller Markussen, who drafted the consultation response submitted by the AIDS Foundation, took this line of argument further. He asked what it meant to insert a diagnosis in statutory legislation:

> you are actually putting a diagnosis into the law for the first time in Danish history [...] So it's a quite a landslide in the way you make legislation concerning health [...] [And] the diagnosis is so unclear [...] with all the debates on what transgender is, what gender is [...] and what it means to be a woman and a man, in society.
>
> (Ole Møller Markussen, AIDS-Foundation)

Markussen went on to stress how understanding the inclusion of this diagnosis as marking a break from the "old-fashioned" wording of 'suffering souls' might obscure the underlying premise it shares with the transsexualism diagnosis:

> The diagnosis itself seems to be based on a very Cartesian body-soul religious understanding. And I keep having these images of angels dropping the wrong soul into the wrong body – a pink soul into a blue body – and that's basically the understanding people have of this: "Okay, you have these two genders and then ah! They've switched!"
>
> (Ole Møller Markussen, AIDS-Foundation)

Important insights can be obscured when amendments are understood to merely update an antiquated or "old-fashioned" provision. This risks obscuring how the term originally came to be included in the Health Act. The history of the 'suffering souls' requirement does not have to be traced particularly far to gain insights which are interesting from a contemporary, and bio-political, perspective. Before it was inserted into the Health Act in 2005,[70] the 'suffering souls' requirement appeared in a 1994 administrative order concerning how sterilisation and castration ought to be conducted.[71] The language of this order is strident; with terms such as *sindsyg*, *åndsvag*, and *svag begavelse* (which literally translate as 'mind-sick', 'weak of spirit', and 'of low intelligence') used to identify the patients who might be sterilised or castrated.[72] That special needs are still portrayed in these ways in the mid-1990s harks back further to the genesis of this legislation – introduced to facilitate Denmark's active 20th century eugenics programme.[73]

70 L 546 Health Act (24 June 2005) (*Sundhedsloven*) (DK).

71 Order on sterilisation and castration (12 July 1994) (*Bekendtgørelse af lov om sterilisation og kastration*) (DK), s 13.

72 ibid. s 7.

73 The possibility of compulsory sterilisation and castration was removed from this law in 1967; BS Hansen (n 66) 63.

Though Denmark has projected a 'liberal and tolerant' outlook to the world, involving itself in the promotion of humanitarian activity overseas, its quest for racial and genetic purity saw it implement sterilisation programmes in what has been described as 'state-sanctioned 'ethnic hygiene''.[74] The link to eugenics in the 2014 reforms raises questions about how these procedures have been mobilised as part of political agendas regarding reproduction, sexuality, desire, and bodily control. In Chapter 2, I suggested that the benefit of 'propertied or sovereigntist'[75] conceptions of the body, as subject to ownership or control, rests on the extent to which they lend themselves to political struggles for the right for subjects 'to craft their own sense of identity'.[76] Danish eugenics policy used surgical sterilisation and castration to target poor unmarried women that were deemed incapable of raising children due to their 'troublesome' sexual appetite.[77] That it did so in a manner which will in most cases have been at least indirectly coercive,[78] casts doubt on the idea that it might have been used in order to construct any 'stable platform' for the subject to pursue their plans.[79] From a bio-political perspective, the fact that both social and eugenic justifications were permitted for enforcing sterilisation and castration demonstrates how historical subjects who expressed gender and sexuality in non-normative ways have been viewed as both potential threats *and* drains to the Danish state – threats to the 'quality' of the population stock, and drains on the resources of the then nascent welfare state.[80]

Throughout modern history, health policy has been tied to the idea of the nation-state. This is illustrated by Susan Sontag's analysis of the various cultural representations of the syphilis epidemic. Syphilis came to be known as the 'French pox', '*morbus Germanicus*', and 'the Chinese disease' – depending on whether it was viewed from neighbouring England, France, or Japan.[81] Reproduction has also often been tied to the nation-state form.[82] While repro-

74 Wren (n 66) 145.

75 E Grabham, 'Bodily Integrity and the Surgical Management of Intersex' (2012) 18(2) Body & Society 1, 3.

76 N Priaulx, 'Rethinking Progenitive Conflict: Why Reproductive Autonomy *Matters*' (2008) 16 Medical Law Review 169, 183.

77 73% of those legally sterilised in Denmark between 1929 to 1950 were women; BS Hansen (n 66) 18, 60, citing T Kemp, *Arvehygiejne, Københavns Universitets Årsskrift* (Copenhagen University 1951) 45.

78 Though direct compulsion was permitted by Danish law until 1967, authorities have suggested that it was never used. Arguably it would not need to be where permission to be released from an institution was conditional upon having undergone sterilisation or castration; BS Hansen (n 66).

79 cf Priaulx (n 76) 185.

80 Hansen (n 66) 35.

81 S Sontag, *Illness as Metaphor and AIDS and Its Metaphors* (Penguin 1991) 133.

82 This is not to suggest that reproductive agendas passively respond to nation imperatives. Nationalist discourses have also been shaped by reproductive activities, as demonstrated by Fletcher's analysis of the relationship between reproductive rights and nationalist agendas in the Republic of Ireland;

ductive policy has not always been explicitly motivated by bio-politics, it always has bio-political consequences. One example is offered by the prohibition of abortion in Ireland. Until this was legalised in 2018, Irish women were required to travel to England to access abortion services. This associated the practice of abortion with Englishness, ensuring that the abortion ban operated as 'a symbol of Irish post-coloniality', as Ruth Fletcher has noted.[83] The protection of the foetal right to life was thus presented as an Irish national interest, irrespective of the consequences on the woman's health.[84] A similar coincidence between reproductive policy and the nation-state can be identified in the disproportionate targeting of black families by the US child welfare system, which Dorothy Roberts suggests indicates that black motherhood is valued less than the white motherhood which is presented as central to the reproduction of the American nation.[85]

A shift which recalls the paradox identified by Stryker, above, sees the historically anti-natal agenda targeted at promiscuous women and others construed as exhibiting non-normative expressions of gender and sexuality (including the sexually 'troublesome' or mentally 'lacking') developed to a point where trans people are in at least one instance subjected to the same pro-natal agenda as the rest of the Danish population. The difference is that they are now dissuaded from removing their reproductive organs (along with other gendered signifiers) when previously they were required (or at least pressured) to do so. That links have developed between reproductive and national agendas in numerous other post-war contexts is no coincidence. Foucault insisted that the development of the interventionist ideas which spawned the welfare state should not be taken out of the wartime context in which they developed.[86] John Harrington concurs that medical law has been shaped by the broader 'plausabilities of welfarism' in Britain (citing 'professional discretion, the passive client, the male-breadwinner family model and so on').[87] This raises questions as to whether the shift in perception of bodies exhibiting non-normative genders and sexualities might reflect the broader institutional vulnerability of the Danish welfare state.

R Fletcher, 'Reproducing Irishness: Race, Gender, and Abortion Law' (2005) 17 Canadian Journal of Women and the Law 365.

83 R Fletcher, 'Post-Colonial Fragments: Representations of Abortion in Irish Law and Politics' (2001) 28(4) Journal of Law and Society 568, 569.

84 ibid. 579.

85 D Spade, 'Intersectional Resistance and Law Reform' (2013) 38(4) Signs: Journal of Women in Culture and Society 1031, 1043, citing DE Roberts, 'Racism and Patriarchy in the Meaning of Motherhood' (1993) 1(1) American University Journal of Gender and Law 1.

86 Foucault describes the job security, health care, and pensions of the welfare state as 'pacts of war', which involved governments saying to people: 'Now we are asking you to get yourselves killed, but we promise you that when you have done this, you will keep your jobs until the end of your lives'; M Foucault (n 42) 216.

87 J Harrington, 'Time and Space in Medical Law: Building on Valverde's *Chronotopes of Law*' (2015) 23 Feminist Legal Studies 361, 363

With an ageing population and high social security expenditure,[88] an increased birth rate offers a solution to the problem of covering the rising cost of Danish welfare which would allow the government to avoid resorting to the unpopular measure of expanding its population to include racialised migrant workers.[89]

Attempts to reduce the number of migrants and refugees have been a priority for successive Danish governments since the beginning of the 21st century.[90] Denmark is one of the only states to have operationalised the concept of 'attachment' in migration law.[91] In 2000, it replaced the right to family reunification for all Danish residents with a requirement that non-Danish spouses or cohabiting partners' prove that their 'attachment to Denmark' is at least equal to their attachment to any other country.[92] This was extended in 2002 to cover all Danish residents who had possessed residency in Denmark for less than 24 years;[93] and was only abolished in response to a European Court of Human Rights ruling in 2018.[94]

Limiting migration – or 'ensuring that the state's freedom to select outweighs the individual's freedom to move across borders'[95] – continues to feature prominently on the political agenda in Denmark. This is evidenced by the adoption of a string of punitive migration policies by the right-wing government which governed from 2015 until 2019, which included: i) cutting welfare payments available to refugees by 45%; ii) increasing the threshold requirements for applying for permanent residency; iii) delaying the opportunity to apply for family reunification for up to three years; iv) permitting police to confiscate cash and valuables from those seeking asylum; and v) banning Islamic veils such as the niqab.[96] This government even drew up plans to build a border wall to stop refugees from entering from its southern neighbour Germany at the time it took power in 2015.[97] Such policies have since been bolstered by a string of so-called 'ghetto laws' (which have included limiting

88 Denmark has the 5th-highest rate of social expenditure as a percentage of GDP (28.7% in 2016) in the OECD, 'Social Expenditure' <https://stats.oecd.org/Index.aspx?DataSetCode=SOCX_AGG> accessed 10 December 2016.

89 The fertility rate in Denmark fell from 2.6 births/woman in 1960, to 1.7 births/woman in 2014; World Bank, 'Fertility rate, total' <http://data.worldbank.org/indicator/SP.DYN.TFRT.IN?locations=DK> accessed 10 December 2016.

90 M Bissenbakker and L Myong, 'Governing Belonging through Attachment: Marriage Migration and Transnational Adoption in Denmark' (2022) 45 (1) Ethnic and Racial Studies 133, 134–135.

91 M Bissenbakker, 'Attachment Required: The Affective Governmentality of Marriage Migration in the Danish Aliens Act 2000–2018' (2019) 13 International Political Sociology 181, 182–183.

92 Bissenbakker and Myong (n 90) 138, citing L 208 Danish Aliens Act 2000.

93 ibid. citing L 152 Danish Aliens Act 2002.

94 Bissenbakker (n 91) 193, citing *Biao v Denmark* App no 38590/10 (ECtHR, 24 May 2016).

95 ibid. 189.

96 H Eakin, 'Liberal, Harsh Denmark' *New York Review of Books* (New York, 10 March 2016) <www.nybooks.com/articles/2016/03/10/liberal-harsh-denmark> accessed 18 May 2016.

97 M Bissenbakker and L Myong, 'The Affective Biopolitics of Migration' (2019) 9(4) Nordic Journal of Migration Research 417.

social housing and legislating for higher penalties for crimes committed in areas characterised by low income, unemployment, low education, disproportionate amounts of criminal convictions, where more than half the residents are immigrants or descendants of those from 'non-Western countries') that were introduced by the current Social Democrat-led minority government which took power in 2019.[98] The current government has even more recently been threatened with legal action as it attempts to forcibly return refugees to Syria.[99]

As I have noted, the failure to distinguish the CPR law from the oaths migrants are required to take to access citizenship in many western states offers 'inclusion' only with an air of scepticism.[100] While trans people are offered recognition, the safeguarding provision implies that this comes with the assumption that they are 'a potential fraud.'[101] This finding is interesting on a disciplinary, anatomo-political, level. But it also fails to interrogate the biopolitical dimension of Grabham's work. Spade advises scholars to think beyond the immediate and internal power relations of specific legislation, and towards external structures and developments. In the context of Danish (anti-)migration policy, the same analogy between gender and national citizenship highlights that the requirement to declare 'an experience of belonging to the other sex/gender' to amend legal gender status entangles trans people in processes of nation-building. Not only are they required to align themselves with a gender with which they may not completely identify, but they must also engage with a state which reserves citizenship for the racialised few. It is not only that trans people naturalised as Danish will benefit from inclusion more than trans immigrants, but they are likely to do so at the expense of an entire population of immigrants – trans or otherwise.

Attempts to hold out for a reform that challenged systems of identity surveillance *and* diagnostic assessments were foiled prior to the legislative process. Instead trans people were left with a purely administrative amendment of civil regulation which was: i) cheap and easy to implement; ii) contained no new rights (other than the right to engage in the process of self-declaration); and iii) deferred to existing jurisdictional divisions between administrative and medical regulation. Systems of population management based upon identity surveillance were meanwhile bolstered by giving the impression not just of being more 'efficient',[102] but also more inclusive. As the boundaries shift so

98 J Versi, 'Denmark's 'ghetto plan' and the communities it targets' *Al Jazeera* (15 January 2020) <https://aljazeera.com/features/2020/01/15/denmarks-ghetto-plan-and-the-communities-it-targets> accessed 12 May 2021.

99 B McKernan, R Swash, and A Kelly, 'Denmark could face legal action over attempts to return Syrian refugees' *The Guardian* (29 July 2021) <https://gu.com/global-development/2021/jul/29/denmark-faces-legal-action-over-attempts-to-return-syrian-refugees> accessed 18 August 2021.

100 Grabham (n 25) 121.

101 ibid. 121.

102 Bissenbakker (n 91) 189.

that citizenship can include certain trans populations, it is increasingly hostile towards (racialised) others. The groups that are considered natural and surplus populations alter slightly, but processes of racialisation are consolidated and repeated.

To access gender recognition, trans people must take part in exclusionary practices of nation-building. They must make a citizenship-like oath to a gender with which they may or may not personally define, offered to them as part of a public relations management campaign to bolster 'the myth of liberal Denmark'.[103] Disciplinary analysis conducted at the level of the human body has drawn attention to the ways in which certain sub-populations of trans people will benefit from inclusion more than others (for example, depending on intersections such as age, class, disability, ethnicity, gender, and sexuality). Bio-political analysis, which is focused more at the population level, expands this insight further, highlighting how trans populations are 'included' at least superficially at the expense of entire populations (refugees and other migrants) – and not just sub-populations (such as non-binary trans subjects) – of non-Danish 'others'. The admittedly limited form of inclusion that some trans people now enjoy comes with the continuing expense of racialised others.

Karen Wren describes Denmark as having become a fertile ground for 'cultural racism' since unemployment rates rose in the 1980s, and perceptions of migrants shifted from 'temporary stop-gap' labourers to potential financial and social burdens.[104] In a country which has placed great emphasis on values of social equality and cohesion, hostility towards foreigners is best couched in terms of support for Denmark's welfare state.[105] And in a context of relative gender equality, hostility towards 'backward' cultures is excused in Denmark with reference to these cultures' perceived sexism and oppression of women.[106] While Denmark has its own cultural specificities in relation to racism, it is by no means an exceptional case in deploying bio-political techniques of population management. Processes of nation-building have been central to the creation of public health care systems and more general welfare states in countries across Europe. In fact, European states that have excelled in enacting what we may now conceive of as 'negative' bio-power (e.g. racism) have also been highly proficient in their use of more 'positive' forms of bio-power (e.g. health care).[107] Denmark does corroborate this point, as its eugenics programme was introduced and implemented by the very same politicians involved in

103 Raun, 'The "Caspian Case" and Its Aftermath' (n 55).

104 Wren (n 66) 150–152.

105 ibid. 142; AS Nielsen and L Myong, 'White Danish Love as Affective Intervention: Studying Media Representations of Family Reunification Involving Children' (2019) 9(4) Nordic Journal of Migration Research 497, 499.

106 ibid. 147–148.

107 Valverde (n 32) 176.

designing its much-envied welfare state.[108] And in the contemporary context, the 'myth of liberal Denmark'[109] can be promoted at the same point in time as access to body modification technologies is effectively restricted, *and* strict anti-migration policies are adopted. But rather than being unique to Denmark, bio-political and racist techniques of nation-building and population management are common to states across Europe.[110] They may even be inherent in the nation-state form itself.[111]

Consequences for (trans, feminist, and socio-)legal studies

Once bio-political critique takes aim at the nation-state form, a link can be made between critical trans scholarship against reformism and critical legal scholarship against rights. Both express concern about the costs of compromise that must be made by activists when engaging with institutions of the state. Both emphasise the exclusions inherent in every 'inclusion' project, and illustrate how law colonises new forms of knowledge by couching them in legal terminology (including 'rights').[112] Meanwhile, the radical potential for social movements can be lost once activists accept 'meliorist reforms that tinker at the edges of inequality' in lieu of struggles for greater resistance or material change.[113] Spade cites the critical race theory term 'preservation-through-transformation' to describe the process whereby law reform provides 'just enough' transformation to stabilise and preserve existing conditions.[114]

Yet just as attempts to move 'beyond the rights debate' required scholars to avoid making unhelpful generalisations about 'law', 'rights', and 'the state',[115] so critical legal scholars largely accept the impracticality of an absolutist position against legal activism.[116] With the benefit of Foucault's insights, the top-down implementation of 'laws as tactics' can be inverted and mobilised by both

108 KK Steincke, who served as Social Democrat Minister of Justice and Minister of Health and Welfare during his parliamentary career, produced a monograph on 'Social relief of the future' in 1920. This presented 'a general outline for the coming welfare state'; 28 of its 200 pages are said to be 'devoted' to eugenics; Hansen (n 66) 28.

109 Raun, 'The "Caspian Case" and Its Aftermath' (n 55).

110 Lentin (n 62); Lentin (n 61) 487.

111 Spade, 'Intersectional Resistance and Law Reform' (n 85) 1032.

112 C Smart, *Feminism and the Power of Law* (Routledge 1989).

113 C Beasley and C Bacchi, 'Envisaging a New Politics for an Ethical Future: Beyond Trust, Care and Generosity – Towards an Ethic of "Social Flesh"' (2007) 8(3) Feminist Theory 279, 280.

114 Spade (n 85) 1035, citing R Siegel, 'Why Equal Protection No Longer Protects: The Evolving Forms of Status-Enforcing State Action' (1997) 49(5) Stanford Law Review 1111, 1119; and AP Harris, 'From Stonewall to the Suburbs? Toward a Political Economy of Sexuality' (2006) 14(4) William and Mary Bill of Rights Journal 1539

115 D Herman, 'Beyond the rights debate' (1993) 2 Social & Legal Studies 25.

116 Munro (n 1).

scholars and activists to pursue law reforms only as one part of a wider range of resistance and mobilisation strategies.[117] So, while critical of activism that seeks to reform gender classification policies, Spade does not dismiss the potential possibilities of such a strategy outright; noting that law reform tactics merely 'shift', but 'do not disappear', when broader demands emerge.[118] He describes the substance of this shift as resting upon the understanding that when law reform is engaged, this will be with a 'tactical understanding of law' as opposed to 'a belief that changing what the law says about us is the end goal.'[119]

Within such an understanding, resistance is theorised by activists and scholars who pay attention to the impact of legal systems – and particularly administrative rules – on the 'survival and political participation' of the population groups that are subject to heightened targeting within bio-political regulations.[120] More concretely, Spade adds that this 'tactical' form of resistance will

> center on the material concerns of those who are perpetually cast as undeserving, because their demands aim to produce material change in terms of life chances rather than symbolic declarations of equality, and because they conceptualize gender and sexual justice and freedom through the experiences of those who are intersectionally targeted by purportedly race- and gender-neutral systems.[121]

As I have noted, self-declaration in Denmark was implemented in a cheap and limited manner, which minimised state responsibility by ignoring the material concerns of 'intersectionally targeted' populations. It instead took the form of a technical amendment of a population management system which surveys and excludes those deemed threatening to the Danish state. This was made possible by a careful deployment of jurisdiction, which was mobilised to sort and separate different concerns, depoliticising the issues at hand.

A balance was therefore struck between reform and maintenance of the status quo. Such critiques question how far the Danish adoption of self-declaration would sit within a wider strategy of tactical resistance proposed by theorists including Spade, above. At a time when access to hormones and surgeries were being restricted, and migrants punished, the CPR law nevertheless seeks to bolster the myth of liberal Denmark. Hence this particular legal 'victory' can be read as a symbolic declaration – which stabilises the status quo.[122] The same activists who criticised the 2014 reforms have also dismissed a more recent development – which saw the diagnosis of 'transsexualism' moved to its

117 Spade (n 29).
118 Spade (n 85) 1032.
119 Spade (n 29) 60.
120 ibid. 60–61.
121 Spade (n 85) 1033.
122 ibid. 1047.

own section of the Danish diagnosis code – as primarily symbolic.[123] Resisting 'preservation-through-transformation' and bio-political co-optation is a political consciousness that is being raised in the Danish context. As hostility towards trans people and migrants abounds, this type of intersectional activism may have to broaden among and beyond feminist activists and scholars in Denmark and elsewhere – if an effort is to be made to ensure that the political gains sought by one marginalised constituency are not made on the back of increasingly marginalised others.

This book has demonstrated that jurisdictional analysis of the governing assemblages regulating legal embodiment illustrates how gender is affected by institutional power-knowledges. When combined with a governmentality perspective attentive to the bio-political mobilisation of these forms of regulation at the population level, this offered various critical insights into the Danish reform project. As I have demonstrated in this chapter, a regulatory perspective enables a form of critique which goes beyond the problems related to individual discrimination and the exclusion of specific sub-populations. It draws attention to limitations and counter-currents, situating law reform projects in relation to wider developments. The main finding of my embodiment analysis is that those unwilling or unable to gain authorisation for body modifications at the Danish health care system's approved clinics continue to be effectively excluded from legal gender recognition even after law was reformed. The affirmative implication of this critique would be to grant the opportunity to self-designate legal gender status to any Danish resident. This would help those who struggle for approval within psychiatric clinics, at least on an anatomo-political level which seeks to understand which norms and subject positions are included or excluded within a governance project such as the Danish reforms of 2014. But a bio-political perspective asks us to look further – at what else the Danish state, and other states, are doing. This raises challenges for the scholars and activists confronted with law reform proposals.

As well as summarising the findings of this book, this chapter included theoretical reflections upon several bio-political insights which were shown to have emerged out of that analysis. This has involved me working at a slightly more abstract and theoretical level than I have done previously. My justification for making this shift was that I felt that it could be useful to supplement this grounded analysis by at least touching upon some of the broader political implications that the limited implementation of self-declaration had brought about. By bringing different socio-legal and feminist theoretical literatures

123 See A Minor, 'Removing the diagnosis: Not the answer?' (*Killjoy.dk*, 1 March 2016) <http://killjoy.dk/en/Opinion/Not-The-Answer> accessed 25 September 2016, and; LM Tams and A Minor, 'Danish Minister of Health To Push For De-Psychiatrization Of Transgender Persons' (*Killjoy.dk*, 12 May 2016) <http://killjoy.dk/en/Report/Minister-Of-Health> accessed 25 September 2016.

together, I have noted that as (inter)subjective experience is an important aspect of embodiment, and legal embodiment and legal consciousness are mutually compatible. This book has also demonstrated that institutional aspects of embodiment could be illuminated by jurisdictional analysis. Drawing from governance studies, this analysis was mobilised to test the limitations of self-declaration in the Danish context, for the benefit of scholars, activists, and policymakers involved in responding to proposals to reform gender recognition law. I found that civil and medical reforms had been separated, to the detriment of trans people and their embodied concerns. The jurisdictional literature was then supplemented with insights from affect literature and institutional vulnerability, to offer broader perspectives on why these boundaries were drawn between institutional power/knowledges, and what effects this had in practice. Broader points were made questioning the utility of visibility and progress narratives, and a normative case was made for properly funded health care (and other) state institutions instead.

While in the previous chapters of this book a disciplinary perspective proved perfectly viable for detailing self-contained critiques of civil and medical regulations of legal embodiment, a regulatory perspective attentive to bio-political population management has been shown, in this concluding chapter, to demand broader contextualisation and more careful thought. In the context of the migrant crisis, and the Danish Government's hostile response to this, a governmental-embodiment perspective casts doubt onto whether any form of self-declaration or gender re-classification could be positioned alongside, and not in opposition to, wider strategies of resistance to existing power structures engaged in the production of 'killable populations'.[124] It is certainly difficult for trans people and activists to stand in solidarity with racialised and marginalised populations when, in order to access gender recognition, they are required to align themselves with a state which, like most others, reserves residency and citizenship for the naturalised few. By supplementing disciplinary critique of how the CPR law promotes certain types of conduct and subject positions with a bio-political critique of how it contributes to wider concerns about population management, I cast further doubt over how 'optimal' self-declaration of legal gender status is and can be.[125]

Looking beyond structures internal to the legislation, I argue that requiring trans people to undertake a declaration of citizenship to amend their legal gender status can see them entangled in exclusionary processes of nation-building. My intention in doing so is not to pass judgement upon those who make such a declaration for personal or strategic reasons. I merely wish to draw attention to the fact that they are required to do so – by purportedly 'progressive' legislation – or face the consequences of exclusion, themselves, from legal

124 Spade (n 29) 70.
125 Dunne (n 10) 539.

recognition. By bringing disciplinary and bio-political critique together, I have demonstrated that trans people are positioned at a disadvantage in relation to cis people – in that it becomes harder for them to resist complicity in the bio-political reproduction of populations which are surplus to the requirements of the nation. In this respect at least, self-declaration of legal gender status is no magic bullet. It is not an all-encompassing solution to the everyday problems faced by trans and other gender diverse people. This is an important point that all feminist and trans legal scholars ought to be wary of, even if they – like me – would ultimately still support the adoption of self-declaration law reforms over more bureaucratic gender recognition laws in most instances in which these are mooted.

Meanwhile, jurisdictional limitation has been shown to have been highly useful for micro-managing the production of boundaries between life and death, allowing regulators to pre-empt controversy by restricting change to one particular area of reform. Broader contexts and developments external to the structures of the CPR law were left unchallenged; notably including the reforms of the medical guidelines, which I described in Chapter 5. This analysis raises critical questions that must be answered by trans activists in the UK and elsewhere, particularly when they are confronted with reform proposals from a government committed to reducing both migration and public expenditure. My advice to activists, and trans people generally, would be to be wary of any form of gender recognition that can be implemented at so little expense, and in such a limited and compromised manner. Trans people have material needs and concerns, a small point which is so often ignored.[126] Like cis people, they face challenges in accessing health care, employment, housing, and migration – only more so, in many instances, as their gender status makes accessing material support in these contexts more complex.

Whether legal policy and reforms are well-placed to address these concerns remains a moot point. What to do to make them so goes beyond the scope of this book. But those who have faith in self-declaration as a mode for reforming the legal recognition of gender have been warned that this offers no panacea. As research conducted in Denmark demonstrates, self-declaration – for all its benefits – will only ever amount to a partial solution to the problems faced by trans and other gender diverse people. As a model of gender recognition, it is also flexible enough to be subsumed within other political projects – from neo-liberal responsibilisation, privatisation, and bio-political nation-building. For these reasons, I have in this book sought to give its proponents at least pause for thought. Meanwhile, I hope those on the receiving end of their promises will be better placed to assess how far self-declaration is compatible with the immediate needs and priorities raised by their own (inter)subjective experience of material, symbolic, and institutional embodiment.

126 Though see JJ Gleeson and E O'Rourke (eds), *Transgender Marxism* (Pluto Press 2021).

Bibliography

Beasley C and Bacchi C, 'Envisaging a New Politics for an Ethical Future: Beyond Trust, Care and Generosity – Towards an Ethic of 'Social Flesh'' (2007) 8(3) Feminist Theory 279

Bissenbakker M, 'Attachment Required: The Affective Governmentality of Marriage Migration in the Danish Aliens Act 2000–2018' (2019) 13 International Political Sociology 181

——— and Myong L, 'The Affective Biopolitics of Migration' (2019) 9(4) Nordic Journal of Migration Research 417

——— and Myong L, 'Governing Belonging through Attachment: Marriage Migration and Transnational Adoption in Denmark' (2022) 45 (1) Ethnic and Racial Studies 133

Conrad R (ed), *Against Equality: Prisons Will Not Protect You* (AE Press 2012)

Cowan D, 'Legal Consciousness: Some Observations' (2004) 67(6) Modern Law Review 928

Duffy N and Cohen B, 'Maria Miller: The Law, the NHS and Public Services Are All Letting Trans People Down' *Pink News* (London, 14 January 2016) <http://www.pinknews.co.uk/2016/01/14/maria-miller-the-law-the-nhs-and-public-services-are-all-letting-trans-people-down> accessed 20 April 2016

Dunne P, 'Ten Years of Gender Recognition in the United Kingdom: Still a 'Model for Reform'?' [2015] Public Law 530

Eakin H, 'Liberal, Harsh Denmark' *New York Review of Books* (New York, 10 March 2016) <http://www.nybooks.com/articles/2016/03/10/liberal-harsh-denmark> accessed 18 May 2016

Fletcher R, 'Post-Colonial Fragments: Representations of Abortion in Irish Law and Politics' (2001) 28(4) Journal of Law and Society 568

——— 'Reproducing Irishness: Race, Gender, and Abortion Law' (2005) 17 Canadian Journal of Women and the Law 365

Foucault M, *The Will to Knowledge: The History of Sexuality Volume One* (first published 1976, Hurley R tr, Penguin 1998)

——— *The Birth of Biopolitics: Lectures at the Collège de France 1978–1979* (Senellart M ed, Burchell G tr, Picador 2008)

Fox M and Murphy T, 'The Body, Bodies, Embodiment: Feminist Legal Engagement with Health' in Davies M and Munro VE (eds), *The Ashgate Research Companion to Feminist Legal Theory* (Ashgate 2013)

Gleeson JJ and O'Rourke E (eds), *Transgender Marxism* (Pluto Press 2021)

Government Equalities Office, 'Government Responds to Gender Recognition Act Consultation' (2020) <https://gov.uk/government/news/government-responds-to-gender-recognition-act-consultation> accessed 17 June 2021

Grabham E, 'Governing Permanence: Trans Subjects, Time, and the Gender Recognition Act' (2010) 19(1) Social & Legal Studies 107

——— 'Bodily Integrity and the Surgical Management of Intersex' (2012) 18(2) Body & Society 1

Hansen BS, 'Something Rotten in the State of Denmark: Eugenics and the Ascent of the Welfare State' in Broberg G and Roll-Hansen N (eds), *Eugenics and the Welfare State: Sterilization Policy in Denmark, Sweden, Norway and Finland* (Michigan State University Press 1996)

Harrington J, 'Migration and Access to Health Care in English Medical Law: A Rhetorical Critique' (2009) 4(4) International Journal of Law in Context 315

——— 'Time and Space in Medical Law: Building on Valverde's *Chronotopes of Law*' (2015) 23 Feminist Legal Studies 361

Herman D, 'Beyond the Rights Debate' (1993) 2 Social & Legal Studies 25

Hines S, *Gender Diversity, Recognition and Citizenship* (Palgrave Macmillan 2013)

Ingerslev R, 'Årets laks går til CPR-kontoret' *Out and About* (Copenhagen, 17 August 2015) <http://www.out-and-about.dk/visnyhed.asp?id=6270#.Vz3hMvl97IV> accessed 19 May 2016

Lamble S, 'Queer Necropolitics and the Expanding Carceral State: Interrogating Sexual Investments in Punishment' (2013) 24(3) Law and Critique 229

Lentin A, 'Racial States, Anti-Racist Responses: Picking Holes in 'Culture' and 'Human Rights'' (2004) 7(4) European Journal of Social Theory 427

——— 'Europe and the Silence about Race' (2008) 11(4) European Journal of Social Theory 487

McKernan B, Swash R, and Kelly A, 'Denmark Could Face Legal Action over Attempts to Return Syrian Refugees' *The Guardian* (29 July 2021) <https://gu.com/global-development/2021/jul/29/denmark-faces-legal-action-over-attempts-to-return-syrian-refugees> accessed 18 August 2021

Ministry of Justice, 'Rapport fra arbejdsgruppen om juridisk kønsskifte' (27 February 2014) <http://justitsministeriet.dk/sites/default/files/media/Pressemeddelelser/pdf/2014/Rapport%20om%20juridisk%20k%C3%B8nsskifte.pdf> accessed 21 July 2016

Minor A, 'Removing the Diagnosis: Not the Answer?' (*Killjoy.dk*, 1 March 2016) <http://killjoy.dk/en/Opinion/Not-The-Answer> accessed 25 September 2016

Munkholm NV, 'Legal Status of Transsexual and Transgender Persons in Denmark' in Scherpe JM (ed), *The Legal Status of Transsexual and Transgender Persons* (Intersentia 2015)

Munro V, *Law and Politics at the Perimeter: Re-Evaluating Key Debates in Feminist Theory* (Hart 2007)

Nielsen AS and Myong L, 'White Danish Love as Affective Intervention: Studying Media Representations of Family Reunification Involving Children' (2019) 9(4) Nordic Journal of Migration Research 497

Nord I, 'Routes to Gender-Affirming Surgery: Navigation and Negotiation in Times of Biomedicalization' in Griffin G and Jordal M (eds), *Body, Migration, Re/Constructive Surgeries: Making the Gendered Body in a Globalized World* (Routledge 2019)

OECD, 'Social Expenditure' <https://stats.oecd.org/Index.aspx?DataSetCode=SOCX_AGG> accessed 10 December 2016

Patients' Ombudsman, 'Kritik for Behandling – speciallæge i plastikkirurgi Jens Pilegaard Bjarnesen' (1 November 2012) <https://www.patientombuddet.dk/Afgoerelser_og_domme/Afgoerelser_fra_Sundhedsvaesenets_Disciplinaernaevn/Afgoerelser_med_navn/2012/1294528.aspx> accessed 16 September 2015

Priaulx N, 'Rethinking Progenitive Conflict: Why Reproductive Autonomy *Matters*' (2008) 16 Medical Law Review 169

Raun T, 'The 'Caspian Case' and Its Aftermath: Transgender People's Use of Facebook to Engage Discriminatory Mainstream News Coverage in Denmark' in Björklund J and Lindqvist U (eds), *New Dimensions of Diversity in Nordic Culture and Society* (Cambridge Scholars Publishing 2016)

Sedgwick EK, *Touching Feeling: Affect, Pedagogy, Performativity* (Duke University Press 2003)

Sharpe A, *Sexual Intimacy and Gender Identity Fraud: Reframing the Legal and Ethical Debate* (Routledge 2018)

Smart C, *Feminism and the Power of Law* (Routledge 1989)

Sontag S, *Illness as Metaphor and AIDS and Its Metaphors* (Penguin 1991)
Spade D, *Normal Life: Administrative Violence, Critical Trans Politics, and the Limits of Law* (South End Press 2011)
——— 'Laws as Tactics' (2011) 21(2) Columbia Journal of Gender and Law 40
——— 'Intersectional Resistance and Law Reform' (2013) 38(4) Signs: Journal of Women in Culture and Society 1031
Stryker S, 'Biopolitics' (2014) 1(1–2) Transgender Studies Quarterly 38
Tams LM and Minor A, 'Danish Minister of Health to Push for De-Psychiatrization of Transgender Persons' (*Killjoy.dk*, 12 May 2016) <http://killjoy.dk/en/Report/Minister-Of-Health> accessed 25 September 2016
Valverde M, 'Genealogies of European States: Foucauldian Reflections' (2007) 36(1) Economy and Society 159
——— *Chronotopes of Law: Jurisdiction, Scale and Governance* (Routledge 2015)
Versi J, 'Denmark's 'Ghetto Plan' and the Communities it Targets' *Al Jazeera* (15 January 2020) <https://aljazeera.com/features/2020/01/15/denmarks-ghetto-plan-and-the-communities-it-targets> accessed 12 May 2021
World Bank, 'Fertility Rate, Total' <http://data.worldbank.org/indicator/SP.DYN.TFRT.IN?locations=DK> accessed 10 December 2016
Wren K, 'Cultural Racism: Something Rotten in the State of Denmark?' (2001) 2(2) Social & Cultural Geography 141

Index

Note: Page numbers in *italics* indicate figures, **bold** indicate tables in the text, and references following "n" refer notes

For Product Safety Concerns and Information please contact our EU representative GPSR@taylorandfrancis.com
Taylor & Francis Verlag GmbH, Kaufingerstraße 24, 80331 München, Germany

www.ingramcontent.com/pod-product-compliance
Ingram Content Group UK Ltd.
Pitfield, Milton Keynes, MK11 3LW, UK
UKHW020137200926
475702UK00005B/795
* 9 7 8 0 3 6 7 2 5 5 1 6 9 *